# Meeting Homeless People's Needs

Service development and practice for the older excluded

# Meeting Homeless People's Needs

Service development and practice for the older excluded

Anthony Warnes and Maureen Crane

LEARNING RESOURCES CENTRE
Havering College
of Further and Higher Education

King's Fund

Published by
King's Fund Publishing
11–13 Cavendish Square
London W1M 0AN

© King's Fund 2000

First published 2000

ISBN 1 85717 253 1

A CIP catalogue record for this book is available from the British Library

Available from:

King's Fund Bookshop
11–13 Cavendish Square
London
W1M 0AN

Tel:   020 7307 2591
Fax:  020 7307 2801

Printed and bound in Great Britain

Typeset by Peter Powell Origination & Print Limited

# Contents

# Acknowledgements

We are exceptionally indebted to our contributors, for without their help this book would not have contained such rich illustrations of, and insights into, services for older homeless people. The contributors have shared both the achievements and the difficulties of their work. Although most have heavy workloads and few had previous experience of writing for publication, they willingly accepted the challenge to contribute to this book. Secondly, we thank the many older homeless people who shared their experiences, thoughts and opinions during innumerable contacts with Maureen Crane. Without their co-operation, our understanding of their situations, problems and needs would be much less complete.

Particular thanks are due to Charles Fraser, Andy Shields and many of their colleagues at *St Mungo's*, which established and developed the *Lancefield Street Centre*, the innovative project for older homeless people that was the main inspiration for this book. They share many of our ambitions regarding services for older homeless people and have shown strong support for our monitoring and evaluation work by allowing free access to the Centre and inviting Maureen Crane to join the Steering Group. We also thank particularly Maggie Giles-Hill and her team at *St Anne's Housing and Action* in Leeds and Sheffield for consistent encouragement and support. Many other staff of several projects working with homeless people in the UK and the USA have gone out of their way to provide information and advice.

Virginia Graham and the Trustees of the *Henry Smith's Charity* enthusiastically supported the Lancefield Street project from its inception, and we are indebted to them for their consistent encouragement of Maureen Crane's research and particularly for funding the second year of the Lancefield Street Centre evaluation. We also thank the Trustees of the *Sir Halley Stewart Trust* for funding Maureen Crane's research on homeless sector services over several years and *The King's Fund* for funding the initial year of the Lancefield evaluation.

Mrs Kate Smith at the Sheffield Institute for Studies on Ageing, University of Sheffield, has provided invaluable help: her considerable secretarial expertise has greatly eased the tasks of compiling and writing this book.

# Preface

## Aims

This book is intended as a guide to effective ways of helping older homeless people. We hope to raise awareness of the problems and needs of a generally neglected group of seriously disadvantaged people, to demonstrate that, contrary to widespread assumption, many of them will accept and respond to help, and to provide evidence-based advice on the delivery of practical help. The emphasis is on the development and delivery of 'second-stage' services. These are distinguished from the interventions and forms of help that meet people's basic needs for food, clothing and shelter and are available on the streets or from temporary or 'first-stage' hostels. In contrast, 'second-stage' interventions aim to make a fundamental difference to the health, morale, attitudes, aspirations and long-term housing careers of a homeless person. They address deep-seated problems and disaffection and therefore commonly require sustained contact, great patience, and sensitive assessments of a person's attitudes, mental state and problems, and they normally have to be provided in an individualised and intensive way. The overall aim is to encourage and enable the individual not only to aspire and prepare for a return to conventional accommodation but also to be equipped mentally, materially and in their living skills to adjust to a housing setting that is carefully matched to their needs and abilities.

## Why *older* homeless people?

The focus of this book on the older person and, by extension, any mature adult homeless person needs explanation. It is partly because we came to the issues as gerontologists with an interest in (conventionally defined) older people, partly because older homeless people have distinctive problems, and partly because recently in Britain the emphasis of policy and services has been on young people. If 30 years ago the stereotypical homeless person was an itinerant or transient labouring man, today's tabloid stereotype is of a young adolescent who is vulnerable to pimps and drug dealers. The Government's perspective is firmly if not exclusively focused on ending the social exclusion of young homeless people. The reasoning is that each day they spend aimlessly on the streets is another that deflects them from acquiring job skills and work habits and, the longer they are homeless, the more likely they are to waste their lives and to become a long-term charge on the public exchequer.

However estimable this concern, an unfortunate effect may be further to marginalise older homeless people. Because they are unlikely to acquire new job skills, their social exclusion has no simple remedy and the policy urgency is low. But, as the following chapters show, they have special problems, some associated with the unusual duration and 'entrenchment' of their homeless state. Older rough sleepers are exceptionally disadvantaged, and no other social group has higher rates of morbidity and lower life expectancy, nor is more detached – if not wilfully excluded – from social and health services.

Neither this book nor our programme of research seeks exceptional help for homeless people over a certain age. We fully support the overall goal of preventing homelessness at all ages, and we recognise that homeless adolescents are exceptionally vulnerable and that society's response should be fast, protective and tenacious. One way to reduce the number of people on the streets is to shorten the duration of 'episodes' of homelessness – to get people of whatever age into accommodation as quickly as possible. Another way is to encourage, help and support formerly homeless people to move from hostels into 'permanent' accommodation, and to maximise their settledness and chances of *not* returning to the streets. This requires more than finding housing vacancies or putting 'roofs over heads'. More understanding of homeless people's problems and a more systematic approach to resettlement preparation and continued support is required. Many of the principles and lessons to which we draw attention are applicable to all age groups of homeless people and to other marginally housed people. It is, however, an account which focuses on more than 20 innovative projects that have explored and implemented ways of helping into conventional housing and lives people who characteristically have either been in and out of homelessness for decades or have deep-seated mental health and addiction problems. Many of the lessons can be applied more widely: it is our and our collaborators' long-term goal to discover and to disseminate effective ways of helping homeless people of any age.

## Origins and sources

The contents of this book have two sources – our own research and the experiences, opinions and recommendations of people who have worked in recent imaginative and innovative projects. Maureen Crane's (1997) pioneering ethnographic study of older homeless people in London, Sheffield, Leeds and Manchester (the Four-City Study) and her close involvement with the conception and experience of an experimental multi-service project in London, the Lancefield Street Centre, have been the foundation of this book. Lancefield Street's work is outlined in Chapter 2 and referred to in several later chapters, and some of its distinctive achievements and problems are described in the contributions from its manager and staff. This book is not, however, an evaluation or comprehensive audit of Lancefield Street's work: fuller reports are available (Crane and Warnes, 1998; 1999).

The second distinctive source is 27 contributions from 20 experimental and pioneering projects in Britain, the USA and Australia. These derive from a wish to set Lancefield Street's achievements and problems against other experience, which led us to comparable projects wherever they could be found. Many projects have been visited in Great Britain, New York City, Boston (Massachusetts), Chicago, Washington DC, Milwaukee and San Francisco, and discussed with their champions and staff; other projects have been read about. We were impressed by what we saw, read and heard, and believed that it would be valuable to compile not just a catalogue, directory or cento of project descriptions, but a reflective and partly prescriptive commentary. The collaborators were enthusiastic and speedy in their co-operation and their descriptive and evaluative essays enrich this book. The case studies have been far from randomly selected but are drawn from projects that:

- are dedicated to the problems and needs of older homeless people
- have specifically addressed homeless people's deep-seated problems such as alcohol addiction and mental illness
- have specifically explored or evaluated more effective ways of resettling formerly homeless people or those with deep-seated problems.

## Structure of the book

The first chapter reviews the current understanding of the circumstances, needs and problems of older homeless people, particularly in Great Britain but also with material from the USA. The subsequent core of the book has two main sections. The first concentrates on 'ways of working', with chapters on helping homeless people leave the streets, first-stage accommodation and related services, providing specialist help, and preparation for resettlement. The second section concentrates on 'service development, organisation and management', and includes chapters on the policy and institutional frameworks that support (and sometimes restrain) service development, the initiation of a service, and the promotion of good practice. Brief appendices contain directories of projects and useful contacts for those who wish to learn more.

## The contents of the chapters

Many of the chapters follow a standard sequence of topics. They open with a general exposition of the aims and requirements of the specific service or service development task, normally drawing from an understanding of the problems and needs of the client group. These abstractions are followed by descriptions of and commentary about actual projects, including our collaborators' contributions. From the accumulated material, we put forward generalisations about the necessary and desirable characteristics of well-conceived interventions, the necessary conditions for effectiveness, and commonly experienced problems and mistakes. If we believe there is sufficient experience and evidence, the chapter concludes with recommendations about the setting up and delivery of the particular service. None of our prescriptions can be definitive, but however provisional our understanding and recommendations, we hope that this exercise in dissemination is as useful to others as it has been to ourselves.

## The international content

To be of practical value, any approach to good practice in the housing, health and social services has to be grounded in the policy, organisational, funding and even welfare ethos of a country or other administrative domain. Most of the evidence and many of the recommendations in this book are specific to the UK, although one should note immediately that the arrangements for approving and publicly funding homeless projects differ even between Greater London and other parts of the country. We have however been keen to represent the experience of imaginative and innovative projects in the USA and Australia (although it should be understood that for neither the UK nor any other country do we claim a comprehensive knowledge of innovative and distinctive projects). We have learned much from these invited reports of the problems of homeless people and the service responses in different nations, and we hope therefore that readers beyond our country will find this book of value.

*The views expressed in this book are those of the principal authors (and of our collaborators in their contributions) and not necessarily those of the organisations that employ us, the service providing organisations that we cite, the project or study funders or The King's Fund.*

Chapter 1

# The needs of older homeless people

This book is about the development and delivery of services for single homeless older people. An appropriate starting point is the formulation of the objectives for a service, which normally would refer to one or more priority needs in a city or local area. These in turn will be a function of both the characteristics of the local homeless population and the strengths and gaps in existing provision. This introductory chapter is therefore about the baseline for all service development and change – the characteristics, problems and needs of the client group. It focuses successively on the concept of need, which has distinctive nuances when applied to the homeless population, on the prevalence of single homeless older people, on their demographic and personal characteristics, and on their problems.

## The interpretation of the needs of single homeless people

The concepts of 'need' and 'unmet need' and conventional measures of housing and quality-of-life outcomes should not be applied to single homeless people without critical inspection, for in this social group 'need' is less related to either expressed demand or service utilisation than is usual in the housed population. This is because single homeless people make non-standard self-evaluations of their physical health and quality-of-life, and many do not solicit help with any of their income, housing or health problems, at least in appropriate or sustained ways. For street people, there is an unusually large difference between their *subjective* need assessments and both *objective* and (professional or societal) *normative* evaluations. The discrepancies combine with a little-remarked weakness of British welfare 'safety nets', that by and large they assume that people in need will seek help or that proxies – relatives and the emergency services – will ensure that help is engaged, which creates among single homeless people a high if unquantified level of *objectively assessed unmet need*. None of the key services of primary health care, acute hospital and local authority housing and social services, nor social security income support has a responsibility to seek out clients, as through outreach work, and in general the statutory mental health services operate under the same principles with respect to single homeless people.

This structural flaw manifests as a distinction in Britain between the 'official' homeless, who are recognised by local authority housing departments as having priority housing need, and the 'unofficial' homeless. One difference in the populations is that the former has presented itself to a housing department and been accepted for priority housing, while the other has either not presented or not been accepted as deserving priority. As 'old age' is a stipulated basis of priority housing need, no person of pensionable age should be unofficially homeless. All this leads to the attitude that, if an older person is homeless, he or she has no need to be and it is entirely his or her own fault. So not only do the statutory services have no explicit responsibility to help single homeless people, but quite often antagonistic attitudes are displayed, as in primary health care centres and hospital A&E departments (although to be fair, most often for practical reasons rather than from prejudice). Hence, single homeless people have tended to be neglected by mainstream services, and we have had to nurture voluntary and charitable organisations into specialist agencies to address their housing and welfare needs.

This analysis has been expressed in the terms of formal social welfare and health care, but as we all know there are other dimensions to society's response to homelessness and particularly 'rough sleeping'. Broader humanitarian, altruistic, moral, aesthetic and ideological considerations are engaged in the social construction of 'needs' among single homeless people. The attitudes of the public, media and politicians towards single homeless people are exceptionally divergent, and display sympathy alongside repugnance, empathy alongside blame. Similarly, one hears prescriptions variously: for greater tolerance *versus* more coercive measures 'to get them off the streets'; for more help with immediate needs (amelioration) *versus* greater attention to people's fundamental problems (rehabilitation); for more preconditions before support is given *versus* more comprehensive unconditional help; and for a more energetic approach to fundamental prevention, as opposed to 'even more' help to the currently homeless. Despite this Babel of conflicting views and recommendations, and the fringe cultural relativist view that those who choose street living do so legitimately, the assumptions and direction of current policies (which are broadly similar in all the developed English-speaking countries) suggest that there are elements of consensus: firstly, that people who live on the streets should be helped; and secondly, in contrast to the normal practice three decades ago, that they deserve more than 'warehousing' in the most rudimentary lodgings but should be encouraged and helped to regain self-worth and the motivation to live in conventional accommodation.

## The dualism in British policies towards homeless people

The *Housing (Homeless Persons) Act 1977* imposed a duty upon local authority housing departments to house homeless people who applied for help, were 'unintentionally' homeless, and in 'priority need' (Jacobs *et al.* 1999). There was, however, no duty to anticipate cases, find homeless people, or help those who had volitionally abandoned accommodation. The effect was to dichotomise 'official' homelessness (usually of families or older people) from the problems of unregistered 'single homeless people'. Ever since, British academic and applied debates on homelessness have been confused by inconsistent definitions (for more detailed comments see Crane, 1999). Housing departments helped low income and vulnerable people whose housing was insecure or terminated, including the cases arising from housing shortages, mismanaged slum clearance programmes, and the actions of irresponsible and inadequately regulated private landlords.

Following considerable protests in response to the anticipatory consultative Green and White Papers, these policies were modified by the *Housing Act 1996* (DoE, 1994; 1995). The new legislation was designed to prevent homeless people having preferential treatment over others on housing waiting lists. The local authority's responsibility to find permanent housing for homeless people was altered to a duty to provide temporary housing, and the definitions of priority need and eligibility were tightened (Lowe, 1997; Somerville, 1999). One consequence of the changes is that the trends in new 'officially' homeless households are now confused.

## Continuity and change in the single homeless population

The decades immediately following the Second World War were associated with historically low levels of vagrancy and rough sleeping in Britain (although the numbers living in lodging houses and direct-access hostels remained high), but from the 1960s homelessness increased substantially and the age structure and backgrounds of the single homeless population changed. Until a generation ago there was a high demand for semi-skilled and unskilled manual labour in mines, construction, docks and the merchant marine. This created many types of temporary accommodation for the large population of migratory labouring men: direct-access lodging houses, seamen's missions, miners' hostels, and railwaymen's overnight kips. These diverse hostels were rudimentary, and their institutional regimes and communal socialising did little to prepare the men for either family-based or self-reliant home-based lives. Although the majority of this 'reserve army of labour' settled in later life into conventional housing and family settings, some worked well past today's retirement age. Others, when temporarily or finally unemployed, became single homeless (and a proportion also transient) men. They were the main users of temporary hostels and lodging houses. A National Assistance Board survey (1966) of lodging houses, hostels and shelters found that among the 25,490 residents whose age was established, 59 per cent were aged at least 50 years, 35 per cent were 60 years or more, and only 10 per cent were less than 30 years of age. Five years later, Lodge Patch (1971) found that 18 per cent of rough sleepers were aged 60 years or more.

From the 1960s, as that labouring population declined, a different but highly visible homeless population grew, of adolescents and young adults sleeping on the streets. Most were estranged from their parents, and many had been in social service care. Being young, single and childless, they were ineligible for local authority housing but their plight, and the nuisance and embarrassment they caused (or were perceived to cause), led to emotive debate and vigorous policy responses (which are detailed in Chapter 7). The substantial change in the age structure of the single homeless population is indicated by surveys during the mid-1990s of the temporary hostel, day centre and outreach teams' client populations (Figure 1.1). At least a third were less

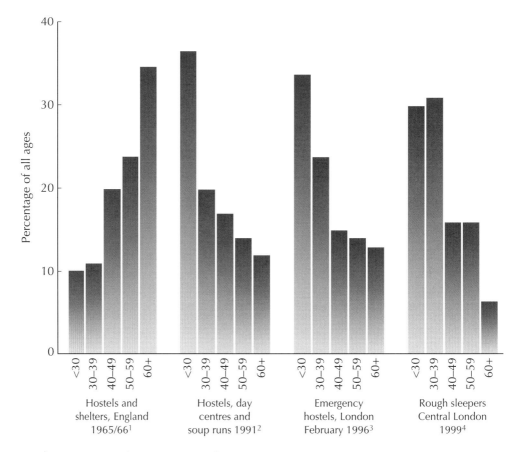

Sources:    1. National Assistance Board (1966)
            2. Anderson *et al.* (1993) (in five London boroughs and Bristol, Manchester, Birmingham, Newcastle and Nottingham)
            3. Harrison (1996).
            4. Homeless Network (1999)

Note:       The sources use irregular and different age groups. The numbers in those age groups have been apportioned to the standard age groups employed in the chart.

**Figure 1.1**  The age structure of single homeless people by age groups: four enquiries in England, 1965–99

than 30 years of age: no wonder the focus of homeless policies, services and agencies switched to young people. It should be noted, however, that even those surveys found that a fifth to a quarter of the single homeless population were aged 50 years or more, and moreover that a recent London street count of rough sleepers found that 38 per cent were aged 40 years or more (Homeless Network, 1999).

## The extent of homelessness among older people

### The 'official' homeless

In 1996–97, local housing authorities in England accepted 110,810 households as homeless, an increase from 53,100 in 1978 but down from the peak of 145,000 in 1991–92 (Bramley, 1993; DETR, 1998; Hawes, 1999). Each year during the early 1990s, between 6600 and 7400 households throughout Great Britain were accepted by local authorities as homeless on the grounds of old age (Table 1.1). The number had fallen slightly since 1985 and by 1998 'the total number of homeless families [in England] accepted under the new Housing Act was down by 25 per cent on the peak year of 1991–92. The percentage of those accepted as vulnerable due to old age, having increased in the subsequent three years, steadied at around 4 per cent of the annual total. This means that 4000–5000 older people [in England] still lose their home each year' (Hawes, 1999, p.200).

**Table 1.1:** Households accepted by local authorities as homeless and vulnerable due to old age

| Year | England[1] Number | %[4] | Wales[2] Number | %[4] | Scotland[3] Number | %[4] | Total Number |
|------|---------|------|--------|------|----------|------|--------|
| 1985[5] | 6579 | 7 | 322 | 6 | 740 | 5 | 7641 |
| 1991[6] | 5860 | 4 | 326 | 3 | 920 | 3 | 7106 |
| 1992[6] | 6230 | 4 | 359 | 3 | 792 | 3 | 7381 |
| 1993[6] | 5920 | 4 | 335 | 3 | 910 | 3 | 7165 |
| 1994[6] | 6050 | 5 | 348 | 3 | 875 | 3 | 7273 |
| 1995[6] | 5890 | 5 | 303 | 3 | 845 | 3 | 7038 |
| 1996[6] | 5510 | 5 | 309 | 3 | 825 | 3 | 6644 |
| 1997 | 4230 | 4 | 224[7] | 5 | n/a | n/a | n/a |

*Notes:*
1. Tables 1 and 12 (Bramley *et al.* 1988) and Table 3 (DETR, 1998).
2. Table 7.4 (Welsh Office, 1997).
3. Tables 6a, 6b, and 6d (Scottish Office, 1998).
4. Percentage of total households accepted as homeless.
5. Represents 1986–87 for Scotland.
6. For Scotland, figures are from April to March of the following year.
7. Verbal report from Welsh Office.

## The 'unofficial' or single homeless population

The number of single homeless older people is unknown, for many do not register with a general practitioner, appear on electoral rolls or official housing and social services departments lists, or receive social security benefits. Some even avoid the outreach teams, day centres and shelters provided for homeless people. In 1989, a count in 17 London boroughs found 226 rough sleepers aged over 50 years (Moore *et al.* 1995). During 1992–96, six-monthly counts of rough sleepers in central London, the City and 'East End' found 80–140 people aged 50 years or more (Homeless Network, 1996; 1995; Randall and Brown, 1996). These counts covered only a small area of the city, excluded isolated and hidden homeless people, and provide only partial evidence of the problem.

To estimate the number of single homeless older people in England requires many assumptions and interpolations, and produces no more than a broad indication. The exercise was attempted for the early 1990s by Crane (1999, pp.33–35). Assembling various counts in central London, outer London and the rest of England and Wales produced an estimate of 570–800 rough sleepers aged 50 years or more on an 'average night'. The second step was to estimate the older share of the 60,042 hostel residents in England (Randall, 1992) and of the 76,680 people who, while not accepted as homeless by local authorities, had been placed in 'bed-and-breakfast' accommodation in England and Wales (Carter, 1997). The best guide was that between 26 and 35 per cent of the hostel populations of London, Glasgow, Birmingham, Bristol and Manchester were aged at least 50 years. Combining all this information, the approximation was reached that between 36,000 and 49,000 people aged 50 years or more were unofficially homeless in England and Wales in the early 1990s. That number implies that only 11–14 per cent of older homeless people were 'officially' homeless.

The most detailed recent evidence of the scale of rough sleeping among older people in London comes from the *Lancefield Street Centre*'s two outreach workers. Between February 1997 and November 1998, they found 491 people aged 50 years or more who were sleeping rough and without housing. Some had been on the streets for years, others for just a few nights. The team was told of others but were unable to find them. Turning to Glasgow, an enumeration in early January 1997 of people staying in temporary hostels and 'welfare hotels' found that 600 men and 41 women were aged 55 years or more, and that they formed 35 per cent of the hostel population (Crane and Warnes, 1997a).

# The biographies of older homeless people

Crane's (1997; 1999) recent research enables a detailed picture of the characteristics, life histories, problems, behaviour and needs of older (55 years and over) homeless people who sleep rough or stay in hostels to be built from two samples: an ethnographic field investigation during 1994–95 of the causes of homelessness among 225 men and women in London, Sheffield, Leeds and Manchester (the Four-City Study), and a longitudinal study of pathways into homelessness and the effectiveness of resettlement through in-depth interviews in 1997–98 with 88 residents at the Lancefield Street Centre (this Centre's genesis and services are described in Chapter 2).

The ages when older people first become homeless span most of the life course. Some have been homeless for years and have become elderly while homeless; others have become homeless for the first time in old age. Among the Four-City Study sample, 24 men and two women were aged under 21 years when they first became homeless, whereas five men and four women were aged in their seventies when this occurred. The simple conclusion is that men are more likely to become homeless at all ages and women more likely to become homeless after the age of 50 years (Table 1.2).

The most frequently reported life events that preceded homelessness among older people are: broken and disturbed childhood homes; the death of the last parent, which raises problems of adjustment for people who have never lived independently and are 'under-socialised'; the ending of a partnership through death or separation; and the onset or increased severity of a serious disorientating mental illness. These antecedents are common to men and women, but gender-specific risk factors

**Table 1.2:** The age when the Four-City Study subjects first became homeless

| Age (years) | Men | | Women | |
|---|---|---|---|---|
| | No. | % | No. | % |
| Up to 21 | 24 | 19 | 2 | 5 |
| 22–29 | 18 | 15 | 2 | 5 |
| 30–39 | 21 | 17 | 2 | 5 |
| 40–49 | 24 | 19 | 8 | 22 |
| 50–59 | 24 | 19 | 10 | 27 |
| 60+ | 14 | 11 | 13 | 35 |
| **Total known** | **125** | **100** | **37** | **99** |
| Not known | 30 | | 24 | |
| Total experienced homelessness | 155 | | 61 | |

*Note*: All the subjects were aged at least 50 years when interviewed. The average ages at interview of the men and women were similar. It is not implied that all subjects have been continuously homeless since they first entered the state. For further discussion see Crane (1997).

are also found: older homeless men are more likely to have been in transient and casual work or in the armed forces, to have lived in impermanent lodgings or barracks, and to have become homeless in early or middle adulthood; older homeless women are more likely to have become homeless late in life having married, raised families, and lived in conventional housing.

By first categorising the subjects in the Four-City and the Lancefield Street Centre studies according to their sleeping arrangements, personal characteristics, behaviours and problems, it was possible to identify combinations of attributes and identify categories of older homeless people's biographies and current behaviour. It was not possible to classify all cases, but 207 in the Four-City Study and 65 in the Lancefield Street Centre Study were placed in seven groups (Table 1.3).

The *Withdrawn Rough Sleepers* were 28 men and 22 women who regularly slept rough in isolated spots, and were characteristically elusive and hostile to the researcher. Over a third of the women in the entire sample were in this group. Many of both sexes had a poor standard of hygiene and dirty clothing, and 16 (five men and 11 women) were typical 'bag people' who hoarded rubbish in luggage trolleys and old carrier bags. The majority had apparent yet unreported mental health problems, and some displayed disturbed behaviour. They tended to remain in one area, seldom used soup kitchens or day centres, and rejected help. They often had long histories of homelessness and rough sleeping and only one person had ever been rehoused. Because they seldom used soup kitchens, they were not in contact with services and few received welfare benefits.

The *Convivial Rough Sleepers* were 47 men and three women who were heavy drinkers and tended to congregate in busy public areas and remain in one town. Many socialised with other drinkers but a few drank alone and 14 occasionally used soup kitchens. They slept rough most of the time, although 29 intermittently stayed in hostels. Eighteen had marked memory difficulties, possibly related to heavy drinking over many years. They had long histories of homelessness and rough sleeping. Six had been rehoused but had soon become homeless again.

The *Active Rough Sleepers* were 18 men and one woman, most under 65 years of age, who stayed in one town. They sometimes worked casually or made money in marginal occupations, such as trading phone-cards and collecting luggage trolleys at railway stations. They slept in secluded locations and went to great lengths to protect themselves. Eleven used soup kitchens. Mental health problems were rare but a few were binge drinkers. Five had been rehoused in the past. All in the past had found either private, rented or tied accommodation or had cohabited, confirming their relatively independent and capable traits.

**Table 1.3:** Dominant sub-groups of older homeless people[1]

| Sub-group | Sex | Sleeps rough | Uses hostels[2] | Uses day centres | Works casually[3] | Social-ises[4] | Mental illness | Heavy drinking | Transient[5] | Receipt of benefits | Rehousing attempts |
|---|---|---|---|---|---|---|---|---|---|---|---|
| I Withdrawn rough sleeper | M + F | Yes | No | No | No | No | Yes | No | No | Rare | No |
| II Convivial rough sleeper | M | Yes | Some | Some | No | Yes | Some | Yes | No | Some | Rare |
| III Active rough sleeper | M | Yes | No | Some | Yes | No | No | Rare | No | Yes | Some |
| IV Transient rough sleeper | M | Yes | Some | No | No | No | Some | Some | Yes | Some | Yes |
| V Settled hostel resident | M + F | No | Yes | No | No | Some | Some | Some | No | Yes | No |
| VI Recently homeless | M + F | Some | Some | No | Some | No | Some | Some | Some | Some | No |
| VII Symptomatically homeless | M + F | No | No | Yes | No | Yes | Some | Some | No | Yes | Yes |

*Notes:*
1. Includes housed people displaying homelessness behaviours.
2. Includes former Resettlement Units.
3. Includes occupations remunerated by gratuities, e.g. collecting luggage trolleys at railway stations.
4. With homeless people.
5. Frequently moves from town to town.

The *Transient Rough Sleepers* were 30 men who moved around the country, generally sleeping rough or using hostels for brief spells. They were estranged, seldom mixed with homeless people or congregated in public places, and travelled alone. They rarely used soup kitchens. Twelve were heavy drinkers and another six had once been so. Ten said that they had suffered from depression for years. They were difficult to trace except when they booked into temporary accommodation. Seventeen had been rehoused, mostly in shared houses or in independent accommodation but had soon became homeless again. Some had been resettled on several occasions.

The *Passive Hostel Residents* were 22 men and 12 women who had stayed in hostels for years. Most of the women (10) and four of the men were mentally ill, and nine men were heavy drinkers. They generally kept away from other residents and did not use soup kitchens, although a few socialised. They had 'settled' in a hostel and only four had been rehoused for a short time.

The *Recently Homeless* were 29 men and eight women who had been homeless for less than 12 months. Some used hostels, others slept rough. Thirteen had mental health problems, and eight were heavy drinkers. None had been resettled as yet.

The seventh group, the *Symptomatically Homeless*, were 36 men and 16 women who had permanent housing but were isolated or estranged from relatives and congregated on the streets with homeless people and regularly used soup kitchens. Thirty-five reported or had apparent mental health problems, and ten were heavy drinkers. The majority had once been homeless. They were living alone, and said that they were lonely, unsettled in their accommodation, and were finding it difficult to manage at home. Generally, they were willing to use services and make known their health, welfare and housing needs.

## The problems of older homeless people

### Physical health problems

A striking characteristic of older homeless people, and the one that supremely demonstrates their extremely disadvantaged state, is their high mortality. The average age of death of people recorded as homeless on coroners' reports varies between 42 and 53 years, which compares with the late seventies in the general population (Grenier, 1996; Keyes and Kennedy, 1992). Confirmation of the low age of older rough sleepers was provided by the Lancefield Street Centre outreach teams' records of the ages of their street homeless clients. Figure 1.2 contrasts the age structure with that of the England and Wales population in 1991. Just under a half of the people they contacted aged 50 years or more were aged at least 60 years, compared to more than 70 per cent of the general population of England and Wales in 1991.

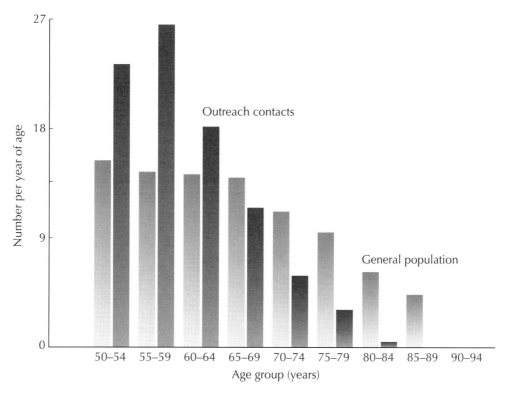

**Figure 1.2**  Age structure of the Lancefield Street Centre outreach contacts with people aged 50+ years compared to England and Wales, 1991

Health problems are exacerbated by age, lack of treatment and the lifestyle, with its risks of assault, exposure, hypothermia and frostbite. Although some wear several layers of clothing and use blankets and cardboard to keep warm, others are inadequately dressed and lack bedding. Many live in insanitary conditions, some eat from litter-bins and have poor diets, and a few use crowded and badly ventilated soup kitchens and day centres. Infections are widespread and the group is susceptible to gastroenteritis, tuberculosis, malnutrition and skin infestations, particularly scabies and lice (Connelly and Crown, 1994; Jahiel, 1992; Brickner *et al.* 1986). In the early 1990s, high rates of active tuberculosis were reported among homeless people in London, the most vulnerable being middle-aged and elderly men who were heavy drinkers and slept rough or stayed in hostels (Citron *et al.* 1995). Poor nutrition increases the risk of infections and can lead to cognitive disabilities, loss of energy and retardation (Balazs, 1993; Belcher and Di Blasio, 1990). On admission to the Lancefield Street Centre, several clients had untreated life-threatening problems such as carcinomas, tuberculosis and renal failure. A strong and statistically significant association was found between physical illness and heavy drinking.

## Alcohol and mental health problems

Mental health and alcohol-related problems are also common among older homeless people. Older homeless men are more likely than women to be heavy drinkers, whereas women are more likely to have mental health problems. In the Four-City Study sample, only 12 per cent of the women but 42 per cent of the men drank alcohol most days or heavily two to three days a week. Some of the men had been drinking heavily for more than 25 years and in the past a few had drank methylated and surgical spirits. At interview, nearly three-quarters of women and two-fifths of men in the Four-City sample had manifest but unacknowledged mental health problems. They were hallucinating and 'answering' imaginary voices, expressing paranoid and persecutory ideas, or disorientated and confused. Although drug abuse is rare among older homeless people, a small number have dual problems of heavy drinking and mental illness. This applied to one-tenth of the women and a quarter of the men in the Four-City Study. Those with dual problems tended to be sleeping rough and had long histories of homelessness.

Three-tenths of the men in the Four-City sample who had been in the armed forces (28 of 94 who provided details) reported horrific experiences during active service, which, by their accounts, had had a profoundly destabilising effect. They described the fear of being under attack, the horror of seeing their comrades badly injured, and the revulsion of killing the enemy, and many still experienced nightmares and panic attacks.

## Social isolation

The majority of older homeless people have been estranged from their family for years or have no known relatives. Among those who are sleeping rough, many are reluctant to use services, claim no welfare benefit entitlements, receive minimal help and support, and their health and social problems continue unresolved. Older female rough sleepers are particularly distrustful and alienated. Despite repeated contacts over many months with outreach workers, some remain hostile and a few refuse to converse.

Homelessness among older people is often a hidden problem and many who patronise soup kitchens or congregate on the streets are not themselves homeless. Apart from those who are heavy drinkers and are visible in public areas, those sleeping rough are not readily found. They are either secluded or frequently move between towns – behaviour that maximises detachment and anonymity. Among rough sleepers, while many men are heavy drinkers and socialise with others, the women are generally isolated, have mental health problems, and are rarely transient.

## Conclusions

While much more can be learned about the most common causes and current situations of homelessness among older people, it has been shown by the broadly corroborative American and British evidence that many who reach this state have both acute immediate needs and deep-seated behavioural, morale, mental health and social problems (Cohen *et al.* 1997; Cohen and Sokolovsky, 1989; Douglass *et al.* 1988; Kutza, 1987; Rossi *et al.* 1986). Malnourishment, exposure, deficient clothing and poor hygiene contributes to very high rates of morbidity and mortality among rough sleepers. If the population is to be helped and the 'problem' reduced, the service response requires more than the provision of a dwelling.

This chapter has described an overview of the problems of older homeless people. Much more detail will be provided in later chapters when the needs of the group will be identified and ways in which they are being helped. Homelessness among older people is not common and the numbers are not large, but older homeless people are seriously deprived and neglected and the problem is one that reveals the flaws and frailties of society's supposedly lavish welfare state.

Section I

# Working with older homeless people

Chapter 2

# Service and practice responses to single homeless older people

## Introduction

Having broadly established the problems and needs of single homeless older people, this chapter turns to the policy and service responses in Britain and other countries. Here we focus on the principles and aims that have underlain the far-reaching developments in the publicly supported services for homeless people over the last quarter of the 20th century. Later chapters will describe in detail specific services and interventions, while the second part of the book will thoroughly examine current policy trends and debates.

As the social histories of vagrancy amply show, legislative and administrative responses to indigence and homelessness have vacillated between empathetic support and punitive sanctions. The approaches of governments, city councils and professional elites have sometimes criminalised, medicalised and stigmatised homeless people, but at other times have offered minimal support. At the end of the 1990s the revival of coercive policy proposals is reverberating among the British homeless agencies: 'third way' thinking has not only opened up debate about the prevention of homelessness and how to get homeless people into work and settled housing, but is also exercised by questions of the morally correct and electorally astute level of 'toleration' of street living.

Policies and services for single homeless people have two overlapping sets of objectives. One primarily promotes the well-being of the individual; the other advances the interests and sensibilities of society or, more specifically, landowners, traders, elected representatives and the general public. The former are founded in humanitarian concern and empathy and tackle many dimensions of holistic 'well-being', from the need for food and shelter to morale and social relationships. The societal objectives may also be presented as humane but, in discouraging aberrant behaviour that is damaging to commerce, public order or the public's equanimity, they have elements of control and proscription. While the class-based critiques and controversies that surrounded homeless interventions a generation ago are less strident in London today, they may quickly revive. However widespread the consensus that rough sleepers who are seriously ill should be helped even when they demonstrate no motivation or effort to help themselves, society's responses to homelessness will never be entirely a matter of technical social administration. There will always be conflicting conceptions and understanding of homelessness, and therefore alternative pronouncements about the types of help that are required.

As for ourselves, three straightforward beliefs have been the foundation and inspiration of this book. Firstly, that there are many single homeless people in Britain who for various reasons are unable to help themselves and are woefully neglected by the mainstream housing, health and social services; secondly, that, as innovative projects are demonstrating, when concerted and systematic efforts are made to engage with and help homeless people, many will gladly accept and work towards more conventional lives; and thirdly, that too little is presently done to disseminate the experience of effective ways of working.

## The growing emphasis on treatment and rehabilitation services

Into the first half of the 20th century, homelessness was still regarded by some as criminal behaviour that policies of restraint were required to 'correct'. The *Vagrancy Act 1824* continued to be used to imprison people for sleeping on the streets or in hedgerows, barns and derelict buildings (Chambliss, 1964). At the same time, homelessness was seen as a moral and spiritual weakness and some religious organisations provided services for homeless people with salvation in mind. Soup kitchens, missions and hostels required the users to attend a religious service in return for help. Homelessness was also regarded as a social problem and homeless people as socially inadequate individuals who should be encouraged 'to relearn the habit of work' (Rose, 1988, p.85).

A high proportion of homeless people at the time were transient labouring men or vagrants, hobos and tramps. They were accommodated in Britain in rudimentary large hostels, reception centres (funded by central government) and lodging houses, in the USA in skid row missions and single-room occupancy hotels, and in Australia in large hostels and night shelters. Many lodging houses provided only overnight accommodation and few offered individualised and intensive help, counselling or treatment programmes, or rehabilitation and rehousing support. Many had been developed by voluntary religious and charitable organisations. Interest was also shown for a short while in replicating the labour and detention colonies that operated during the late nineteenth century in Belgium, Switzerland and Germany. The *Salvation Army*, which set up its first hostel in 1888, for a few years ran a labour colony at Hadleigh in Essex (Rose, 1988).

By the 1960s, though vestiges of these attitudes and practices continued, the emphasis on restraint, correction, religious observances and salvation had lessened greatly. At the time, the British welfare consensus was critical of the custodial care of vulnerable people in institutions such as mental hospitals, and increasingly favoured individualised interventions and rehabilitation (Rogers and Pilgrim, 1996). Accordingly, programmes were established to close large hospitals for mentally ill and handicapped people and to resettle the patients in supported housing. The *Mental Health Act* had become operational in 1959; it gave powers for petty offenders to be referred by law enforcement officers to mental hospitals for treatment, and a number of homeless people were admitted for mental health problems, alcohol addiction and petty offences (Archard, 1979). Hence, a medical model was introduced into the field of homelessness, which became associated with people who were inflicted by the 'diseases' of mental illness and alcoholism and required treatment and rehabilitation in detoxification units, specialist hostels and half-way houses.

By this time, a new generation of homeless sector voluntary bodies was growing up in the UK, stimulated by the creation of the *Housing Corporation* in 1964 and the *Housing Act 1974*, which introduced a range of capital and revenue social housing subsidies (Malpass and Murie, 1994). Housing associations were founded to work with single homeless people, such as *St Anne's Shelter and Housing Action* in Leeds, *St Mungo's* in London, and *The Talbot Association* in Glasgow (Spiers, 1999). Many started as a hostel or day centre to meet local needs and characteristically they developed detoxification centres, special needs hostels and supported housing schemes. The large traditional hostels were castigated for their low rate of resettlement and for promoting a 'circuit of homelessness' (Deacon *et al.* 1993). Teams were set up to rehouse hostel residents with help from local authority social services and housing departments (Dant and Deacon, 1989; Duncan and Downey, 1985; Duncan *et al.* 1983).

Since then the consensus has grown that we should provide specialist and supportive services to encourage rehabilitation and the return to independent living. It is increasingly acknowledged that the way forward is not simply to provide basic shelter and food and to maintain people in a state of homelessness, but to provide small transitional hostels and specialised interventions such as health care, job training and counselling. Organisations have expanded their range of provision and developed more focused and specialised services. The Salvation Army, for example, had 62 hostels and just over 8000 bed spaces nationwide in the early 1960s (National Assistance Board, 1966). Many had been built before 1914, were large establishments with 100 or more beds, and had dormitories and inadequate bathing facilities (Digby, 1976). By the mid-1990s, the organisation had closed most of its large hostels and developed smaller hostels designed to rehabilitate and resettle homeless people. Similar changes have been in progress in Australia and the USA where, arguably, the less comprehensive statutory provision and a more flexible and entrepreneurial approach to social service delivery has enabled more experimentation in rehabilitation and support services.

Until less than a decade ago, there was still a wide gulf between models of good practice and the generality of services on the ground. Large spartan lodging houses continued to operate, and many had no resettlement service. Even today, many day centres provide only for the most basic of needs and operate with a minimum of staff. In the late 1980s, in some British hostels, a large number of residents had mental health problems, the staff were not trained to manage their care appropriately, the residents were ignored by mainstream psychiatric services, and 'mini-institutions' were being created and a 'medical model of homelessness' being reinforced (Craig and Timms, 1992; Marshall, 1989).

Undoubted improvements to services over the last decade have been made possible by new government funding programmes: in London the *Rough Sleepers' Initiative* was launched in 1990; in Australia the *Supported Accommodation Assistance Program* was introduced in all states and territories in 1985; and in the USA the *Stewart B. McKinney Homeless Assistance Act* was initiated in 1987. (These are described more fully in Chapter 7.) As services have focused less on the containment of homelessness and more on helping homeless people find ways out of the lifestyle, it has become clear that some groups have protracted problems and special needs, and that older homeless people are among such groups.

## The recent development of services dedicated to older homeless people

Since the mid-1980s, it has become recognised in the UK, the USA and Australia that the needs of older homeless people are inadequately met by generic homeless services. While most day centres and hostels for homeless people cater for all ages, their facilities and outreach and resettlement work are usually dominated by the needs of young homeless people. Many older homeless people refuse to use hostels and day centres as they dislike the noise and overcrowded conditions, and they fear violence and intimidation from young users (Cohen and Sokolovsky, 1989; Crane and Warnes, 1997a; Doolin, 1986; Douglass *et al.* 1988). A few organisations have responded by developing services dedicated to older homeless people. They include drop-in and day centres, temporary accommodation with rehabilitation and resettlement programmes, and various long-term housing options (Bisonnette and Hijjazi, 1994; Doolin, 1986; Hallebone, 1997).

Services specifically for older homeless people are not however widespread, for several reasons (Cohen, 1999). Firstly, only a few studies have identified the circumstances and unmet needs of older homeless people, and hence many service providers are unaware of the problem. Secondly, despite the recent development of policies and services for homeless people, older homeless people are not regarded as either numerous or a 'special needs' group, so no dedicated funding programmes have been created. Designated services have instead developed through the initiatives of the existing providers of homeless people's services, and through the formation of new non-profit organisations for the specific purpose, e.g. the foundation in 1991 of the *Committee to End Elder Homelessness* in Boston, Massachusetts (Boxes 6.3 and 8.3). Furthermore, although several innovative projects have been developed for older homeless people, there have been few formal evaluations and reports of the schemes. As a result, the outcomes of different types of interventions are unknown, and lessons and achievements are rarely disseminated.

## Principles underlying current practice

Two broad principles underlie current practice in helping older homeless people. Firstly, *social norms* about older people are used to make assumptions about the needs of homeless elders and the type of help they need. It is generally accepted by policy-makers, service providers and practitioners that people should not be homeless, particularly that they should not be sleeping on the streets, and that they should be living in customary types of housing and conforming to conventional lifestyles and social norms. As summarised by Wiseman (1979, pp.217–18) in her study of homeless alcoholics, 'the primary purpose of the rehabilitation of all social deviants [is] to return them to the community, much in the way the Biblical prodigal son returns to his father, somewhat the worse for wear, but contrite and reformed ... re-entry into society is thought not to be possible unless the person is sober and "in contact" with others ... [but] how does a person who has "checked out" for several years, as many alcoholics have, gain readmittance and eventually long-term acceptance in this society?'. A deviancy approach is, however, gradually being moderated by experience and evaluated practice, which brings us to the second, increasingly influential, principle.

There is an increasing adoption from medicine into the homeless and special needs housing sectors of the merits of *evidence-based practice* – the most direct route being through the community psychiatric services. Four consensual assumptions and shared objectives for working with older homeless people can further be identified. They arise from both the evidence of needs among the group and the embryonic accumulation of practical experience and of formal service evaluations.

The first is the need for progressive *rehabilitation and resettlement* services that help homeless people move from the streets to temporary accommodation and eventually into permanent housing. Many require step-by-step help to combat basic problems such as poor nutrition, lack of sleep, and unsettledness, followed by gradual and more intensive help with intricate health and behaviour problems, and finally the building or rebuilding of social, daily living and household management skills. Individuals' needs differ and the benefits of individualised and holistic programmes of care and support guide the necessity for key workers and well-formulated care plans that are regularly reviewed and updated.

The second emergent principle is that there is a need for a *linked pathway of services* for homeless people from the streets to long-term housing (Crane and Warnes, 2000a). Its steps include outreach teams, day centres, temporary or 'first-stage' accommodation, services to combat health problems and heavy drinking, benefits

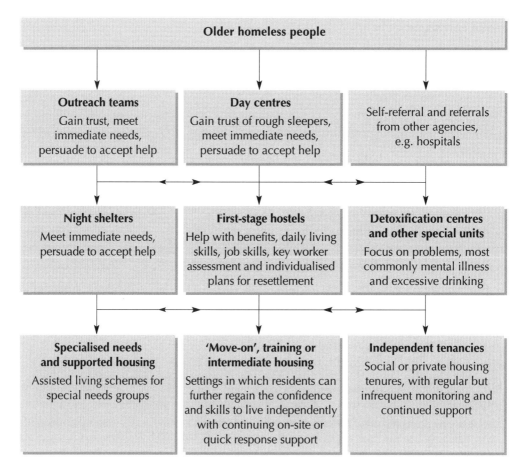

**Figure 2.1** Pathways from homelessness to permanent accommodation

and living skills advice, training in job skills, resettlement programmes, long-term housing options, and continuing support for the rehoused (Figure 2.1). Consideration has also to be given to the distinct needs of groups of homeless people who may require dedicated services. A spectrum of specialist services may be required to meet the needs of young and old homeless people, the physically frail and disabled, and those with mental health, alcohol and drug problems. Within the spectrum, the services need to be well co-ordinated, and they also require good linkages with various community groups, voluntary organisations and statutory agencies, including the health, housing and social services providers.

An example of a linked pathway of services was the *Lancefield Street Centre* in west London. It was established as an experimental project for two years in January 1997 and was managed by St Mungo's. It provided a linked series of services for homeless men and women aged 50 years or more who were sleeping rough: tenacious street outreach work with two dedicated workers; a 24-hour drop-in centre where users could become accustomed to the project and be encouraged to accept help; a 33-bed temporary hostel, where individualised and relatively intensive work was conducted with the residents to meet their basic needs and address deep-seated problems; and resettlement in long-term housing. The Centre was based on outreach work and day centres in New York City and Boston (Cohen *et al.* 1993; Doolin, 1986). The provision of an integral first-stage hostel was however unprecedented and proved an invaluable complement to the services. The Centre is referred to many times throughout this book.

A third principle, that a welfare service should be *effective for the clients and efficient in its use of resources*, is now well rooted in the homeless sector, although most organisations have little time or resource to contribute to the accumulation of rigorously evaluated evidence. Some elements are firmly in place, such as the desirability of clear objectives, good management, setting standards and working to appropriate performance and outcome indicators. It is increasingly realised also that an evaluative 'culture' can not only improve the efficacy of the services but also be vital to secure renewed or increased funding.

Effectiveness and efficiency also makes imperative the good management and support of staff. They must have clearly defined roles and the motivation and skills to ensure that the objectives of the service are met. Hostel work is particularly demanding, for balances have to be struck between complex and sometimes contradictory roles: as 'landlords' in managing the premises and controlling behaviour; as 'social workers' in assessing needs and implementing care plans; as 'care assistants' in assisting with personal care tasks; and as 'guardians' in advocating for services and entitlements and promoting the best interests of the residents.

The fourth emergent principle is the *superiority of prevention over rescue*. The British Government has recently made clear the importance it attaches to prevention (DETR, 1999a). The problem is that there is only a general understanding of the causes of and risk factors for homelessness, and in most organisations there are too few resources to reduce substantially the proportion of the residents of hostels and special needs housing schemes who return to homelessness. Prevention is the least well implemented of the four shared objectives and principles. A policy statement adopted by the governing council of the *American Public Health Association* in November 1997 noted that, 'there have been considerable achievements in terms of providing services to homeless people, but little or no progress in preventing homelessness ... there needs to be greater emphasis on prevention ... methods must be developed to identify individuals at risk' (Anon, 1998, pp.519–20). Primary prevention requires the identification of people at risk of becoming homeless for the first time for reasons of 'housing vulnerability', deteriorating personal relationships, isolated living, depression and the increased severity of a psychotic illness. This requires (i) more understanding of the 'risk factors' or markers for a high likelihood of unsettledness, poor household management, and wilfully abandoning one's home or being evicted; (ii) evidence about interventions that effectively ameliorate these problems and help people to cope at home; and (iii) implementing an 'early warning' system that identifies people at risk, and practical and effective procedures to combat the problem (Crane and Warnes, 2000b).

## Conclusions

If, at the beginning and at the end of the 20th century homelessness produced discordant policy responses, it brought great strides in elaborating and improving service practice. The vanguard organisations have moved a long way towards providing helping, rehabilitation and resettlement services, although implementation is far from universal. Some local authorities and businesses choose to ignore or deflect the problem of homelessness: they 'move' homeless people from their area and oppose plans for shelters and services for the group (Cavell, 1993; Crane and Warnes, 1998; Randall and Brown, 1996). Although for most of this century policies of restraint and imprisonment for rough sleeping have rarely been used, in Britain and North America that situation may now be reversed. The *Social Exclusion Unit* has suggested that coercion may be used to move rough sleepers into hostels (Social Exclusion Unit, 1998), echoing the stance in New York City of Mayor Rudolph Giuliani, who has vowed to clear the city's streets (*Metro London*, 1999, p.14).

Few agencies now see homelessness principally in terms of moral and spiritual weakness, though a few religious organisations still compel homeless people using their services to attend a religious service in return for help. On the other hand, the importance attached to getting people into work as the answer to the problem has grown. The current British Government strongly supports schemes to help homeless people return to work through employment and training schemes (DETR, 1999a). Within the specialist homeless services, however, over the last two decades there has been a substantial move to supplement the traditional role of meeting basic needs with the goals of treatment and rehabilitation. This requires the creation of a spectrum or pathway of services that reaches to several different kinds of specialist and intensive help, and to several levels of supported housing, and that in turn makes essential an ever-more complex network of complementary and collaborating providers. At the turn of the century, we are seeing in Britain the overturning of a long-established assumption about homeless services – that they can operate outside the majority providers of housing, health and social services. As their work moves from meeting 'first' to 'second'-stage needs, a more accomplished and professionalised sector will emerge and increase its standing in the welfare complex.

Chapter 3

# Providing basic help for older rough sleepers

Persuading older people who sleep on the streets to move into hostels is the usual first step in changing their circumstances. It is extremely difficult to meet people's requirements while they are sleeping on the streets, for they tend to be exclusively concerned with their immediate needs for food, shelter and warmth. Their physical and mental health problems cannot be properly assessed or tackled on the streets (or even in the majority of day centres), nor is it possible to determine people's capabilities for self-care or in daily living skills. This chapter discusses the ways in which older rough sleepers can be helped to leave the streets. It has contributions from two outreach workers attached to the *Lancefield Street Centre* in London, and from workers at two day centres in the USA that have been developed specifically for older homeless people.

Older rough sleepers should be encouraged to leave the streets without delay. The lifestyle is degrading and stressful and it leads to or exacerbates physical illnesses, mental health problems, heavy drinking, demoralisation, low self-esteem and depression. People sleeping rough become 'entrenched' or 'engulfed' in homelessness with time (Snow and Anderson, 1993; Grigsby *et al.* 1990). Many become detached from conventional social relationships and roles, and increasingly isolated and dysfunctional. It is therefore generally easier to persuade someone to accept help when he or she first sleeps rough and before they become accustomed to living on the streets, although it is also the case that persistent and intensive work is effective for some long-term rough sleepers (Craig, 1995; Sheridan *et al.* 1993; Wasylenki *et al.* 1993). There are two approaches to the delivery of basic helping services to older rough sleepers: to take services on to the streets through outreach work; and to encourage people to attend day and drop-in centres at which more intensive help can be arranged.

## Aims and methods of street outreach

The aims of street outreach work with older rough sleepers are:

- to identify as quickly as possible older people when they first begin to sleep rough and to link them to services

- to find, engage, and persuade long-term older rough sleepers to accept help, particularly to move into accommodation
- to meet some of the most pressing needs of older rough sleepers on the streets until they can be persuaded to move into accommodation.

These are not simple tasks. Some rough sleepers are 'difficult to serve' or 'hard-to-reach' (Sheridan *et al.* 1993; Susser *et al.* 1990). They have been on the streets for years, are entrenched in the lifestyle, have severe mental health or substance abuse problems, and resist help. Some have been helped by outreach workers in the past, have moved into hostels or night shelters, but have later returned to the streets. Some with mental health problems are unable to comprehend the precariousness of their situation, while many are so depressed and demoralised that they do not believe that their problems can be resolved. Nancy Rotem, a *St Mungo's* outreach worker who spent 30 months working with older rough sleepers in London, has perceptively described a syndrome of 'outreach contact fatigue' among homeless people:

> *Many older homeless people have spent years on the streets, during which time they have been approached by countless workers. This leads to 'outreach contact fatigue' and an unwillingness to engage or access available services. Previous negative experiences, often with authoritarian 'old-school' hostels and other street-based social and welfare services, compound their intolerance, resistance and lack of trust.*

There are four basic steps to outreach work with older rough sleepers: locating them; approaching and making contact; engaging and responding to immediate needs; and developing care plans and linking people to services, particularly accommodation.

## Locating older rough sleepers

Finding older rough sleepers is not easy. Many stay in secluded and hidden places, some on the outskirts of cities, and are unknown to local statutory and voluntary service providers. In London they have been found sleeping in old cars, phone booths, sheds, disused toilets, cellars, subways, woods and parks on the fringe of the city (Crane and Warnes, 1999). Some move around the country and stay in a town for only a few days, while others remain in one town but linger in public libraries and cafes during the day and walk around the streets at night or ride on night buses. Some are seen on the streets at night but deny that they are homeless to deter questioning, to preserve their anonymity, or because they are distrustful and fearful.

One way to find older rough sleepers is to search systematically the streets and secluded places. Contacts are most likely in the early morning and late evening, when most elderly housed people are at home, many older rough sleepers have 'bedded down' in doorways and other sleeping sites, and most public places are closed and so those without a refuge will be wandering the streets. This method is time-consuming and requires careful attention to the safety of the searchers. A second way is to become acquainted with those who use day centres and soup kitchens, and who frequent the street sites where food and clothing are handed out. Although some of the users may have hostel places or tenancies, others will be rough sleepers. A third way is to seek information about older rough sleepers from local statutory and voluntary agencies, religious organisations, the police, staff at train and bus stations and in public libraries and cafes, street vendors, public toilet attendants, and park keepers.

## Approaching and making contact with older rough sleepers

It is not easy to approach street people on their 'home territory' and to start a conversation. A few might be found receptive and eager to talk, but many will be suspicious or frightened. Some deliberately avoid contact and hide. The worker therefore needs to approach the person cautiously and in a non-threatening way. In Richmond, Virginia, outreach workers made contact with mentally ill homeless people by 'hanging out' on the streets, by sitting beside potential clients, and by sharing meals, so that the client became familiar with the worker (Sheridan *et al.* 1993). Some older rough sleepers are hostile or aggressive when first approached but, as Nancy Rotem describes (Box 3.1), this should not deter the worker from making further contacts and trying to initiate conversation, as patience and persistence can be effective.

## Engaging with older rough sleepers and responding to immediate needs

Once contact has been made with an older rough sleeper, the next step is for the outreach worker to build rapport and trust, as a first step towards eventually persuading him or her to accept help. The process can last many months, and no particular approach is known to guarantee results, although consistent and persistent contact brings familiarity and demonstrates to the rough sleeper that the worker is dependable, trustworthy, wishes no harm, and is interested in his or her well-being. Visiting at regular times and flexible and imaginative ways of working can be beneficial (Box 3.2). Outreach workers need to learn about each client's daily habits, preferences and needs, so that they can respond appropriately without unduly disrupting a person's routine. The Lancefield Street Centre team, for example, took books and magazines to one elderly rough sleeper, and other clients to a cafe for breakfast. It is essential that outreach staff work at the client's pace and are not intrusive. Many clients will be unaccustomed and unwilling to divulge personal information. Initial contacts should be short, and conversation general and not probing. From these, a person's tolerance for more intense contact can be gauged (McQuistion *et al.* 1991).

**Box 3.1:** MAKING CONTACT WITH OLDER ROUGH SLEEPERS THROUGHOUT LONDON

*Nancy Rotem (née Smith) worked for St Mungo's as a street outreach worker with older rough sleepers in London for 30 months. In this, the first of a sequence of three contributions, she describes strategies she used to make contact with homeless people who were difficult to engage in conversation.*

Initiating dialogue with new clients for the first time can be awkward; offering tea or cigarettes may reduce suspicion and tension and facilitate introductions. To explain the role and purpose of an outreach worker and to ask the person if he or she is aware of anyone sleeping rough has proved successful - this approach reduces the risk of offending the client. Although it is not always the case, new clients are often willing to enter into general conversation from which a pattern of contact can gradually be established. An elderly woman who was sleeping rough, for example, was known to sit daily on the same park bench but would not talk to outreach workers. In order to reduce her fears and suspicions, I asked if I could sit on the bench beside the woman but did not attempt further conversation. After five minutes I thanked the woman and left. This was repeated at regular intervals until gradually the woman became accustomed to my presence, conversation began and a dialogue was established.

This approach is time-consuming but a more direct introduction would have alienated the client and ended the opportunity to engage with her and develop a relationship. Patience and persistence are essential, as initially a client may not be receptive to an outreach worker. It is important that a worker is not deterred by a client's negative response. If a client is unresponsive or abusive, it is best to withdraw but return the following week and so on until a dialogue is established. Similar patience and persistence is required for those individuals who refuse to acknowledge that they are sleeping rough.

Outreach workers also need to respond to an older rough sleeper's immediate needs. Rough sleepers who are difficult to engage are most likely to accept help when it is offered rather than imposed, and when it is perceived as useful (Susser *et al.* 1990; Cohen, 1989). Mentally ill homeless people, for example, are more likely to accept food, clothing and cigarettes than help with mental health problems (Sheridan *et al.* 1993). Older rough sleepers' pressing concerns tend to be food, blankets, sleeping bags and physical safety. Meeting these needs and assisting with claiming benefits may be a useful first step in getting a person to accept further help. Once a person is successfully engaged, then more complex physical health, mental health, alcohol, and accommodation problems can be tackled.

**Box 3.2:** Engaging with older rough sleepers on London's streets

*Nancy Rotem's second contribution describes the various ways in which the St Mungo's outreach team for older rough sleepers in London built rapport and trust, and illustrates well the long time that the process can take.*

Once an outreach worker has established a dialogue with a homeless person, it is important that the objective – to help him or her to access appropriate services – is made clear. It is essential, however, that the client dictates the speed at which he or she progresses from conversation to a service. Trust needs to be developed with the client and is promoted by regular contact at acceptable times, and by providing hot drinks, food, blankets and clothing. Remembering a client's likes and dislikes demonstrates attention to and recognition of his or her wants and needs. Contacts that begin with the offer of a cup of tea can, over time, lead to a careful assessment of a person's housing requirements.

As recognising a client's privacy is paramount to building trust, avoiding unnecessary questions is most important. An outreach worker needs to distinguish between essential and 'interesting' information. Through years on the streets and contact with countless outreach workers and service providers, many homeless people have been asked time and time again to divulge personal and often painful information. There is a fine line between directing a conversation to compile a personal history and pressing for non-essential information that creates a barrier and meets with resistance. As trust is established, much of the required information will be volunteered in general conversation. When unknown details are required later for a specific purpose such as a referral to a housing provider, these are more likely to be offered because their use will be clear.

This gradual approach to the development of rapport and to the creation of trust proved successful when our outreach team worked with a previously unknown elderly gentleman. He was sleeping rough, had mental health problems, was disheveled and had poor self-care. When approached he would neither talk to nor look at us. Despite his disregard, we introduced ourselves, explained our purpose, and then withdrew, leaving cigarettes beside him. We returned the following week, received a similar response but repeated our purpose, this time leaving a bottle of water and cigarettes. This pattern continued for some weeks and over time he accepted food and cigarettes directly from us. He still refused to engage in conversation, but had not discontinued contact by leaving his site. In time, a dialogue began: his responses were monosyllabic, the conversation was kept deliberately brief, but he gave his first name. He accepted blankets, which he had previously been unwilling to do, and agreed for his two thermos flasks to be taken away and filled with soup. Eventually he looked pleased to see us when we visited.

After many months, the gentleman began discussing his physical and mental health problems and housing options. A mental health worker from one of the *Homeless Mentally Ill Initiative* teams accompanied me when I visited him on the streets. With assistance and support, he agreed to begin a welfare benefit claim and to provide a personal history. This facilitated a referral into supported housing with input from social services. For this man and many other older rough sleepers, building trust is based largely on simple gestures, mannerisms, time and attention to detail. A consistent approach affords the client the stability necessary to recognise and challenge his or her situation.

## Developing care plans and linking people to services

Once a worker has successfully engaged with an older rough sleeper, the final stage is to link that person to temporary accommodation and other services. This requires several intermediate steps: assessing needs; formulating a care plan; and persuading the person to accept help by breaking down any resistance to receiving services. In large cities like London, several outreach teams work on the streets and this can lead to a homeless person receiving duplicated and confusing contacts. As Nancy Rotem makes abundantly clear in a further contribution, it is preferable for one outreach worker to be the 'key worker' who builds the relationship with the older person and co-ordinates his or her care:

> *Only this worker should initiate responses to the client's housing, social and welfare needs. This will minimise the risk of the client experiencing further 'outreach contact fatigue', and will prevent duplication of work and conflicting care plans. Other workers may monitor changes in the individual's health or behaviour and alert the key worker as necessary. Liaison between organisations and outreach teams is therefore essential.*

Assessing people's problems and needs while they are sleeping on the streets is difficult. They are living in exceptional and stressful circumstances and only preliminary assessments can be undertaken of their physical and mental health states and welfare needs. If a street homeless person is accommodated and has time to recover, good food, regular sleep and social contact, his or her physical appearance and mental state may improve and behaviour change (Snow *et al.* 1988; Koegel and Burnam, 1992). The high care needs of some older rough sleepers and their inability to manage personal care and daily living tasks may become apparent only when they move into accommodation.

Assessments on the streets should be carried out at each contact so that, over time, detailed information is gathered about a person's problems and needs, e.g. whether that person is well nourished, is managing to keep warm, has suitable clothing and shoes, has adequate bedding, and has a safe sleeping site. In effect, various risk assessments should be made, and if it is thought that the rough sleeper is in imminent danger, assistance should be summoned or an 'avoidance' intervention made. Careful observation will enable subtle signs of mental health problems to be detected, and engaging a person in conversation will often reveal signs such as delusions (Morse *et al.* 1996). Assessments also involve prioritising a person's long-term needs, and developing an understanding of what it will mean for that person to leave the streets. Decisions need to be made about the timing of help, as premature interventions may scare away clients.

From these assessments, individualised care plans with realistic goals should be developed collaboratively with the older person. Linking some clients to formal sources of help may be protracted, and may require increasing help and support on the streets. Nancy Rotem gives a further account in Box 3.3 of how innovative and creative ways need to be devised to gain their interest and persuade them to accept help. She and her colleagues escorted some to appointments with doctors, chiropodists and opticians. They made arrangements for an optician to see on the streets an elderly man who refused to attend a clinic. They distributed clean clothes to those with poor hygiene, cut a few clients' hair on the streets, and escorted some to day centres where they helped them bathe. As described in Box 3.4, some older rough sleepers need multiple services from several agencies. In such instances, care plans should be co-ordinated by the key worker, with regular reviews of the care plan and liaison between agencies.

**BOX 3.3:** DEVELOPING CARE PLANS AND LINKING OLDER ROUGH SLEEPERS

TO SERVICES

*Linking rough sleepers to services is the ultimate goal of outreach workers. Nancy Rotem describes how care plans can be designed with this objective in mind.*

Once trust has been established the outreach worker can begin to challenge a person's reluctance to accept help and his or her misconceptions about available services. An assessment of the person's welfare and housing needs can also be made, and an individualised care plan devised. Care plans must have realistic objectives and timetables, and be flexible enough to respond to changed circumstances. It may take many months (in some instances years) to achieve the objectives, but care plans must be drawn up without delay and be capable of implementation at a moment's notice.

It is unrealistic to expect an entrenched rough sleeper to accept an offer of accommodation immediately: the care plan should include intermediate steps. Personal hygiene, substance misuse, and primary and mental health care issues can be addressed in the interim. Referral to specialist workers within these fields is part of the key worker's role, and should be followed-up by introductions. It is important to be aware that there is a fine line between outreach work that encourages a person to accept help as a preliminary to leaving the streets and that which enables continued street living.

Once the client is amenable to a discussion about housing and a suitable option has been identified, showing photographs of the project can fuel their interest and give them the confidence to visit. Many older entrenched rough sleepers in London have experience only of 'cold-weather shelters' to which they have retreated during extreme winter weather. If the individual can be persuaded to visit a less chaotic hostel environment for a meal, and is then returned to his or her site without any pressure to move in, he or she is often thereafter more willing to consider accommodation. In order to make an accommodation visit less traumatic, it may be preceded by visits to a familiar local cafe for a cup of tea, and later by journeys to the same cafe in a vehicle. Visits to a day centre, preferably when the centre is 'closed', to use the bathing and laundry facilities are also advised. The client gradually becomes used to leaving his or her sleeping site with the worker, and in addition becomes accustomed to the mode of transport. Visits should initially be kept short, and lengthened progressively over time.

One client had been in contact with generic outreach workers for some time but could not break out of homelessness despite her desire to find accommodation. It was an approach by an older person's outreach worker that enabled her to overcome the ideas that were preventing her from accepting help, and which provided the support to make the change. Initially, the worker allocated considerable time for each contact (often up to two hours), giving time to establish trust and for her to feel that she was being listened to and understood. It became apparent that her inability to access accommodation stemmed from a resistance to claim benefits. At each contact she devised additional difficulties. By consistently challenging the way she saw the welfare system and presenting her with an alternative construction, the outreach worker eventually persuaded her to make a claim. This enabled referral into accommodation. Many older rough sleepers have low self-esteem, but the extended periods that the worker spends with a homeless person helps to re-establish that person's self-respect and willingness to engage.

**Box 3.4:** Collaborative first-stage work with homeless people – London case study

*Jeanette Reed, an accredited social worker, has been working in the field of homelessness, addiction and mental health for 20 years. Now employed by St Mungo's, her work focuses on older homeless people in touch with London's homeless services. In the following case study, she describes the collaborative response among several agencies to help an elderly woman who had been living on the city's streets for years.*

Ethel, a 67-year-old woman, had been sleeping rough for more than 20 years. Raised in Belfast, she described her childhood as 'a difficult time'. From the age of four, she and her siblings were raised by their father following the death of their mother. She left school in her early teens and worked in a local factory. She said, 'all us kids did it ... we brought money into the house for my father but he drank it'. She moved to London in her early twenties, married and shortly afterwards had two sons. Her marriage lasted just a few years, leaving Ethel to raise her sons single-handedly. 'I was working, cleaning, washing and raising my two sons; as they grew up, the police were always around as they were constantly in trouble.' During this period, she suffered from depression for which she received medication. She found it hard to cope and began drinking heavily. She received no support and eventually lost her job and home.

Several outreach workers in London knew Ethel, who over the years had occasionally used night shelters and the local day centre. She was frail and neglected her personal hygiene but had no apparent mental health problems. She sometimes drank heavily and behaved anti-socially, but also had periods of sobriety. When the Lancefield Street Centre opened in January 1997, Ethel was encouraged by other outreach workers and myself to use its drop-in centre. She agreed but stayed only a few nights before returning to the streets. She refused to return to Lancefield Street, and I took on the responsibility to support her on the streets until she could be persuaded to accept further help. I assessed Ethel's problems and needs, paying careful attention to her health and welfare. Ethel had not received Social Security benefits for years, and I helped her to make a claim. Because Ethel was unable to manage money, an appointee relationship was secured on her behalf, ensuring that she regularly received the payments.

Regular contact was maintained with Ethel on the streets, providing her with practical and emotional support, and her situation was continually reviewed. Over the months and with Ethel's agreement, a care plan was drawn up which involved other local agencies. The first goal was to persuade Ethel to leave the streets and become used to accommodation. Because she had remained in one locality for years and had become accustomed to that area, a local night shelter, a residential home for formerly homeless women, and a day centre agreed to help.

The night shelter manager agreed that Ethel could stay at the shelter each night. Because Ethel was reluctant to sleep in a room with other residents and could not manage stairs, and because her personal hygiene was very poor – she had head lice and suspected scabies which she refused to have treated – the staff allowed her to sleep on her own in a ground-floor room that was adapted for her use. This arrangement was acceptable to Ethel and allowed her to adjust to accommodation.

The night shelter closed during the day and it was therefore agreed with the day centre that Ethel would use it during the day. The night shelter staff accompanied Ethel each morning to the day centre. It closed at 2 p.m. and it was arranged for Ethel to stay at a women's residential home nearby each afternoon and until the night shelter opened. At the time, Ethel was physically unwell and was unable to find her way from the day centre to the home. A rota was therefore drawn up among a few agencies to take Ethel each day from the day centre to the residential home. This arrangement lasted a few weeks, worked relatively well, and enabled Ethel to stay indoors for long periods during the winter.

Ethel was referred to social services and assessed by a care manager (a social worker) who recognised that she was unable to live alone and needed care, and on these grounds secured funding for her move into the same residential home that she was accustomed to using. Ethel moved from the night shelter and stayed at the home for two months but there were problems: she refused to accept help for her personal hygiene and to have treatment for her head lice and suspected scabies. This may have been due to her lack of understanding of the consequences or to her stubbornness, but it jeopardised the hygiene of the home and the health of the residents and staff. It also meant that Ethel could not be encouraged to mix with the other residents. Each time the staff tried to address the personal hygiene issues, Ethel left the home and slept rough for a few nights. On these occasions the staff informed me and the agencies that work on the streets, and we traced her and persuaded her to return.

A meeting was held with Ethel, her care manager from social services, the manager of the home and me to discuss Ethel's hygiene. She was informed that her lice needed to be treated if she wished to remain in the home, as they were placing the other residents at risk. She refused treatment, left the home, and returned to the streets. Her bed was reserved for several weeks in the hope that we could encourage her to return. Contact was maintained with her on the streets and she was informed many times that she could go back to the home if she agreed to address her hygiene. She still refused and finally her place in the home had to be relinquished.

I will continue to support Ethel on the streets until she is ready to try again to settle. Her return to the streets was partly due to her inability to adjust to more settled living, and partly because pressure was put on her to address personal hygiene issues. A solution was not found that was satisfactory to Ethel and which ensured that the other residents and the staff were not put at risk. Several workers from statutory and voluntary services, and from generic and specialist teams, are collectively trying to help Ethel. It appears that with Ethel, as with many other long-term rough sleepers, a great deal has yet to be learned about their needs, how they can best be helped to leave the streets and adjust to more settled living, and how different skills and agencies should work together to achieve the best outcomes.

## The provision of outreach work for older rough sleepers

In several towns and cities in the UK and the USA, outreach teams are linked to voluntary organisations that provide a service to rough sleepers of all ages. However, generic services have their limitations. Their clients include young homeless people who tend to be visible, assertive and demanding: sometimes they dominate the service. Few teams provide a service specifically to older rough sleepers, who tend to be more isolated and difficult to engage. Street outreach workers in Richmond,

Virginia, noted that many older rough sleepers 'were likely to avoid contact with both service providers for the homeless and other homeless persons. Their extreme isolation, in a population that is generally fearful and withdrawn, required a longer and more persistent period of engagement and relationship building than was needed with most younger clients.' (Sheridan *et al.* 1993, p.414)

Wherever *older* people are known or suspected to sleep rough, a dedicated outreach team is required for at least a few hours of the week. In London two outreach workers have since 1997 been employed by St Mungo's and are fully occupied in work with older homeless people (Crane and Warnes, 1999). But in an area with few rough sleepers, although it will not be a sensible use of resources to do the same, there will probably be a strong case either for generic outreach workers to devote some hours each week to older and entrenched rough sleepers, or for some day centre or hostel staff hours to be dedicated to this work. *Project Rescue* in New York City and the *Oasis Senior Center for the Homeless*, Washington DC, are day centres for older homeless people (Boxes 3.5 and 3.6). At both, the staff have conducted outreach work to encourage older street people to use the facilities. The best arrangement depends on the extent of the problem and the availability of staff: street-work during the early mornings and the evenings has been found to be most productive. One advantage of having designated street-workers is that their time is not diverted by day centre or hostel work, but on the other hand if rough sleepers are introduced to day centre and hostel staff while on the streets, the relationship established can be an asset.

---

**BOX 3.5:** PROJECT RESCUE – A CENTRE FOR OLDER HOMELESS PEOPLE, THE BOWERY, NEW YORK CITY

*Following several research projects that demonstrated a need, Project Rescue in The Bowery, New York, was established in 1985 as a day centre for men and women aged 60 years and over. Its work is here described by Professor Carl Cohen of the Department of Psychiatry, Health Science Center at the State University of New York, Brooklyn. He has been involved with the centre for nine years as psychiatrist and researcher. His contribution describes the programme during 1985–92. The programme continues to assist older homeless persons, but during the past decade the population of the neighbourhood has changed and the programme now serves a large indigent but domiciled (often in overcrowded conditions) elderly Chinese population.*

The centre operates six days a week and is staffed by several case workers, a kitchen worker, a homebound worker, and volunteers. It is located one block from *The Bowery* and across the street from the *Bowery Residents' Committee (BRC)*. It offers diverse services to older homeless people although clients often require encouragement to use them. One of its more important functions is to provide a haven from the dangers of the streets and flophouses[1] and an alternative to taverns and drinking groups. Project Rescue teams foray daily into local parks, subways and flophouses, to provide information about services and to encourage people to attend. The outreach teams estimate that nearly 90 per cent of those contacted on the street eventually come to the project.

The centre serves nutritionally balanced breakfasts, lunches, and snacks to between 100 and 125 homeless older people six days a week. A part-time psychiatrist is available to clients through the BRC, which also operates a large alcohol rehabilitation programme. Project Rescue runs several groups for older people, such as an alcohol group, an art group, a gardening programme, and a writing group. A multidisciplinary health care team, sponsored by *Health Care for the Homeless*, visits the BRC two days a week, and a nurse comes one day a week. The staff help clients obtain government entitlements and, for those who are able, jobs or vocational training. They work closely with the flophouse managers to help homeless seniors obtain shelter and forestall their eviction. Incapacitated flophouse residents can receive daily meals from the centre.

Project Rescue is an informal multi-service agency offering free food, clothing, and a warm place to hang out. It attracts vulnerable people, including many who are mentally ill. Service provision is a three-tiered process of making contact, providing basic necessities such as food, clothing and showers, and providing specialised services including psychiatric evaluations and housing and health care referrals. An extensive evaluation after three years of 130 people who attended the centre indicated that a majority of both the mentally ill[2] and non-mentally ill clients had obtained temporary or permanent housing, improved their physical health, and secured entitlements. However, persons with mental illness received significantly fewer services than those without mental illness (3.2 vs 7.2) and had significantly fewer successful outcome categories (2.5 vs 2.9, based on a maximum of seven outcome categories). A multivariate analysis indicated that the type of presenting problem – either health or need for entitlements rather than requests for food – and the number of services received were significant predictors of successful outcome. The work at Project Rescue demonstrated that:

- a generic programme can attract and effect substantial improvements among homeless and marginally housed seniors, for both those with and without mental illness
- more and sustained encounters with staff are likely to lead to improvement in many outcomes
- no single demographic or health variable predicted service engagement or outcome. Rather, the type of presenting problem was a key determinant of engagement and outcome. It is likely that the type of problem reflected the motivation and desire for help as well as indicating the level of services required
- although Project Rescue clearly benefited seniors with mental illness, their poor outcomes compared to those of the clients without mental illness may have reflected a combination of their disordered thinking or motivation, the staff's inability to respond appropriately, an inadequate programme mix, and insufficient levels of staffing and community resources.

*Notes*
1. Flophouses are lodging houses with sleeping cubicles measuring 4 × 7 ft, separated by a low partition and wire-netting to the ceiling.
2. Mentally ill is defined as currently psychotic or having a history of psychiatric hospitalisation.

## Outreach practice

Through intensive case work over many months, it is possible to engage and build trust with some older long-term rough sleepers and persuade them to accept help. It is not, however, a straightforward process. Some can readily be engaged and persuaded to move into hostels, while for others it takes months and progress is slow. In London, the older rough sleepers who most readily accepted help tended to be those who had recently become homeless, while the most resistant to help were women and those with long histories of homelessness or mental health problems (Crane and Warnes, 1999). As shown with the case of Ethel (Box 3.4), rough sleepers may link to services and move into accommodation, but then return to the streets. Outreach workers need to have low caseloads. A ratio of 10–15 clients to one worker has proved effective when working with both hard-to-reach homeless people and those with severe mental illness who are equally difficult to engage (McMurray-Avila, 1997; Sainsbury Centre for Mental Health, 1998; Sheridan *et al.* 1993).

Being able to distribute beverages, food, clothing or blankets or take a person for breakfast, is a useful way of developing rapport. Funding should therefore allow for the required time and incidental expenses. Persuading an older rough sleeper to accept help is the first step towards settled living, and an outreach team's efforts are 'only as successful as [its] ability to offer immediate access to the services desired by the client' (Williams, 1992, p.25). In every district there needs to be a range of services to which older rough sleepers can be referred, and there should be at least one facility, such as a 24-hour shelter or hostel, to which a client who agrees to accept help can immediately be taken. Some older entrenched rough sleepers will accept help only when their physical health deteriorates or after some other crisis. When this happens, it is important that the outreach worker is able to respond promptly and that the person is immediately linked to services.

### Required skills of the staff

To work effectively with older rough sleepers, outreach workers need to be able to work patiently, persistently, creatively and flexibly, and have the skills to engage people who are withdrawn or display disturbed behaviour. They need to be able to carry out assessments on the streets, to use tact and discretion in offering advice and in timing interventions, and to have a good knowledge of the local homeless, mental illness, substance abuse, and specialist services and their admissions procedures. In Richmond, Virginia, it was found that the outreach staff who worked most effectively with clients were particularly skilled in: (i) communication, listening and the ability to be empathetic; (ii) building trusting and collaborative relationships; and (iii) thorough monitoring and making prompt interventions in individually sensitive ways (Sheridan *et al.* 1993). The observance of health and safety rules and adherence to good practice guides are vital in outreach work. Staff should work in pairs and take no unnecessary risks like entering structurally unsafe buildings, and there should be reporting systems before and after street-work. Mobile telephones are valuable, while a vehicle enables a team to cover a large area and is useful for taking clients to view hostels, to day centres for showers, and to clinics and hospitals.

In England and Wales, the Department for the Environment, Transport and the Regions (DETR) has developed performance indicators and targets for outreach workers which focus on the number of rough sleepers who move into hostels (DoE *et al.* 1996; Randall and Brown, 1995). But work with entrenched rough sleepers is time-consuming, progress is made in very small steps, and other changes in a person's situation are made before a housing outcome is achieved. Useful work is not measured entirely by the housing outcomes. A similar problem was noted in a review of care for people with severe mental illness who are hard to engage: 'services are driven to look at short-term outcomes in order to show that they are ... valuable and effective ... success should perhaps be measured in terms of achieving initial engagement and gaining acceptance of what may seem to be fairly low-level interventions' (Sainsbury Centre for Mental Health, 1998, p.33).

## Responding to older rough sleepers in severe neglect who resist services

A dilemma for an outreach worker is how to respond to an older rough sleeper who is in a neglected state, or has severe mental or physical health problems, but refuses to access services and help. As psychological or physical health problems intensify, some rough sleepers become more depressed and demoralised or psychotic, and more neglectful of their personal care. They become less amenable to formal services, from which they are often excluded because of poor hygiene and self-neglect. Some die on the streets, others are admitted to hospital only when illnesses have become so severe that they require urgent treatment. On occasion it may be imperative for their survival to help clients against their wishes. As noted by the US *Federal Task Force on Homelessness and Severe Mental Illness* (1992, pp.36–37), 'street outreach must include the capacity for an emergency response [and] back-up medical and psychiatric support is essential to ensure access to involuntary treatment when it is needed'.

The need for imposed treatment would be less if health care for homeless people was more widely available and provided in more imaginative ways. In several American cities, mobile health units provide medical care to rough sleepers (Stinson *et al.* 1998). The vans are staffed by doctors and nurses who conduct health assessments and medical screening, dispense medication, administer basic treatments such as dressings, and transport clients to hospitals and clinics. A similar scheme used to operate twice weekly in inner London. It served many isolated homeless people, some of whom agreed to attend a medical centre (staffed by the same medical team). It acted as 'a link between those sleeping rough and formal medical services' (Ramsden *et al.* 1989, p.374). The service was discontinued through 'lack of use'. In London and other large British cities, mental health and alcohol teams work on the streets, but not primary health care or social services teams. They could draw on the trust that homeless service organisations' outreach workers have built. In New York City, the *Homeless Emergency Liaison Project* runs a mobile outreach unit which provides crisis medical and psychiatric services to rough sleepers who are mentally ill, resistant to services, and at risk of physical harm (Marcos *et al.* 1990). It does take people to hospital against their will, and some have been aged 50 years or more. Two years after being hospitalised, 298 cases were followed-up and 55 per cent were living in the community or in institutions. Such involuntary measures are essential if a person is seriously disabled with mental illness and needs urgent care and attention (Lamb, 1990; Susser *et al.* 1990).

## Day centres and drop-in centres

There are day and drop-in centres for homeless people in many European and American cities. In Britain, only seven existed before 1970 but they have multiplied rapidly and there are now more than 250 used by approximately 10,000 people on an average day (Cooper, 1997; Llewellin and Murdoch, 1996). Their premises, objectives and services are exceptionally variable: some began and continue as soup kitchens in church crypts, provide only food, clothing and showers, and depend heavily on volunteers; others have salaried and trained staff and deliver rehabilitation, group therapies, health care and resettlement programmes. Some have good links with statutory and voluntary agencies, while others are proudly independent; some open for long hours including at weekends, while many open for just a few hours only on weekdays. The majority do not allow drinking on the premises, and most provide a service for people of all ages. Many have an 'open door' policy and are used by homeless people, formerly homeless people, and vulnerable people who have never been homeless. A rising number of users in many day centres has brought overcrowding and increased violence (Waters, 1992).

A principal goal of day centres and drop-in centres should be to link rough sleepers to services and specialist help. In Britain and the USA, however, many older rough sleepers do not use these centres (Cohen and Sokolovsky, 1989; Crane, 1999; Doolin, 1986; Douglass *et al.* 1988). Some are unaware of the facilities, some are confused and unable to appreciate the help, and some are paranoid and delusional about the centres and the staff. Others refuse to use them, as they dislike the crowded conditions and fear violence and intimidation from younger users. Some who do patronise the services are unassertive, undemanding, do not make known their needs, and their presence tends to be overshadowed by those of younger users who are often more demanding. In a crowded centre, older users may obtain food or drinks and leave without being engaged by the staff.

To counter these problems, day centres specifically for older homeless people have been established in a few US cities. The *Cardinal Medeiros Center* in Boston, Massachusetts, opened in 1984 for people aged 45 years and over, and provides food, company, case work, access to medical and psychiatric care, substance abuse programmes, social services, and housing advice to around 150 people each day. Similar help and support is provided at Project Rescue in New York City, and at the Oasis Senior Center for the Homeless in Washington DC (Boxes 3.5 and 3.6).

---

**BOX 3.6:** THE OASIS SENIOR CENTER FOR THE HOMELESS, WASHINGTON DC

*Robin Vazquez, Director of the Oasis Senior Center for the Homeless, Washington DC describes in this contribution some special dimensions of the homelessness problem in Washington DC – the high number of very disadvantaged and excluded older people in the city, the sensitiveness of the problem in the nation's capital, and the relative availability of intervention funds. She has been the Director of the centre for 14 years.*

The Oasis Senior Center for the Homeless was established in 1987 by the *Greater Washington Urban League,* with funding from the *District of Columbia Office on Aging,* to provide services for older homeless people in the city. It is obligated by federal law to serve any senior who is aged 55 years or over. We received a dispensation from the City Council to lower the age limit from 60 to 55 in our second year. We have few rules but refuse services to anyone who is intoxicated to the extent that their behaviour is inappropriate.

The centre is open eight hours a day and five days a week. Its services include a nutritious midday meal that guarantees one-third of the recommended daily allowance for older persons, recreation and socialisation activities, mental health counselling, health promotion activities, social services counselling and referrals, day trips, seminars by outside speakers, and a safe haven where older homeless people can relax among their peers. Its staff comprise a director, a mental health counsellor, a recreation co-ordinator and a food services co-ordinator, with the addition this fiscal year of a fitness co-ordinator.

It is used by 30–40 people on an average day. When it first opened, the staff conducted outreach work on the streets to encourage older homeless people to attend. Close to 2000 clients, mostly men, have sought services at the Oasis since its inception. Their presenting problems usually include untreated mental illness or substance abuse. Many of the veterans were on active duty during the Korean and Second World Wars, and there seems to be a link between homelessness and combat. Many of our clients were born into poverty and have little education, and many have been in prison. Further, most earned low wages as labourers during interrupted working years, so they have small social security stipends and no supplementary savings. As the Washington metropolitan area has little very low-cost housing, its 'single room occupancy' hotels have almost disappeared and no other local programme that serves older people can assist those aged under 60 years, helping the clients find affordable housing is one of our greatest challenges.

The programme has existed long enough to show a rather disturbing recidivism rate among the clients who move to independent housing. Many formerly homeless individuals return to the shelters and our programme after only a few years. Sobriety is also short-lived. Having become thoroughly acclimated to the streets, the regime of the shelters, and homelessness's freedom from responsibilities, many are unprepared for the demands of a tenancy, e.g. paying the rent on time. They allow friends to squat and create problems for themselves that are resolved only when they are evicted. Mental illness complicates this process. The provision of alternative housing is indicated.

## The requirements of day and drop-in centre services

In Britain, the evolution of day centres and drop-in centres has been 'subject to individual whims, quirks and funding availability', and generally has paid little attention to supply and need (Waters, 1992, p.7). There are 37 listed day centres for single homeless people in London, and a further 46 drop-in centres (Jacobs *et al.* 1998). They exist in small towns like Boston in Lincolnshire, but there are few in Wales and, whereas Lowestoft, Gloucester and Stevenage have recognised problems of homelessness, they have no day centres (Pleace, 1998). Their accessibility to clients is a function of the location and opening hours. The majority open only during the day and there is little provision for rough sleepers in the evening. An exception is in Glasgow, where *The Wayside Club Day Centre* and the *Glasgow City Mission* are open until late evening.

The effectiveness of day and drop-in centres in encouraging homeless people to leave the streets is associated with the objectives, skills and resources of the management, staff and volunteers. A *National Homeless Alliance* study in 1996 of 51 British day centres found that those which helped their users most effectively 'devoted time and energy to building effective links with other voluntary and community organisations, and with local statutory services' (Cooper, 1997, p.47). Some, however, relied on inexperienced staff and volunteers, struggled to cope with a huge workload, and operated in isolation with few links to statutory and voluntary services. The attractiveness or 'acceptability' of day and drop-in centres to older homeless people depends upon the facilities and the attitudes and behaviour of staff and other users. Although the benefits of centres dedicated to older homeless people have been demonstrated in the USA there are few examples in Britain, although several centres for young homeless people exist (Jacobs *et al.* 1998). Four London day centres that found that older homeless people were staying away have introduced dedicated workers and sessions once or twice a week (*St Martin-in-the-Fields Social Care Unit, North Lambeth, The Passage* and *St Giles*) (Crane and Warnes, 1997b). The staff's role is to engage with isolated older users, carry out preliminary assessments of their needs, and advocate for services on their behalf. If one of these centres targeted *older* rough sleepers, more intensive work could be carried out.

It is important to find ways to persuade older rough sleepers to attend day centres. The evidence from Project Rescue and the Oasis Senior Center for the Homeless shows that outreach work on the streets is useful. Another approach is to provide centres that are easily accessible and place few demands on their users: these attract rough sleepers who are unsettled, mentally ill, distrustful, and unable to tolerate the protocol of formal services. Described in the USA as 'community living rooms' or 'street centers', they provide a safe haven until users are ready to accept more structured help and support (Pollio, 1990; Segal and Baumohl, 1985). An example is *Peter's Place* for homeless people in New York City aged 60 years and over, which is open 24 hours and 365 days a year. Up to 120 people use the centre daily, and between 20 and 50 at night. Besides offering continuous shelter and support, 24-hour centres are a great help to older homeless people who have memory difficulties or disturbed thoughts or do not follow conventional quotidian routines.

In large towns it may be practical to have a separate facility, but in small towns such units could be attached to hostels. The 24-hour drop-in facility at the Lancefield Street Centre functioned as a refuge, a 'transit lounge' and a half-way house, enabling wary users to become accustomed to the hostel residents and the idea of further help (Crane and Warnes, 1999). Some users moved between the streets and the drop-in centre many times until they were ready to accept a hostel place. It also functioned as an assessment centre in which the staff became acquainted with the users and their needs, and linked them to medical, psychiatric and alcohol services, and to the welfare benefit system.

## Conclusions

This chapter has described several ways in which older rough sleepers can be given 'first-stage' help. As the contributions from various projects in different countries have explicitly argued, outreach and drop-in services specifically for older homeless people are needed. The reasons are that many in this group tend to be withdrawn, have multiple and chronic problems, and require extended interventions on the streets before they will enter temporary accommodation. The evidence from a number of pioneering projects shows also, however, that when homeless service staff engage with even the most damaged and most entrenched older rough sleepers in dedicated, determined and flexible ways, at least some will eventually accept help, leave the streets, and begin to adopt less arduous, healthier and more conventional ways of living.

The basic principles of good practice in providing 'first-stage' help to the most resistant homeless people are becoming clear. The first, expressed formally, is to carry out *early diagnosis and interventions*. Evidence is accumulating that those who have only recently become homeless are on average easier to help than those who have been living rough for years. In this context it should be noted that approximately every other person aged 50 years or more found sleeping rough in London has *not* had a lifetime history of street living, but has became homeless following a relatively recent estrangement, bereavement, redundancy, illness or mental trauma (Crane, 1999). One way to reduce the prevalence of homelessness is to identify newly incident cases more promptly and to shorten the duration of first-time homelessness.

The submitted contributions and other reports from projects in the field show considerable agreement on the approaches that service delivery should follow, which can be summarised as *individualised, holistic and progressive*. To provide help to single homeless people who have become entrenched in the lifestyle and have multiple problems, repeated and extended contact is required and several kinds of specialist help – particularly emergency shelters, mental health services and direct-access accommodation. Unconventional ways of working are sometimes required to engage with people who have been detached from services and support for many years, as well as exceptional quotients of empathy, patience and persistence.

The second element of a rational service network is the provision of a full spectrum of the required services from street outreach, through specialist health care and addiction programmes, to a variety of special needs housing schemes (to be described more fully in later chapters). Working intensively with homeless people on the streets or in day centres without adequate next-stage placement opportunities will lead to disappointment and broken promises and is counter-productive. First-stage workers must have a good knowledge of the follow-on options where more intensive and structured support towards long-term goals can be organised, and most of all they must have the co-operation of and good standing with the hostel, health and housing providers.

A third principle can be extracted from the experience of recent projects – the importance of *rationally organised case working*. This refers to the preconditions for the effectiveness of help and support: that it is based on a careful assessment of the individual's background, problems and needs; that the interventions are progressive and staged; and that there is an expectation and tolerance of 'backsliding'. The implication is that a programme of help for a client should be managed by one worker, or in other words that best practice requires a *key worker*, not least to co-ordinate the inputs of several agencies. If this approach is not followed the client can become confused and successive interventions can be wasteful and conflicting, and on occasion may cause more harm than good.

Presently *rationally organised case working* is rare, and in all but a few cities the availability of help and its fitness for purpose is a lottery, not least because dedicated services for older and entrenched rough sleepers are still scarce, but also for organisational reasons. The homeless services are non-traditional components of the health and welfare professional complex and have an uneasy and contested existence at the margins of mainstream housing, medical, mental health and social services. At various times each of the traditional sectors has developed services for single homeless people, but none has taken them as their own. Specialist housing, primary care, mental health and social work agencies have all experimented with specialist provision, but all show ambivalence and reserve about their role. The consequence is a multitude of debilitating inter-professional and inter-agency ills: lack of understanding and ignorance of each other's ways of working, workloads and practical constraints; misunderstanding and distrust of each other's goals; and professional suspicion, disdain and prejudice. The organisational and policy implications of these conditions will be elaborated in the final chapter, but the pertinent consequence for client–worker practice is that the *key worker role* is ill-defined, open-ended, unaccredited and unprofessionalised. It is performed largely by exceptionally dedicated and subtle people with a huge commitment to their tasks, but for the most part they have to work from first principles and receive neither guidance from good practice models nor systematic training and managerial support. Moreover, their low standing in the traditional professional and organisational hierachies reduces their ability to secure the co-operation of specialist providers. Sometimes they are forced to make interventions beyond the boundaries of their competence, annoying accredited professionals in those fields, and sometimes the lack of support means that they have to take personal risks that we should neither expect nor allow.

An issue has surfaced in this chapter that will echo to the last page of this book, namely the timeless but also newly topical policy and practice debate around *empathetic support or coercion*. Its contemporary expression is in prescriptions about the appropriate *level of tolerance* of rough sleeping, and as applied to first-stage services the argument is whether they should be available only to people who enter residential hostels or also provided on the streets and in day centres (Casey, 1999; Ghosh, 1999). Distributing food, bedding and clothing on the streets can of course sustain the street lifestyle and discourage rough sleepers from entering temporary accommodation, thereby avoiding contact with assertive helping services. As this chapter's project reports have amply demonstrated, however, the problem is that a minority of single homeless people, among them many of the most disadvantaged and damaged, are alienated from residential hostels and in a few cases all mainstream services. The most extreme individuals will not go to day centres for food, and choose rather to scavenge in litter-bins or go without. An outreach worker who demonstrates interest and concern can engage them, while mobile food runs attract some older isolated rough sleepers, and therefore create opportunities to contact some who are otherwise unknown to services. Street-work and purposeful, individualised interventions in day centres are therefore vital as the first step in the progressive engagement with some rough sleepers, and for some are a precondition for helping them make positive changes in their lives.

Chapter 4

# First-stage accommodation and meeting basic needs

Temporary (first-stage) accommodation is required for homeless people until their needs can be assessed and their problems stabilised, and until they can be helped to settle in long-term housing. Over the last three decades, the available temporary accommodation has changed markedly in Britain, the USA and Australia. Large old hostels and night shelters have gradually been replaced by small hostels with improved standards and amenities, though many traditional hostels and much poor standard accommodation remain. This chapter outlines the basic needs of *older* homeless people when they enter temporary hostels, describes innovative schemes for the group in the UK and the USA, and discusses the main requirements of such accommodation for older homeless people. There are contributions from a nurse practitioner who works in homeless hostels, and from the manager of the *Lancefield Street Centre*.

## The basic needs of older homeless people

When older homeless people first move into a hostel, some require minimal help besides shelter, warmth and food until long-term housing can be arranged, while others need intensive help and support with everyday tasks. Many have mental health, alcohol abuse, and psychological problems, but until their more basic needs are met, they are unlikely to accept help with these deep-seated problems.

### Help with settling in accommodation

Some older homeless people have been on the streets for years and are very unsettled when they first move into a hostel. Entering a hostel disrupts their daily street routine, and breaks social ties with other street people. Moreover, most rough sleepers have no responsibilities except daily survival. Moving into a hostel implies simple responsibilities, such as claiming Housing Benefit, attending to personal hygiene, and behaving in a way that it is acceptable to the staff and other residents. While on the streets, the days are occupied in finding food, shelter, warmth, clothing and bedding, whereas in a hostel these necessities are provided and there is more 'free' time. A resident may then reflect more on why he or she became homeless and his or her current circumstances, and this may increase unsettledness and unease.

The first task for the hostel staff with new residents is to persuade them to stay. New residents need to feel safe and comfortable and to have their anxieties about accepting accommodation and other residents allayed. They should not initially be questioned at length about their histories, and hostel staff should distinguish between the information that is essential on admission, e.g. current health problems, and that which informs rehabilitation and resettlement and can be gathered over time. Several hostel staff who work with entrenched rough sleepers point out that some clients must be allowed to return to the streets at will and return to the hostel, for their adjustment to accommodation is protracted and slow. Once a new entrant has been encouraged to stay, then help can be given with nutrition, income, personal hygiene, and physical health problems. The needs of older rough sleepers when they first move into a hostel and the diversity of the work is described by Andy Shields, the manager of the former Lancefield Street Centre (Box 4.1).

**BOX 4.1:** THE BASIC NEEDS OF OLDER HOMELESS PEOPLE IN FIRST-STAGE

ACCOMMODATION

*Andy Shields was the manager of the Lancefield Street Centre in inner west London throughout its 23 months of operation by St Mungo's. He describes the needs of older rough sleepers when they first move into a hostel. He has worked with homeless people for 10 years, and is now the Capacity Building Project Co-ordinator for St Mungo's.*

Although older homeless people are no less diverse than others, they have common basic needs, i.e. shelter, warmth, and food. They are often wary of accessing services for, although they may not enjoy being on the streets, many find that environment less threatening or worrying than an institution. They often report fear – of intimidation, extortion and violence from younger homeless people – as being a major reason for remaining on the streets and keeping away from hostels. It was for such reasons that *St Mungo's* developed and managed the outreach, hostel and 'drop-in' services for older rough sleepers at the Lancefield Street Centre.

From my experience of working with St Mungo's, older rough sleepers must feel in control of the first move into accommodation. It is therefore desirable to allow people to try a service in an unconditional way, minimising the initial paperwork and changes to welfare benefit claims. The Lancefield Street Centre allowed the clients to try the service without making a commitment. When an older homeless person first arrives at a hostel, it is very important for the staff to concentrate on the welcome: simple things such as introducing a new resident to his or her fellow residents are beneficial. There should be regular contact with the client in the first 24 hours to check that he or she does not feel lost and uncomfortable.

An assessment should be made of the individual's immediate needs. As well as the staff's observations, information can be obtained from the resident and from referring agencies such as outreach workers. Identified needs have to be dealt with sequentially, starting with the most pressing. Warmth, food, clean clothing, a bath and sleep diminish a wide range of problems and should usually be provided before looking at issues of physical health, mental health, or alcohol and drug abuse. It is important to help residents sort out their benefits once they have settled, as the interruption in the payment of benefits can cause considerable stress. The staff therefore require expertise in this area.

Older homeless people often present in a very poor state of health and frequently exhibit challenging behaviour. A care-planning approach is best used to help residents begin to overcome their needs; the action priorities have to be agreed with the resident. Flexibility is required – what may appear to be a pressing need to the staff may not seem so pressing to a resident. It is crucial that first-stage projects have access to a GP, preferably conducting a regular surgery at the project. A nurse is also a useful resource for projects for older rough sleepers. Good access to local detoxification facilities and regular contact with alcohol workers are essential, as is input from the local mental health team. Regular contact with the local social services department is also of great importance as many older rough sleepers have personal care needs that cannot be met in a first-stage hostel; their need is for a community care assessment with a view to being moved into a registered care home.

**Key lesson**
While all the noted services are needed in a hostel for older homeless people, the experience of St Mungo's is that key factors in holding a new resident are that the welcome is friendly and that the first 24 hours is unobtrusively but resolutely attentive and well-designed. A cheerful welcome, checking back, introductions to other residents, and tackling the person's immediate practical needs, all help the new resident see an immediate improvement in his or her quality-of-life. This reduces apprehension about moving from the street. If the first 24 hours is well-managed, there is a significant reduction in the number of people abandoning the accommodation.

## Encouraging better nutrition

While sleeping rough, many older homeless people have very poor diets. Some scavenge in litter-bins or eat sandwiches at day centres and never have hot meals; some heavy drinkers do not eat for days. It is therefore important that good eating habits are encouraged and nutritional assessments made. Three nutritionally balanced meals (or two meals and a snack) should be available daily. In 1996, only 16 per cent of 49 direct-access hostels in London provided three meals a day (Harrison, 1996). Some hostels have self-catering facilities and provide no meals. This is unlikely to be adequate for people with a long history of homelessness unless staff give daily help with shopping and preparing food. For some with severe mental health or alcohol-related problems, such support is essential. Many older homeless people need prompting to eat, and some with memory problems have to be reminded when meals are being served and taken to the dining room. Others are heavy drinkers, have poor appetites, and need persuasion to eat. In some hostels, the staff buy meal-tickets for the week when a vulnerable resident receives his or her weekly benefits, to ensure that he or she does not spend all the money on alcohol.

## Help with claiming welfare benefits and budgeting

Many older rough sleepers claim no benefit entitlements and have no income. Some have allowed their claims to lapse while they have been on the streets, but others have not claimed benefits for years and are unaware of their entitlements. Some are illiterate, have learning difficulties or mental health problems, or have formerly relied on partners or relatives to deal with their finances. Others are unable or unmotivated to find benefit offices, arrange appointments, and complete complex forms. In the UK, most homeless people can draw Social Security Housing Benefit (HB) and when they enter a hostel this pays the rent. HB thereby becomes essential revenue for hostels.

To make a claim for benefits, people need proof of identity. The Westminster Benefits Office, for example, requires a valid passport, driving licence or pension book to establish identity, but accepts any two of the following: a birth certificate, bank statement, utilities bill, or a benefits book if the client's address on the book had been changed by the Department of Social Security (Crane and Warnes, 1999). Few older rough sleepers possess such documents. For those with no proof of identity, the hostel staff will be required to obtain birth certificates and occasionally letters from social workers. At the Lancefield Street Centre, several hostel residents came from travelling families in Ireland and their births had never been registered. Sorting out the residents' HB alone involved approximately 1.5 project workers' overall time throughout the Centre's life, and it sometimes took months for claims to be processed.

Many older homeless people have poor budgeting skills. Some have lost these skills while sleeping rough but can re-learn: others are unable to manage because of mental health problems, illiteracy or heavy drinking. Some require budget agreements to be drawn up by which their money is distributed day-by-day, and some need escorting to a post office to draw pensions, to help them open savings accounts, and to make deposits. These forms of support require the staff to act as 'guardians' and carry out tasks that are normally undertaken by family and close friends.

## Assistance with personal hygiene

Some older homeless people, and a majority of those who have habitually slept rough, have poor personal hygiene and need repeated prompting or assistance to wash, bathe and change their clothes. Some have scabies or head and body lice. Neglected hygiene is associated with mental health problems, heavy drinking and low morale. It also arises when people have no access to washing facilities and lose habits which for most of us are unconscious. Incontinence of urine or faeces is also relatively prevalent for three reasons: some who have slept rough for years are accustomed to urinating or defaecating in public places and have lost conventional toileting skills; for some, incontinence is related to physical health problems; and for others it is associated with a lack of motivation or inability to use the toilet when drunk.

Persistently poor hygiene renders a hostel not only odorous and undesirable to current and potential residents, but also a health risk through infestation and contagion. At the same time, some residents may leave and return to the streets if pressure is placed on them to bathe or change their clothes (as with the lady described in Box 3.5). Broaching the topic requires tact, sensitivity, and discretion, e.g. the best time to ask a resident to bathe is *not* when they are extremely unsettled or intoxicated. Some hostels develop simple hygiene rules for the residents, such as expecting them to wash and dress before breakfast and having a day fixed every week for each one to clean his or her room and launder his or her clothes. By involving all residents, no individual feels targeted. In the UK, local authority social services departments sometimes fund care assistants to provide daily personal care in hostels to residents who are incontinent.

## Managing physical health problems

Many older homeless people have physical health problems, and it is important that *all* residents see a doctor or nurse and have a medical check-up soon after admission to a hostel. Commonly the problems are not apparent. At the Lancefield Street Centre in London, some residents had tuberculosis, jaundice and ascites from liver and renal failure, carcinomas, severe anaemia, and fractured limbs, while others had less critical problems such as diabetes, arthritis and bronchitis. Some with severe problems had not sought medical care while sleeping rough. Two men collapsed only a few hours after admission, were taken to hospital, and died shortly after. Another man had a carcinoma of the mouth, while another had cataracts in both eyes and was nearly blind. Several other residents required medication but had not seen a doctor for some time and had no prescriptions.

In hostels that accommodate older homeless people, the incidence of physical health problems will remain high and there will be a frequent need for medical care and treatment. Characteristically, the residents' multiple health problems are complicated through chronicity and poor management. Treating the illnesses is problematic because many residents are unable to provide a medical history and have little insight into their health problems. Physicians therefore have great difficulty in determining past illnesses, investigations and treatments. Many residents require extensive hospital investigations but, if they stay in a hostel only briefly, it is difficult to arrange out-patient appointments and provide continuity of care, and the work becomes crisis management rather than controlling illnesses.

Many older homeless people who enter hostels require continuing supervision with their health care. Some are unmotivated or unable to self-medicate and the staff will have to remind them to take medication. Some are reluctant to accept medical care and treatment and will not report their illnesses. The staff become responsible for detecting problems, arranging doctors' appointments, escorting the residents to medical and hospital appointments, and ensuring that they comply with treatment. In the London boroughs of Lambeth, Southwark and Lewisham, a joint primary health care team works with homeless people in hostels and day centres (Crane and Warnes, 1997b). Its nurses have found that they have to escort confused and forgetful older clients to hospitals and clinics to keep appointments, and that others have low self-esteem and fear being stigmatised by health care workers.

In Britain, health care is provided to hostel residents in various ways. Some hostels have a nurse practitioner on site and a designated GP visits and accepts responsibility for all the residents. Peripatetic teams of nurses and doctors provide sessions at some hostels, but at others no health care professional works on site and medical care is provided at a local health centre or general practice. Having a nurse practitioner in a hostel team brings several benefits, as the nurse can: (i) detect symptoms of physical and mental illness, and refer the residents for medical care using her or his knowledge of hospital and community practices; (ii) ensure that medication and other treatments are complied with, and provide care to those residents who initially refuse but later are persuaded to accept treatment; (iii) build a relationship with those residents who are fearful or suspicious of accepting medical help, and escort them to appointments; (iv) promote health and hygiene in the hostel; and (v) explain to the hostel staff about the signs and symptoms of illnesses, treatment programmes, and behaviours associated with conditions such as dementia.

At St Pancras Way, a hostel in London for heavy drinkers managed by St Mungo's, a nurse practitioner works two days a week and a GP provides a session fortnightly. Box 4.2 describes the hostel nurse role. With the nurse in-house, the residents rarely need to use the GP's surgery except in an emergency. Likewise, in London and Edinburgh hostels which have access to adequate primary health care services, the residents rarely use inappropriately the accident and emergency departments of local hospitals (North *et al.* 1996; Powell, 1987).

**Box 4.2:** The role of a nurse practitioner, St Mungo's hostels, London

*Noreen Kerrigan has worked for the last nine years as a clinical nurse specialist in St Mungo's Endell Street and St Pancras Way hostels for homeless men in central London. She has specialist training in nutrition, counselling, stress management, substance misuse, depression, and the management of tuberculosis: all are essential to enable her to provide a safe and professional service. Being employed by a charitable housing association (not a health provider), her account of her work with a general medical practitioner in a hostel for heavy drinkers is of great interest.*

Homeless people have multiple health care needs. I work with male hostel residents who have tuberculosis, respiratory problems, liver and pancreatic disorders, gastric ulcers, vitamin deficiencies, malnutrition, alcoholism, and mental illness. Some are depressed and isolated, have learning difficulties, and have injuries and fractures from road traffic accidents and falls. In particular my work involves addressing physical trauma that is directly related to alcohol addiction and the chaotic lifestyle of homeless men. The work is invaluable to homeless people who do not access statutory services, and it prevents them using hospital emergency departments inappropriately. Photographic profiles are kept as a way of assessing and recording changes. One elderly resident was found shortly after admission to be emaciated, and to have active tuberculosis, a fractured shoulder and cataracts on both eyes. He also had learning difficulties and a speech defect. I help the residents to register with general practitioners; conduct general health care assessments including checks on blood pressure, weight and urine; promote health education among the residents; and counsel those who are distressed or want to discuss their problems. I advocate for health care services and other help on behalf of the residents, and liaise with day centres, GPs, and hospital wards and accident & emergency and out-patient departments. An important part of my work is regular liaison with outside agencies and a visiting GP for specialist services.

**The benefits of an on-site nurse in hostels**
Many homeless people do not access mainstream health care services. Their common experience is to have been referred here, there and everywhere; and to meet different professionals at each appointment; and to be treated with disdain and to come away feeling 'less than human'. They tell me, `I prefer *no* service if the option is a conveyor belt approach, or lengthy waiting lists which I may never survive'.

The presence of a sensitive professional with multiple skills who intervenes promptly redresses some of these problems. I work flexibly and holistically. It is virtually impossible to deliver a meaningful service to a homeless person by treating one problem such as alcohol abuse, tuberculosis, or mental illness in isolation from others. The homeless person is often unaware that TB is associated with the lifestyle, and many alcoholics do not understand that excess alcohol consumption damages the liver. My work accordingly extends well beyond the traditional 'nurse' role, for effectively I have a 'caseload' or 'patient list' that involves working consistently with the residents, building relationships and rapport, and offering support and counselling if required.

The aim and effect is to improve their well-being and self-esteem. For example, if a resident comes to see me with a fractured shoulder, I am also in a position to give advice and support about his tuberculosis, cataracts and substance misuse. If someone is sad, lonely, angry, or confused about his situation, I use my counselling and stress management skills to help him.

The main difficulty is to overcome the residents' chaotic lifestyles, e.g. ensuring they attend follow-up appointments with TB clinics, out-patient departments, physiotherapists, chiropodists, diabetic clinics, and psychiatric departments. More often than not, this is achieved by sitting down with the resident, listening to him, and finding out why he repeatedly fails to keep his appointments. Usually there is a reasonable explanation, but it takes time to surface. Giving the resident time to explain empowers him and raises confidence. He begins to trust me, and will then explain the real reasons. Some are depressed in the mornings and stay in bed. Some have started to drink heavily again: one explained that it was his baby's first birthday. Some are hiding from other residents to whom they owe money. Homeless people, like the rest of us, experience all sorts of trying incidents that trigger all sorts of reactions and lead to a sense of being unable to cope.

**Lessons learned**
Many lessons have been learned during the nine years' work. I regularly review the work I do and modify its objectives and intended outcomes. This ensures that a safe service with high professional standards is delivered to the residents. The service seeks constantly to improve existing practice and to promote health education and awareness in our hostels. Small, consistent interventions lead to positive and sustained changes in homeless people's lives. It is important that homeless people receive help and support, not only with physical health problems but also with the unresolved psychological problems that lead to anger, guilt, pain, regret, isolation and low self-worth.

## The provision of temporary accommodation for older homeless people

In many cities, most hostels and shelters accommodate homeless people of all ages, but it has been found in Britain and the USA that many older people will not use the facilities for fear of violence and intimidation from younger residents (Coalition for the Homeless, 1984; Crane and Warnes, 1997b). A few service providers in Europe and elsewhere have therefore developed hostels specifically for older homeless people. The following are examples of schemes in the UK and the USA.

### The Zambesi Project, Birmingham

The *Zambesi Project* opened in 1988 and is managed by *Focus Housing Group*. It provides temporary accommodation in several houses to older homeless men over the age of 45 years. Three adjacent Victorian houses have been converted into one large home which accommodates 16 men in single rooms. It has a sitting room and a dining room, and there is a separate dining room for the 12 residents of a second house opposite. The residents include men with long histories of homelessness and unsettledness, and a few who have recently become homeless after being evicted or leaving private rented accommodation. Both houses have staff on duty 24 hours. The management and support staff work at both, but each has its own night staff and cleaners. An internal telephone links the two houses and a resident can summon help at any time. In 1998, a third house nearby became a rehabilitation house for 18 older homeless men (see Box 5.3).

## The Dwelling Place, Washington DC

Some organisations have developed small-unit temporary accommodation for older homeless people. One example is *The Dwelling Place* in Washington DC, which was established by *SOME (So Others Might Eat)* with a grant from the *District of Columbia Office on Aging* in 1986. It accommodates seven people aged 60 years or more in single rooms and targets those who have been abused, neglected, exploited or displaced. It is the only shelter in the city specifically for older homeless people. Some residents have mental health problems and have been evicted for rent default, some are armed service veterans who have failed to claim appropriate benefits, and some have been financially abused by their sons or daughters who have drug problems. The shelter is staffed 24 hours, the accommodation and its services are free, and three meals a day are provided. By providing rent-free accommodation, time is created to sort out the residents' Social Security benefits. When these are received, the residents are required to open a bank account and to save for eventual rehousing.

The residents stay on average for three months, during which time they receive help with claiming benefits, medical and psychiatric problems, and housing. The staff work with the residents to restore independent living skills. All residents must wash and dress before breakfast and all are involved in a weekly cooking group. The shelter is on the first-floor of a large house, and on the ground-floor there is a day centre managed by SOME for local elderly housed people and which the residents are encouraged to use. It offers exercise groups, health education programmes, trips to the shops and the cinema, discussion groups, and dancing and sewing classes. Once the residents are rehoused, the staff provide follow-up support for one year. A reunion for all former residents is held each summer.

## The role of an assessment flat, Trafford Housing Aid, Greater Manchester

In some rural areas, small towns and suburbs there may be only a few homeless older people and there will be insufficient need even for a temporary hostel with a handful of beds. An interesting facility for such a situation, which provides a stepping stone from the streets, has been developed in Partington, a suburb of Manchester, by *Trafford Housing Aid* in conjunction with the Borough of Trafford's housing and social services departments. It is an 'assessment flat' in *Cecil Walker House*, a sheltered housing scheme for homeless people aged 60 years or more. The flat is furnished and has a fully equipped kitchen and bathroom. The resident receives support from the warden on site, is registered temporarily with the local GP, and can participate in the social activities arranged for the other tenants. If needed, meals can be provided by an adjacent residential home and home-help can be arranged.

The scheme started in 1995 and has since accommodated 11 older homeless people. Some became homeless following domestic violence and marital breakdown, and some when they returned to England after living abroad. Following their move in, assessments are carried out of their housing and social care needs, and after a few weeks or months most have been rehoused in sheltered accommodation or independent tenancies with mobile (visiting) wardens, while two moved to residential homes. Difficulties have occasionally arisen because the resident older homeless person has had mental health problems or been a heavy drinker. For this type of scheme to work, the collaboration of housing aid, warden services and social services is crucial, and weekly review meetings of all agencies are held (Iqbal, 1998).

## The requirements of first-stage accommodation for older homeless people

Temporary accommodation for older homeless people has to be attractive and accessible as well as fit-for-purpose. It has to meet the needs of both those who have been on the streets for years without service contact, and those who have recently become homeless. From the early 1980s, the accepted practice was that temporary accommodation should be in units for no more than 30 people in single rooms (Consortium Joint Planning Group, 1981). Yet in many cities, hostels and shelters that accommodate more than 100 people continue to operate, and several have dormitories or shared bedrooms which offer no privacy (Crockett *et al.* 1997; Harrison, 1996). At the Lancefield Street Centre, most residents had single bedrooms but there were four double rooms – these were unpopular and most of their occupiers requested single rooms. Some preferred to remain on the streets or in the drop-in centre until a single room became available.

The majority of older homeless people are men and they therefore predominate in mixed-sex hostels, while many older homeless women sleep rough and refuse to enter accommodation. This may be associated with their high prevalence of mental health problems, but part of the explanation must be their fear and reluctance to enter accommodation dominated by men. Some women become homeless following physical abuse by partners and many are physically frail. Those hostels that have been developed specifically for women tend disproportionately to attract adolescents and young adults. In Leeds, the *Over-55s Accommodation Project* lost contact with some older homeless women who had abandoned all-age women's hostels. Older homeless women are an exceptionally ill-served group and, to gain their trust, there is a strong case for experimental dedicated hostels.

## Promoting access and admissions

Hostels for homeless people should be readily accessible but in practice many impose conditions that exclude the most disorganised and disconnected people – among them many older rough sleepers. Some hostels will not accept homeless people who have no proof of identity and are not receiving benefits (Harrison, 1996), but many older rough sleepers claim no benefit entitlements, have no income, and no proof of identity. In 1994, the habitual residence test for the receipt of many Social Security benefits was introduced. To qualify for income support or housing benefit, a person must have a 'settled intention' to reside in this country and have been 'habitually resident' for 'an appreciable period of time' – the terms are not clearly defined (George *et al.* 1997). Having lived abroad for years, some older people return to Britain following a divorce, the death of their spouse, losing their home, or a business collapse. While in the majority of cases people have relatives or friends who will help them, a minority have no contacts. Most returnees fail the habitual residence test, are denied benefits and therefore cannot enter most hostels. The only free accommodation is in night shelters with restricted services (in contrast to most large US cities where more 'emergency' hostels and shelters are free).

Until recently it was rare for hostels to admit known heavy drinkers or to allow the residents to drink alcohol on the premises. Many maintain these rules, but a few recognise that prohibiting alcohol consumption excludes a very needy group of people who need to be accommodated as a preliminary to receiving help in reducing their alcohol consumption. A few hostels therefore admit heavy drinkers and allow alcohol to be consumed in either bedrooms or designated areas, e.g. 'wet' lounges. The rationale is well explained by Portland Jones, the manager of the Zambesi Project of Focus Housing Group in Birmingham:

> *At the Zambesi Project, the emphasis is on good quality accommodation, safe and secure, with food provided. This is a 'wet' house – there is no requirement to give up alcohol before being allowed into the project. We take a non-judgmental approach. We assist someone to a more settled way of life and provide safety, security and food. If the person then wishes, their alcohol problem can be tackled.*

## Fit-for-purpose accommodation

Hostels for older homeless people self-evidently should meet the residents' needs. People require 24-hour shelter and security, yet some night shelters and hostels require residents of all ages to leave the premises in the early morning and not to return until the evening. Those without work have no option but to linger on the streets or move around soup kitchens and day centres all day. This is tiring and demoralising, provokes physical ill health, and increases vulnerability and feelings of unsettledness. It also means that the opportunities to refer or link reluctant residents to non-emergency health and social services are reduced. In 1995, *Crisis* developed an 'Open House' programme in five English towns to provide emergency accommodation for rough sleepers. At four of the shelters, the residents had to leave the premises during the day. A two-year evaluation found that the projects had little success in referring the residents to housing, social and health services (Pleace, 1998).

Many older homeless people have slept rough or moved around hostels for years and it will take time for them to settle and for their problems to be addressed. Temporary accommodation provides stability and enables protracted help. Yet some hostels and shelters impose limits on the number of nights people can stay, while others operate for just a few months. In Britain, cold-weather shelters open only from December to March each winter to encourage people to leave the streets. In 1998–99, only 10 per cent of the 1223 users of London's shelters were rehoused in long-term accommodation on departure; others moved to hostels, other temporary settings, or returned to the streets (CRASH, 1999).

It takes time for projects to identify effective ways of working, to become known, to fit into a spectrum of local provision, and to develop the required range of contacts with specialist alcoholism and mental health services and with diverse general and special needs housing providers. A stable and continuing relationship with a general medical practitioner is also a precondition for the effective management of many of the chronic disorders of later life, e.g. diabetes and arthritis. Continuity fosters successful resettlements, which have a demonstration effect on others. At the Lancefield Street Centre, the proportion of older homeless residents who were rehoused increased from 5 per cent during its first six months (January–June 1997) to 43 per cent during July–December 1998. There was a corresponding decrease (from 79 to 39 per cent) in those who were evicted, left of their own accord, or returned to the streets (Crane and Warnes, 1999). This suggests that the project settled over time and that the staff developed their within-hostel working practice and their relationships with housing providers and other agencies.

The needs of entrenched rough sleepers tend to differ from those who have recently become homeless. The former are more likely to be unsettled, have multiple and severe health and behaviour problems, and to require intensive help and support. In Britain, a few hostels target the group and employ staff who are competent to manage difficult behaviour. In many hostels, however, the staff are untrained to cope with people who are mentally ill or heavy drinkers, and so operate exclusion policies (Ham, 1996; Harrison, 1996). Older men who have been evicted from hostels because of disruptive behaviour associated with heavy drinking and mental illness then move from hostel to hostel or sleep rough, without settling and receiving consistent care and treatment (Crane and Warnes, 1997a; 1999). Many older homeless people have physical health problems that restrict their mobility and require ground-floor bedrooms or accommodation with a lift. At the Lancefield Street Centre, there were no ground-floor bedrooms and there was no lift. As a result, some residents with poor mobility and respiratory problems had difficulties with the stairs, and a few potential users could not be admitted.

## Required skills of the staff

The residents of hostels dedicated to long-term rough sleepers and older homeless people will have a higher prevalence of mental health problems, deficient personal hygiene and heavy alcohol consumption than is normal in temporary hostels. As the care and support needs approach the level of a nursing home for mentally ill older people, the staff–resident ratio and the range of skills should reflect these high demands. The precise staff profile will depend partly on the targeted client group and partly on the availability and responsiveness of the local specialist and intensive support services. At the 'Open House' shelters developed by Crisis, all projects had low staff levels, two were reliant on volunteers and, apart from the project managers, most of the staff 'were not trained in medical care, support or in other fields': with 16-hour shifts being worked, stress was an issue (Pleace, 1998, p.53).

To work effectively with older homeless people who are withdrawn or unsettled, have poor social skills or disturbed behaviour, and mental health or alcohol problems, support and help needs to be persistent and sensitive. Hostel staff also need to be willing to provide high levels of personal care, and at least one of their number must understand the welfare benefits system and be able to negotiate claims. Some hostels allocate to each resident a key worker who is responsible for ensuring that basic needs are met, that more detailed assessments are undertaken, and that care plans are drawn up (described in Chapter 5). *Shroton Street Hostel* in London is managed by *Thames Reach* and provides temporary accommodation for 13 residents who have slept rough for years. The hostel has separated the functions of a 'move-in co-ordinator' (who is responsible for urgent tasks, e.g. sorting out welfare benefits and helping the resident to register with a GP) from 'assessment and the orchestration of care', which is passed on to a key worker after two weeks.

## Conclusions

This chapter has reviewed the necessary and desirable ways by which first-stage accommodation can meet the basic needs of its residents when they first move into the accommodation. Several innovative types of temporary accommodation have been described, from a medium-sized hostel to a single flat. All have similar aims and objectives: to provide shelter, food and warmth; to assess needs and provide or arrange more intensive help and support; and to prepare clients for rehousing in appropriate long-term accommodation. Temporary accommodation for older homeless people has to be financially viable, responsive to local needs and effective. In London, New York City and other large cities, there are many older homeless people and medium-sized projects may be justified. In small towns and rural areas, however, the need may be for just a small project, or even a single flat. The provided accommodation has also to reflect the needs of its intended clients. It is unlikely, for example, that an older entrenched rough sleeper with severe mental health or alcohol problems will manage in accommodation that is not staffed 24 hours and expects the individual to cook and look after him- or herself. On the other hand, such accommodation may be beneficial to a person who is newly homeless and has no mental health or behaviour problems.

# Chapter 5

# Specialist help and the rehabilitation of daily living skills

This chapter discusses the specialist help with deep-seated problems that many older homeless people require before they are ready to be resettled in permanent housing. The first section considers the assessment of needs and the development of individualised care plans; the second discusses the roles of structured activities and counselling in addressing low morale and poor motivation. The next two sections focus on services for heavy drinkers and those with mental health problems, while the last examines rehabilitation programmes and the ways in which older homeless people's daily living skills can be improved. There is a fine line between skills rehabilitation and resettlement preparation, and the two are usually merged. Nonetheless, a detailed review of resettlement preparation is held over to the next chapter.

There is immense experience among mental health and social work professionals of case working with mentally ill people and those with alcohol and hallucinogenic drug addiction problems. Similarly, the nursing and other staff of registered nursing (and care) homes have immense experience of helping older people with restricted abilities in the 'activities of daily living' (eating, dressing, bathing, toileting). We do not claim a comprehensive knowledge of innovations and best practice in these fields. The chapter attempts rather to focus on the key issues associated with mental illness, alcohol addiction and rehabilitation, and the first principles of providing the required help and care. The priorities are to recognise the problems and assess needs. Quite clearly the problems are sometimes insuperable and the best course is to refer on to specialists or to more appropriate accommodation. These eventualities, and the prime mission to help the residents prepare for long-term housing, puts a premium on the quality of a project's collaboration and networks with specialist and housing providers. We are aware of several projects that have shown exceptional flair in working with specialist agencies (and there will be others), and include contributions from managers of such projects in Cardiff, Birmingham and Boston, Massachusetts, and from a development worker who initiated structured activities in London hostels.

## Assessing needs and individual case work

Once an older homeless person has become accustomed to a hostel's staff and regime and his or her urgent needs have been addressed, then assessments of deep-seated problems can begin. There are at least three overlapping purposes of assessment:

(a)   To identify problems with a view to immediate amelioration, correction, treatment or control on three dimensions:

*physical:* needs for medical treatment, nutritional supplements, better clothing and improved personal hygiene

*mental state and emotional:* whether treatment for diagnosed psychiatric disorders is being received, and the probability of undiagnosed psychiatric and affective disorders

*material:* current income and savings, and social security income entitlements

(b)   To make risk assessments, which are critically important for a minority of homeless people. Such assessments require information about the first two dimensions of (a) but have different emphases: on the risks to the survival and health of the client, and the risks to other residents and staff that might arise from the client's physical and mental state and behaviour problems.

(c)   To assess the individual's cognitive deficits, mental state and behaviour problems that are impediments to independent (or shared and supported) living. The topics overlap with those of (b) but the focus is on the medium- and long-term prospects of amelioration or termination of the problems, and on building the individual's skills and confidence to the level required in long-term accommodation. Some of these assessments are estimates of the probability of the success (or failure) of rehabilitation or resettlement – confusingly they are sometimes described as 'risk assessments'.

The range of information that potentially needs to be collected is therefore immense. The following short list adds brief statements (in italics) of the purposes for which the information is collected:

- background, family and social contacts, housing and work histories, and the circumstances that preceded and contributed to homelessness, *to provide indications of the underlying reasons for becoming homeless and the person's principal grievances, anxieties and fears*
- mental health state and morale, and whether there are indications of depression, mental illness, unresolved stresses, or memory difficulties, *to judge (as above) whether diagnosed psychiatric disorders are receiving treatment and the likelihood of undiagnosed psychiatric and affective disorders*
- drinking habits, drug addiction and problematic behaviour, *to judge whether behaviour problems are recognised and being tackled*
- recent accommodation, including durations of stays in hostels and reasons for leaving, and the person's experiences of resettlement, *to provide indications of the attitudes and behaviours that may be critical to the success of resettlement*

- daily-living and personal-care skills, literacy and social skills, and attitudes about and motivation to live more independently and in long-term accommodation, *to judge the preparedness and ability of the person to live without the structure of support and absence of responsibilities of a temporary hostel*.

Given its scale and complexity, assessment must be a sequenced process and cannot be completed at a single interview. Some older homeless people have severe mental health problems or memory difficulties and are unable to give accurate details, while others are reluctant to provide information or deliberately mislead, e.g. by using several names and identifiers. Wherever possible, information should be obtained from other agencies who have had contacts with the individual. Needs, abilities and attitudes will change as problems are resolved or ameliorated, and therefore assessment should continue throughout a person's stay in a hostel.

## Assessment instruments and practice

The quality of the assessments of homeless people varies greatly among service providers. Some hostels have detailed assessment forms that the staff complete, following which a care plan is designed and implemented, but many collect minimal information apart from age, next of kin, and benefit entitlements and receipts. Such routine procedures are unexceptional and the instruments employed rarely become known outside the organisation.

Multi-dimensional and risk assessments require more sophisticated instruments which should have been tested and validated, procedures that in themselves generate a greater awareness of both their strengths and weaknesses and their potential value to others. The *Sainsbury Centre for Mental Health* in London identified five categories of information for assessing the risks associated with mental health problems: (i) an individual's history; (ii) their self-reports; (iii) observations of their behaviour and mental state; (iv) discrepancies between self-reports and observations; and (v) a psychologist's opinion or report (Warner *et al.* 1997). *Thames Reach* in London, which accommodates people with long histories of homelessness and mental health and substance abuse problems, has developed a risk assessment form which covers four main topics: (i) risks associated with behaviour, including violence, self-harm, harassment, 'accidental' dangerous behaviour linked to substance misuse, and annoying behaviour which is likely to provoke attack; (ii) physical health, and risks associated with mobility, weight, personal hygiene and substance misuse; (iii) mental health, and the risks around associated medication and behaviour; and (iv) the person's management of his or her accommodation, including the risks deriving from appliances, hoarding paper in the room, and the kitchen. For each category, the staff identify risks and dangers, who is at risk, and how the staff and the resident can lessen the risk.

## Individual case work and action plans

Once an older homeless person's needs have been assessed, individualised care plans (sometimes referred to as action plans) should be designed which state how the person's problems will be tackled and by whom. It is important that achievable and realistic goals are set, and that the plans are prepared with the full co-operation and understanding of the client. The care plans should initially focus on simple tasks such as personal hygiene, but once confidence, self-esteem and motivation have increased, they may progress to more complex issues, such as alcohol abuse. Care plans need to be reviewed regularly and revised according to changing circumstances.

The value of making a 'key worker' responsible for a client's care has been recognised in clinical psychiatry for many years (Watts and Bennett, 1991). The key worker assesses the needs of a client, develops an individualised package of care, liaises with service providers, co-ordinates the person's care, and reviews the care package and adjusts the help accordingly. Key workers have gradually been introduced into homeless services and are now designated by many hostels, although in 1996 31 per cent of London's direct-access hostels did not operate a scheme (Harrison, 1996).

An advantage of key workers, particularly in hostels with more than a few residents, is that they can ensure that isolated, withdrawn and undemanding residents receive care and attention. Given sufficient time, the key workers are able to build relationships and trust with clients who are suspicious or difficult to engage. They also ensure that programmes of care are implemented, that identified needs are met, and that services are not duplicated. Box 5.1 describes the adoption of individualised social work practice into the distinctive *Grangetown Preparation for the Rehabilitation of Elderly People (PREP)* project in Cardiff.

---

**BOX 5.1:** THE IMPORTANCE OF INDIVIDUALISED ASSESSMENTS AND CARE

PLANS FOR OLDER HOMELESS PEOPLE

*Janice Bell, manager of the Preparation for the Rehabilitation of Elderly People (PREP) projects for the United Welsh Housing Association, Cardiff, describes the importance of developing individualised assessment and rehabilitation programmes for older homeless people.*

The first of the three PREP projects (184) opened in Grangetown, a district of Cardiff, in April 1992. It occupies a terraced (in the USA, row) house, which provides an innovative form of temporary supported housing for four people aged at least 40 years. Its objective was to help formerly homeless people learn living skills to the point that they can enter independent housing and avoid high-cost residential care. The residents receive intensive care and support 365 days a year, but in the evening the staff leave the premises. Thus dependency is not fostered, and the clients become accustomed to being independent.

The three staff at the project are on call 24 hours a day, and hours are worked flexibly depending on the clients' needs.

The 1993 community care provisions of the NHS Act 1990 gave local authorities the responsibility for carrying out assessments of dependent older people and purchasing their care. Earmarked transitional community care grants were available for some years. Many of the clients are referred to PREP by Cardiff Social Services through these arrangements. PREP 184 is a registered care home for people who are dependent through old age, drug and alcohol dependency, mental ill health, mental handicap, and physical disability. Although the other two projects (PREP 197 and PREP 40) are not registered care homes, they use similar referral and assessment processes and the same individual approach to care and support.

Admission to any PREP project is initiated by a completed referral form which covers personal details, housing history, the client's experience and self-assessments of daily living skills, legal and advocacy issues, health and welfare, socialisation, voluntary work, hobbies and knowledge of the local area. The form is usually completed by a professional social worker in conjunction with the applicant. Its submission is followed by an informal visit and interview. The visit is a crucial opportunity for the staff to gain knowledge of the client's experiences, support needs, and motivation – a commitment to becoming independent and regaining skills and confidence is essential. Whether PREP is appropriate is decided jointly by its staff, the client and the other professionals involved. As the first visits are invariably stressful, the clients are given the opportunity to revisit and to become familiar with the project and the tenants before they move in. These visits allow the staff to build up a picture of an individual's capability and hopes, and makes the transition as comfortable as possible for all concerned.

For the residents who move into PREP 184, social workers draw up an initial care plan. This is the foundation for a more detailed care and support plan, which we find can be drawn up only when a client has been resident for at least one month. By this time, the close working and trust that develops from living and working in small friendly environments enables the resident to express openly their aspirations and expectations. We emphasise that goals may change and are not set in stone. Many of our clients have similar aspirations in spite of their varying support needs, but their individuality is never forgotten. It is important to help the clients achieve their goals in their own individual ways and at their own pace. The aspiration to live independently is not a precondition of admission to a PREP scheme. Even a thorough assessment does not always make clear if this will be possible, and they are not under any pressure to adopt this goal. What is right for one person may not suit another. Some clients find the thought of living alone terrifying but are able to cope with permanent shared housing, family care or even permanent residential care.

We have found that it is important to take one step at a time, rather than to stress the long-term goal. A resident's success in small steps, e.g. looking at accommodation options (rather than applying for flats), or making a successful food shopping trip (rather than preparing meals), builds up their confidence. Care plans therefore need to be flexible and reviewed at regular intervals. As all three projects are small, interaction among the residents is supportive. One person's strengths can be another's fear, but by seeing a fellow client enjoy shopping or catching public transport, strength and confidence may be gained. Similarly, seeing someone use his or her time constructively in voluntary work may inspire another to a similar activity.

PREP is renowned for having successfully moved around 70 per cent of its clients into their own flats in the community. The consensus was that this would never be possible with some residents, as with Tom, who was 87 years old. He had been evicted from his lodgings while in hospital and, although alternative accommodation was obviously needed, some professionals and friends assumed that because of his age he should move into residential care. Fortunately Tom's assertive request, and right to choose, was noted by a newly qualified social worker who explored other options. Tom moved into PREP a few weeks later and worked towards achieving his own flat. It was an extraordinarily touching moment some months later when Tom opened the door to his new flat and said, `I can't believe this flat is mine and that I can do whatever I like here'. Until that moment Tom had never had a place of his own and had never lived alone, but this is what he chose to do. Tom died in early 1999 aged 91. If he had not been listened to, his life may have ended earlier. His experience shows how professional attitudes and preconceptions if unchecked can override a person's right to choose.

From the early years of PREP, the staff have grown to appreciate the dangers of their own assumptions, values and prejudices, and the value of questioning them. Our policies and procedures have developed from our experience and guide us in new cases, but are not allowed to curtail our clients' options or to limit who we will help. PREP has become effective because we observe thoroughly and respond patiently to individual needs. Our guiding principle is to help clients achieve their own goals in their own way.

## Addressing low morale and poor motivation

Many older homeless people become demoralised, depressed and have low self-esteem. For some, these negative states preceded and contributed to them becoming homeless. They felt desperate when their wives died or their marriages broke down, and drank heavily, made suicidal gestures, severed links with their family and children, and abandoned their homes. In doing this, they gave up roles, responsibilities and interests. Feelings of desperation, depression and hopelessness continued once they were homeless, so many never tried to secure accommodation and settle down. They had no goals or interests, made no plans, isolated themselves, and did nothing except seek food and a place to sleep at night. Even when older homeless people move into temporary accommodation, many remain poorly motivated, demoralised, depressed and apathetic. Most need help if they are to raise their morale, build self-esteem, and regain interests. This section describes two ways in which services are trying to address these problems: by organising activities that build confidence and interests; and by providing counselling to those who are depressed and distressed as a result of past traumas and losses.

## Structured activities

The value of structured activity for people with mental illness has been well documented, and has led to the development of sheltered workshops and clubhouses to help people achieve or regain confidence, skills, concentration, self-worth and self-satisfaction (Beard *et al.* 1982; Gloag, 1985; Sainsbury Centre for Mental Health, 1998). Among services for homeless people in Britain, however, there has been little attention to the value of organised activities, and only a minority of hostels provide them. Most do little more than provide a TV, a pool table and board games.

In a few hostels and day centres, however, considerable thought has been given to the promotion and support of activities. The *Church Army Day Centre* for homeless women in London has a varied programme including computer classes, aromatherapy and massage, reflexology, make-up and manicure sessions, hairdressing, a video club, and groups for sewing, singing, woodwork, gardening, literacy, cooking, arts and textiles. A few organisations have developed training schemes for homeless people to build self-confidence and self-sufficiency, and to teach work skills. *St Mungo's* in London runs a 'skills training, employment and placement service' (STEPS), which has a vocational guidance team, a job club to help people find work, a training centre with a careers library and computer facilities, a woodwork shop, and a carpet cleaning business scheme.

At the *Lancefield Street Centre*, London, some older homeless people were keen to participate in activities, but many were poorly motivated and showed little interest. The staff arranged twice-weekly bingo sessions, pool competitions, quizzes, discussion groups and barbecues. Outings were popular, but arts and crafts groups had less appeal. The Centre had a large garden and some residents planted flowers and vegetables and maintained the garden. Shortage of time and other duties prevented the hostel staff arranging regular activities. An occupational therapy student, who had experience of working with homeless people, on a two-week placement facilitated discussion groups and quizzes. Because she worked every day, these activities became routine and she was able to persuade some heavy drinkers to participate.

Structured activities can raise morale, motivation and self-esteem but it is a slow process. It requires flexible and creative ways of working, and the activities need to be held regularly and frequently so that the clients become accustomed to them. At the Church Army Day Centre, many users had mental health problems and were apathetic, and several strategies were tried to encourage participation. A discussion group was held first in a group room, then in the main reception area, and then integrated with an informal group, before it gained the women's interest. It was noticed that once interest was achieved, interest and motivation usually persisted. Structured activities in hostels not only help to boost morale among the residents and the staff, they can also subdue a volatile atmosphere, as the contribution of Michael Keen of St Mungo's makes clear (Box 5.2).

---

## BOX 5.2: THE `MAKE-IT-WORK' SCHEME, ST MUNGO'S, LONDON

*Michael Keen set up the Make-It-Work scheme in a St Mungo's cold-weather shelter in London. He explains the value of the scheme for hostel residents and the staff.*

The *Make-It-Work* scheme (MIW) was conceived in the winter of 1993–94 in a St Mungo's cold-weather shelter in central London. Although the residents had accommodation, food, health care and were prepared for resettlement, I was concerned that there was nothing for them to do during the day, as was then characteristic of most hostels for homeless people. Inactivity seemed to me to be a leading cause of the lack of motivation and the volatility and frustration that was prevalent in these projects. I was also concerned by both the custodial nature of such projects and the disempowerment of the residents and their effect on client–staff relationships. There is time and 'space' in hostels for meaningful interaction between people, and for opening up what one might call people's 'secular spirituality' – their ability to understand their existence and to come to terms with their past, their future, their suffering, and their hopes.

This agenda is crucial to understanding MIW. The project was never just about 'things to keep people busy', or 'making things to brighten up the walls'. Nor was it just about developing self-confidence, or getting people to realise that they could do something (rather than nothing), or enabling some people to take a first faltering step towards employment - although these goals are important elements. At the root of MIW was a belief that if human beings are to begin to understand themselves then they need to 'unfold the text' of who they are. Furthermore, for the vast majority of the people in homeless shelters and hostels, this 'unfolding' needs to be a practical activity: doing and making, creating and building, mending and 'messing about with things'.

I set up the first pilot MIW venture in early January 1995 in a winter shelter. It ran on a shoe-string and operated for 2.5 months. Activities included computer basics, creative writing, music and drama, sport, arts, screen printing, crafts, discussion groups, and entertainment. Volunteers and a few paid tutors provided the tuition. By June 1995, art by MIW participants figured in an exhibition held in London's Building Trades Centre to mark *National Sleep-Out Week*, and displays about MIW featured at other events. By the following winter, the volunteers had grown to ten, including former clients and others with experience of homelessness, as well as people with expertise and qualifications in handicrafts, media, education and computers. This team went on to develop with the residents experimental photographic reproductions, graffiti murals, taped radio programmes, a newspaper, making things for sale, and music making.

By 1996 the benefits of MIW on hostel life were becoming recognised. In St Mungo's 1996–97 cold-weather shelter, much of the day-to-day running of MIW passed to the residents (who had an office, telephone, and working rules). The shelter manager attributed the remarkably low level of tension and violence, as well as the generally high level of morale, to the presence of MIW in the shelter's life. Meanwhile, in a small long-stay mental health project, within a week of installing a low-grade computer, eight of the ten residents were using it, and two went on to conventional computer training courses. In 1997, MIW was designated by St Mungo's as one of its priority projects and, in 1998, it obtained major charitable funding to support a team of five full-time workers who were tasked to introduce MIW into all its major hostels.

Being in a hostel for homeless people is often a difficult experience for the staff as well as the residents - and MIW can help both groups. For the residents, the main benefit is that it enables them to strengthen their own identities: 'this is who we are, people who do things and make things'. Displays of activity, pursued with self-confidence can make a strong impression on new residents. The message that is conveyed is: `We belong here, we are doing things, and what we do is legitimate. Join us'.

## Counselling

Before becoming homeless, many older people experienced stresses, losses and traumas such as widowhood, divorce, the death of a child or a parent, physical abuse from a partner or a parent, or disturbing war experiences. Some experienced multiple stresses in a short time. Many become distressed and tearful when talking about the past. Their distress and unsettled behaviour suggest that they have never come to terms with the traumas. It is well documented that some people react atypically to events that require significant readjustment such as widowhood (Parkes, 1986; Stroebe and Stroebe, 1983) and divorce (Duck, 1992; Argyle and Henderson, 1985). Particularly affected are men with weak family and social support networks. Active armed service is recognised to be particularly stressful, and can lead to emotional problems, survivor guilt, disaffiliation, alienation, and heavy drinking (Crocq, 1997; Elder and Clipp, 1988; Laufer, 1988).

In the USA, counselling has been found to be of value to some homeless people who have experienced emotional problems (McMurray-Avila, 1997). Its primary objective is to maintain or enhance a person's quality-of-life, by helping people who are suffering from the impact of traumatic experiences to find ways of resolving or containing their problems, and to look at the present and future with optimism and hope. It must be undertaken by trained workers, who are able to listen and build trust with a person, empathise, interpret reactions, challenge difficulties, and facilitate decision-making. If delivered by untrained people, it can be ineffectual or worse (Hunt, 1997; Scrutton, 1997).

In the UK, counselling is little used with older people and rarely with older homeless people. It may however be of benefit to some who have been distressed by losses and failures. In London, a counsellor works with older homeless people who drink heavily. She has found that some have serious bereavement adjustment and psychological problems, and heavy drinking is a symptom of their distress. From her experiences, it is not beneficial to work with a person while he or she is sleeping rough, as the person's attention is focused on finding food and shelter. She begins to counsel in hostels and continues when a person is rehoused. In hostels, people have more time to think about themselves and their lives. Many react positively and are committed to counselling, and are grateful for help. Through counselling, some have made changes in their lives, developed confidence and self-worth, and have been helped to reduce or stabilise heavy drinking. She works closely with the residents' key workers to develop behaviour and support programmes, which the hostel staff then implement.

Few hostel care staff are trained counsellors, but they can identify and refer onward older residents who may benefit from such help, and support and encourage those who are being counselled. Specialist counsellors are available in some areas to which older homeless people can be referred. In Leeds, for example, a few older women who became homeless after being physically abused by their husbands were referred to counselling programmes for domestic violence.

## Addressing alcohol problems

### The needs of heavy drinkers and service requirements

Many of today's older homeless people, particularly the men, are heavy drinkers. For some the habit dates back to their early adult years in the armed forces, the merchant navy, or as labourers on building sites. Some drink most days, but others binge heavily for a few weeks, abstain for a few weeks, and then resume. Older homeless heavy drinkers tend to have multiple inter-related problems and are often difficult to manage and help. Severe physical health problems, low morale, poor motivation, and behaviour problems are common. Long-standing alcohol abuse, poor nutrition, and self-neglect tends to produce progressive physical and mental health problems and poor functioning. Some heavy drinkers require more intensive help and supervision with personal care and other tasks than can be provided in first-stage general needs hostels. At the Lancefield Street Centre (where residents were allowed to drink in a 'wet lounge' and in their bedrooms), many heavy drinkers neglected their personal hygiene, were incontinent, and needed prompting or assistance with self-care, bathing, and managing finances. The group spent most of the day consuming alcohol. Some fell while heavily intoxicated, sustained injuries, and required hospital treatment. Those who were heavy drinkers were more likely than abstainers to report depression, sleep disturbances, poor appetite, loneliness and pessimism (Crane and Warnes, 1999). Similar problems were reported at a shelter in Seattle that accommodated older male heavy drinkers (Elias and Innui, 1993).

In the USA, the *National Institute on Alcohol Abuse and Alcoholism* has, with funding from the *Stewart B. McKinney Homeless Assistance Act*, supported 23 community demonstration projects since 1988 to identify effective approaches for providing substance abuse treatment to homeless people. Based on the collective experience of all projects, the general lessons were that: (i) treatment programmes should not only focus on addiction problems but also address the material needs of homeless people, particularly for housing, income support and employment; (ii) flexible, low-demand interventions are accepted by clients who will not commit to more extended care, and who can gradually be brought into more intensive treatment programmes; (iii) long-term comprehensive services are needed for some people, and (iv) clients should be matched to appropriate treatment services by the severity of substance use and the level of social isolation (McMurray-Avila, 1997).

## Services for heavy drinkers

Although the association between homelessness and heavy drinking is near universal, paradoxically it produces notably inconsistent proscriptive and helping responses from society and by services. In Britain it used to be rare for hostels to accept homeless people who abused alcohol – many had strict 'no alcohol' policies, searched residents each time they came in, and evicted those who had been drinking or had alcohol in their possession. Since the late 1970s attitudes have begun to change. Detoxification units, counselling services, rehabilitation programmes, and supported transitional accommodation have been established to help people withdraw and abstain from alcohol. A few organisations offer targeted help for homeless people with alcohol problems, including *Equinox* (formerly the *Drinks Crisis Centre*) in London, and the *Homeless Alcoholics Recovery Project (HARP)* in Birmingham. Equinox has outreach workers who contact drinkers on the streets, a detoxification unit to help people withdraw from alcohol, an assessment centre where people stay for up to six months and receive health and social care, and move-on supported accommodation.

By the late 1980s services began to recognise that some heavy drinkers are reluctant to stop drinking and unable to abstain 'by command', as required by detoxification programmes. One response has been the creation of 'wet' and 'damp' projects for homeless people who are heavy drinkers. 'Wet' projects allow drinking on the premises, while 'damp' projects accept drinkers although alcohol cannot be consumed on the premises. The first 'wet' hostel in London was established in 1994 at St Pancras Way by St Mungo's; and the first 'wet' day centre was developed by *Nottingham Help the Homeless Association* in 1991 at Handel Street, Nottingham. 'Wet' hostels have since been developed in Nottingham, Bradford and Carlisle. Some are exclusively for heavy drinkers; others admit homeless people regardless of their drinking habits. Very few other day centres in Britain allow drinking on the premises.

The emphasis of 'wet' schemes is on 'harm minimisation' and progressive change, not enforcing abstinence. They aim to reduce the damage caused by alcohol abuse, to encourage abusers to control their drinking and change to less dangerous substances, and to promote healthier lifestyles (McMurray-Avila, 1997). The *Handel Street Day Centre*, for example, provides nutritious food to heavy drinkers, assisted access to medical and alcohol services, and a small nurse-run injuries clinic (Cooper, 1997). The advantage of 'wet' projects is that the clients have no need to leave the building to drink: they do not therefore generate street drinking and its associated dangers. 'Wet' projects are controversial: they may encourage heavy drinking, but on the other hand they have a useful role to play in controlling drinking, for there are indications that people are more likely to accept help and treatment once their basic needs are met (Oakley and Dennis, 1996). It is therefore essential that the objectives of 'wet' projects, which should emphasise harm minimisation and the control of drinking, are constantly reinforced.

In Britain, the local availability of services for homeless heavy drinkers depends on the attitudes of service providers and the skills and willingness of their staff. Some hostels and most day centres still disallow alcohol on the premises and evict violators. In some cities, such as Leeds and Oxford, all hostels have 'no drink' rules (Carter, 1997). Where specialist services are lacking, some heavy drinkers move between the streets, hostels, health care services, and alcohol services without receiving a comprehensive package of care (Harrison and Luck, 1996).

## Interventions for homeless heavy drinkers

Work with older heavy drinkers has to be incremental. Realistic goals have to be set and the clients should not feel pressurised to make major changes quickly. Useful preliminary steps are to persuade a resident to eat nutritiously, attend to personal hygiene, and pay hostel charges. It is essential that heavy drinkers have access to physical and mental health care services, to alcohol programmes that are able to respond promptly if help is suddenly required or requested, and to social services. Services can be fine-tuned to meet the clients' needs. The *Aspinden Wood Centre* in London, run by Equinox, provides permanent accommodation for heavy drinkers over the age of 40 years. The residents' main meal used to be served in the evenings. It was however found that many residents were drinking during the day and going to bed early, so the main meal is now served at lunchtime. The change has improved the eating habits of a large number.

Several strategies are used by staff at 'wet' projects to tackle the deteriorating health and behaviour problems of heavy drinkers. Setting 'house' rules and clear boundaries have proved useful. At the Lancefield Street Centre, a rule barred the residents who had been drinking heavily and were incontinent from using the wet lounge and the dining room until they had washed and changed their clothes, and the wet lounge was closed whenever the occupants became noisy and argumentative. Similarly, at the St Pancras Way 'wet' hostel, the residents are not allowed to use the communal facilities if they have been incontinent. As the manager explained, 'such action conveys to a resident that this is what that behaviour has cost you – we want you to stay, but will not accept such behaviour'. Having strict budget agreements with the residents is essential, for without them some residents drink excessively when they receive their benefits and behave deplorably and unmanageably. At St Pancras Way, budget agreements are drawn up with the residents and their money is released day-by-day. Some receive £5.00 each day, while some have £3.00 in the morning and £2.00 in the afternoon. The staff have found that when the residents are sober, they are usually grateful for such arrangements, although they do cause tensions when the residents are drinking. There is concern that such a rule places the staff in a guardian role, and that this contradicts the long-term aim of encouraging homeless people to be responsible for their own actions.

Regular and organised activities have been found to be valuable. At St Pancras Way, several residents participate in the Make-It-Work scheme described earlier (Box 5.2). They do not drink alcohol during the sessions, and become interested in other activities. At Burghley Road, London, a permanent residential home for older homeless people with alcohol dependency and other complex needs, there is a full-time activities co-ordinator. The residents are encouraged to participate in various groups and activities, including art and mural projects, woodwork, gardening, bingo, crossword and quiz sessions, and day trips. Many have been drinking heavily for years, have cognitive deficits, short-term memory loss, and low self-esteem. Through the activities, they gradually rebuild their interests, communication skills, and physical co-ordination, and learn to trust each other. During the activities they are distracted from drinking alcohol and, according to the worker, some are now less disruptive and argumentative in the home.

There are no easy answers to tackling heavy drinking among older homeless people. Among those who only recently began to drink, if the instigating factors are addressed then their consumption may reduce, but for others it is an intractable lifetime pattern. A range of specialist services with skilled staff is required, including outreach work on the streets, 'wet' projects, detoxification units, rehabilitation programmes, counselling services, and supported houses for those who have stopped or have controlled their drinking.

## Addressing mental health problems

### The needs of mentally ill people and service requirements

A high proportion of older homeless people have mental health problems. A few have long-standing problems and have had several or lengthy episodes in mental hospitals. Some have severe problems yet have never received psychiatric help. While some willingly accept treatment, many deny their problems, refuse to see a psychiatrist or have treatment, and remain unsettled, distressed by delusional ideas, and extremely difficult to help. At the Lancefield Street Centre, some residents with a paranoid illness or frequent mood swings neglected their self-care, isolated themselves or were aggressive and refused treatment. For some, these problems were exacerbated by alcohol consumption: some used alcohol to combat distressing symptoms of a mental illness; for others heavy drinking induced psychotic thoughts and disturbed behaviour.

Some residents had 'undefined' mental health problems, behaved in strange and difficult ways, yet when assessed by mental health workers were not deemed to be mentally ill and in need of treatment. One woman, for example, believed that neighbours were watching her and trying to harm her. She stayed in her bedroom, refused to communicate with the staff except aggressively, dressed bizarrely, neglected her personal hygiene, and rarely ate. She was diagnosed by a psychiatrist as suffering from a severe personality disorder rather than a mental illness. This meant however that untrained hostel staff had to cope alone with her difficult behaviour. Similar problems have been reported from other hostels.

### Services for mentally ill people

In Britain, the USA and Australia, there have been major changes in the care of mentally ill people during the last three decades, involving the movement away from institutional care to community care, the closure of large psychiatric hospitals, and the discharge of patients into the community. In Britain, 'community mental health teams' have been established in most areas to provide domiciliary care to people with mental health problems. Because these teams have large caseloads that do not allow for intensive contact, and because their style of service delivery is rarely assertive, they are unlikely to respond adequately to the needs of severely mentally ill people who are hard to engage (Sainsbury Centre for Mental Health, 1998). A 'care programme approach' was introduced in 1991 which ensures that generic health and social services are involved in assessments and designing care plans for people with complex and multiple needs. Each client is allocated a key worker (usually a mental health nurse or a social worker) who is responsible for formulating the care plan, for ensuring that the care is delivered and that the plan is regularly reviewed.

Simultaneous with these changes in Britain, the number of homeless mentally ill people has increased, stimulating various responses by policy-makers and service providers. In 1990, the Mental Health Foundation and the Department of Health launched the *Homeless Mentally Ill Initiative (HMII)* to fund services for homeless mentally ill people in London. Since 1996, the scheme has been extended to other towns and cities including Bristol, Bath, Exeter, Leicester and Manchester. *Crisis* has recently funded organisations in some cities to provide outreach services to homeless mentally ill people.

Specialist outreach teams comprising mental health, housing and social workers have been established to work with homeless mentally ill people on the streets, at day centres and in hostels. Dr Philip Timms works for one such team in London, the *South Thames Assessment, Resource and Training Team (START)*. In Box 5.3, he describes the mental health problems of their older clients and the types of help given. Special needs hostels have also multiplied. They generally accommodate 10–20 people for 18–36 months, during which time they participate in treatment and rehabilitation programmes, later to move to independent or supported tenancies. Thames Reach in London have developed two schemes of self-contained flats as temporary accommodation for people with severe mental illness and a history of rough sleeping. These are particularly useful for clients who are withdrawn and deterred by the presence of others, and for those whose behaviour may aggravate others in shared housing. Despite these services, many mentally ill homeless people receive no specialist care but sleep rough or stay in general needs hostels which may not have the support of mental health workers.

**Box 5.3:** WORKING WITH OLDER MENTALLY ILL HOMELESS PEOPLE – THE START TEAM, LONDON

*Dr Philip Timms, Senior Lecturer in Community Psychiatry, at Guy's, King's & St Thomas's School of Medicine, University of London, works for the South Thames Assessment, Resource and Training Team (START). It is funded through the Homeless Mentally Ill Initiative to provide mental health services to homeless people in the contiguous London boroughs of Lambeth, Southwark and Lewisham. He describes the mental health problems of older homeless people, their contact with the team, and the types of help that are given.*

*The START Team* in south east London has been providing psychiatric services to homeless people since 1991. It is one of five multidisciplinary mental health outreach teams established in 1991 as part of the central London Homeless and Mentally Illness Initiative. The objective was to make contact with people who were not in contact with psychiatric services, or who were reluctant to do so. To make this happen, the teams work in hostels and day centres with homeless people of all ages. One may regard homeless people over the age of 55 years as constituting the 'older' group: this is consistent with both the arduous nature of homeless living and the cultural differences between younger and older homeless people.

### Referrals

Of the 3460 people referred to the START Team over seven years, 321 (9 per cent) were aged over 55 years. Men are over-represented in most homeless populations that present to services, and this was a strong pattern in our referred group of over-55s. Only 10 per cent of the referrals were of women, compared with 18 per cent of under-55 years referrals. The oldest clients were more than 80 years of age in both men and women. As might be expected, in London's minority ethnic groups that have recently arrived in this country, only a small proportion of the population is old. The majority of the older homeless group were white British, Irish or European – 81 per cent compared with 66 per cent of under 55s. The major differences were: 12 per cent of the younger group were Black British or Caribbean, compared with 4 per cent of the older group; 20 per cent of the older group were White Irish, compared with 7.5 per cent in the under 55s.

There were no significant differences between the older and younger groups in the referring agencies. For both age groups, the overwhelming majority came from voluntary agencies working with homeless people, and their night shelters, hostels and centres. A local specialist primary care service for homeless people referred equal proportions of younger and older homeless people. Compared with the younger referrals, the older group were more likely to be referred for confusion, alcohol problems, self-neglect, delusional ideas or eccentric behaviour. They were less likely to be referred for depression, self-harm or aggression.

### Engagement

Of the older women referred to the START Team, 17 per cent were never seen, compared with 25 per cent of the older men. A significantly greater share of older men than women were seen at least once, although a higher proportion of women were taken on for long-term work. Compared with the under 55s, both male and female older clients were more likely to be taken on for long-term work. For those who did eventually meet a member of the START Team, the older group were no different from the younger group in terms of the time taken to meet a member of the team following referral. Around two-thirds of each group were seen within seven days of referral. A further quarter were seen within the next three weeks. Older people who had three or more contacts with the service were more likely to stay in contact with the team for a longer period – 81 weeks against 61 weeks for the younger group.

## Diagnosis

Diagnoses were made for only a minority of the clients who saw the team, because of the limited availability of medical time. However, among both the over-55s and under-55s for whom a firm diagnosis was allocated, 50 per cent were of psychotic disorder. Approximately 20 per cent were suffering from depression or manic depression, and 20 per cent had an alcohol or substance abuse problem. In the under-55s this was substantially accounted for by substance abuse, in the over-55s by alcohol abuse. It is important to remember that these figures do not accurately reflect the prevalence of these disorders in the homeless (let alone the general) population, merely of those who were referred to the team and substantially engaged with it. Around one-third were allocated more than one diagnosis, and the majority (80 per cent) of the secondary and tertiary diagnoses involved alcohol or substance abuse.

## Types of homelessness

Older homeless people are no more homogeneous than young homeless people. They include:

- elderly women living solitary lives, sleeping out or in night shelters, often suffering from chronic psychotic disorders and usually having had no previous contact with psychiatric services
- working men who have lived their whole lives in temporary accommodation, and who often suffer from alcohol problems. After retirement age, they have no social network to fall back on
- men with chronic schizophrenia who have spent several episodes in psychiatric units, but who after discharge from hospital often lose touch with services. For them, the homelessness circuit has provided an alternative setting for institutionalisation to occur.

## Use of the Mental Health Act

Around 3.5 per cent of those referred in both the older and younger groups had at some point been assessed for compulsory admission to hospital under the Mental Health Act. However, 13 per cent of the women aged over 55 had been so assessed. The number of clients involved (4 out of 30) is small, but this does perhaps reflect a perception by workers of the particular vulnerability of older homeless women. Two were well-known `bag ladies' and both have subsequently settled successfully into high-support accommodation.

## Summary

Older homeless people seem to be as likely as younger homeless people to be recognised as suffering from severe and enduring mental illnesses. In spite of the chronicity of their disorders and the length of time they have spent leading isolated lives, they seem to be no harder to engage than younger groups. Although anxieties were felt by team members about the impact of intervention and hospitalisation, older homeless people can benefit as much as younger homeless people from psychiatric, social and psychological interventions.

## Interventions for homeless people with mental health problems

Older homeless people who are mentally ill need temporary accommodation in small projects where intensive help can be given and few demands are made. Spaciousness is an advantage. Some who have been on the streets for years become distressed when close to others. Experienced care workers who have the skills to engage the residents and to manage difficult behaviour should staff the projects. Regular input is essential from trained mental health workers who can assess mental states over time, supervise medication, and plan programmes of care in conjunction with the hostel care staff.

In some projects for homeless mentally ill people, activities have been found to be of value in encouraging socialisation, in building social and daily living skills, in raising morale and motivation, and in promoting appropriate behaviour. Aberdour Court in London, managed by Thames Reach, accommodates 10 homeless people with mental health problems in self-contained flats. Barbecues and coffee afternoons are arranged for the residents, as also are art, gardening and cookery groups. The last involves the residents in planning, shopping for and cooking a meal. At Shirland Road, a registered care home in London managed by St Mungo's for 18 residents with mental health problems, a life-skills worker is employed. A weekly programme of activities is arranged which includes art, assertiveness and relationship groups, day trips, household and bills management, gardening, swimming, shopping and cooking. Nearby, there is a lost dogs' home. The staff and residents walk the dogs, and some very withdrawn residents who do not communicate in the home begin to talk while on these trips.

Specialist and intensive services can help homeless people with mental health problems. *Valley Lodge* in New York City, which is managed by the *West Side Federation for Senior Housing* and funded by the City of New York through a contract with the *Department of Homeless Services*, provides temporary accommodation to 92 homeless men and women over the age of 50 years, many of whom are mentally ill or have alcohol problems. The project received funding in 1991 to expand their social care staff, and a study compared the outcomes for the mentally ill clients served in 1991–92 with those served in 1990–91. It was found that the decreased caseload in the second year enabled more intensive work to be carried out and raised effectiveness. For those mentally ill clients who were rehoused, the average length of stay in the hostel reduced from 505 days in 1990–91 to 319 days in 1991–92 (Jorgensen *et al.* 1996). The *Rosati Center* in St Louis, staffed by social workers and a nurse, provides temporary accommodation to 15 chronically mentally ill people. The residents receive medical and psychiatric care, and help or supervision with behaviour problems, obtaining benefits, daily living tasks, taking medication, and arranging and keeping treatment appointments. Of the 228 residents during

1986–91, 78 per cent were housed when they left the project and, of these, 92 per cent remained housed one year later (Murray and Baier, 1995).

An extensive evaluation of services and interventions for mentally ill homeless people is in progress in the USA. Launched in 1994 by the Center for Mental Health Services as the *Access to Community Care and Effective Services and Supports Program* (*ACCESS*), and implemented over five years at 18 sites, it is examining the influence of the integration of services on usage and the quality-of-life of severely mentally ill homeless people who are not receiving community treatment (Lam and Rosenheck, 1999). Funds have been provided for specialist outreach teams to involve severely mentally ill homeless people in services, and for case management teams to provide comprehensive services for up to one year to at least 100 new clients each year. Early findings suggest that where services in a city are well integrated, there is improved access to housing services and better housing outcomes for homeless people who are mentally ill (Rosenheck *et al.* 1998a).

## Interventions for homeless people with mental health and alcohol problems

Since the late 1980s, there has been increasing attention paid to the problem among homeless people of coincident severe chronic mental illness and substance abuse (alcohol or drugs). Although drug abuse is currently rare among *older* homeless people, some have dual problems of mental illness and heavy drinking (Crane, 1999). People with such problems are particularly vulnerable, have multiple, interacting impairments and special needs, and require intensive services (Drake *et al.* 1997). Yet in Britain and America, they are often excluded from services as few offer integrated treatment (more target either mentally ill people or substance abusers) (Oakley and Dennis, 1996; Pleace and Quilgars, 1996; Williams, 1992). As noted by the Sainsbury Centre for Mental Health (1998, p.33), people with these dual problems are 'among the most marginalised of service users'. Three-fifths of the clients contacted by the HMII teams in London had combined problems, yet 'none of the teams was equipped to provide specialist interventions for substance dependency' (Craig, 1995, p.73).

Programmes in the USA that integrate mental health, substance abuse and housing services for dually diagnosed homeless people have been found effective (Drake *et al.* 1997; Rosenheck *et al.* 1998b). 'Mental illness and chemical abuse' (MICA) workers are employed at some shelters and drop-in centres, e.g. *John Heuss House* in New York City, a 24-hour drop-in centre. 'Continuous treatment teams', which provide 24-hour help to people with a dual diagnosis, have been established in New Hampshire. Each trained case manager has around 12 clients and has the time and resources to treat both mental illness and substance abuse (Johnson, 1997). It has been shown that individuals with a dual diagnosis experience little or no change in their substance abuse over time if treated for one disorder only (Block *et al.* 1997), but substance abuse problems do improve for some clients of integrated programmes after four to seven years (Drake *et al.* 1996; Oakley and Dennis, 1996). They require interventions that increase motivation, encourage social networks and activities that are not dependent on substance misuse, promote problem-solving and social skills to negotiate difficult situations without using alcohol or drugs, and allow a greater tolerance of relapse than has been common among conventional substance misuse interventions.

A federal *Collaborative Demonstration Program for Homeless Individuals*, with funds from the *Center for Mental Health Services* and the *Center for Substance Abuse Treatment*, has been established in the USA since 1993 to address the needs of homeless people with dual diagnoses. Innovative intervention and treatment programmes are being monitored and evaluated in New York, Portland, San Diego, Berkeley, Colorado and Bridgeport (Block *et al.* 1997).

## Rehabilitation programmes

The principles of rehabilitation are to build on an individual's capabilities, to promote 'normal' patterns of life through the establishment of appropriate social roles, to help an individual reach a satisfactory quality-of-life, and to maximise the person's independence or autonomy. There is considerable literature on the rehabilitation of people with mental and physical health disabilities (Brown and Hughson, 1987; Liberman, 1988; Pilling, 1991; Shepherd, 1984; Watts and Bennett, 1991), but little on the rehabilitation of homeless people which, in many cases, principally requires training to build or restore an individual's morale, self-esteem, living skills and social skills.

Rehabilitation programmes for homeless people should primarily be a preparation for resettlement and coping in the intended accommodation. The transition from a hostel where meals and services are provided to independent living is daunting for many homeless people, and impossible for some without long preparation. Some have become 'deskilled' while in a hostel or on the streets, and some have never learned the skills of independent living (Vincent *et al.* 1995). Since the 1990s, several organisations have responded to this problem by developing rehabilitation units for homeless people. The clients stay in the units for a few months, receive support from staff to become increasingly responsible for looking after themselves and their own cleaning and cooking, are taught household management and budgeting skills, and are prepared for a move to independent accommodation.

There are several 'models' of rehabilitation units. Some are attached to hostels: as a resident's problems are stabilised and their motivation increases, he or she progresses from the hostel into the units. Several large *Salvation Army* hostels have adopted this model, as in Sheffield and at Edward Alsop Court, London. Some temporary accommodation consists of small homes that encourage the residents to participate collectively in daily living tasks such as cooking and household chores. Box 5.1 details one such scheme in Cardiff, Grangetown PREP. Another interesting scheme is Aberdour Court in London, described earlier, where the residents are accommodated in clustered self-contained flats and receive help from on-site staff.

In Melbourne, Australia, a comparable model is the *Transitional Accommodation Project (TAP)* which prepares homeless individuals to adjust to their choice of independent or shared accommodation. Its emphasis is on community integration, and while restricted to homeless people aged 25–50 years, 'aspects of the model are considered appropriate to the needs and capacities of more active homeless elderly persons, in particular those who have recently become homeless' (Purdon, 1991, p.134). The first stage is a 'redirection house' with five beds where homeless people stay for one month while their needs are assessed and income benefits and health care are sorted out. The house is staffed Monday to Friday from 9 a.m. to 5 p.m., and there is on-call out-of-hours cover. After four weeks, the residents move to one of two 'living skills houses' for approximately six months. Each house has five residents and two workers who help the residents to build daily living skills and community networks. Once a person no longer requires this level of support, he or she moves to one of four 'community houses' which are not staffed but where the residents receive support from a community group. They stay in the houses for 6–12 months, intensify community links, and are then helped to move into independent or shared housing. Not all clients require the three stages: some move directly from a living skills house to independent accommodation.

The first step in planning rehabilitation for older homeless people is a careful assessment of their needs, capabilities and housing preferences. Their ability to manage self-care, daily living tasks and finances varies. Some have been homeless since early adulthood: others who lived with their parents or a partner have never had the responsibilities of a tenancy, household chores and paying bills. Those who intend to live independently will need to be able to shop, cook, clean, budget, pay bills and rent, and manage self-care. No assumption should be made about a person's longer-term housing possibilities until their skills, capacity for learning and preferred housing choice are known.

The second step is to design individualised rehabilitation programmes 'for the [housing] environment in which people will eventually function, rather than simply to achieve good levels of functioning during rehabilitation' (Watts and Bennett, 1991, p.5). Some people prefer to live in shared housing where they have companionship and no responsibility for utility bills (which are paid by the housing provider). Some with severe mental health or alcohol dependence problems may need to be rehoused in a group home where meals and care are provided. The programmes should be reviewed and revised regularly according to changing needs. Box 5.4 describes the work of a rehabilitation house attached to a temporary hostel for older homeless men in Birmingham, England. Box 5.5 describes a project in Boston, Massachusetts, which provides temporary housing in self-contained units and preparation for independent accommodation.

---

### BOX 5.4: THE ZAMBESI PROJECT, BIRMINGHAM

*Portland Jones, the manager of the Zambesi Project of Focus Housing Group in Birmingham, describes the establishment of a rehabilitation and resettlement programme at the project, and the effect that it has had on motivating the residents to settle down.*

*The Zambesi Project* was set up in response to a specific housing problem and a request for help from Birmingham City Council. An elderly man had died in hospital and the coroner was so appalled by his emaciated and flea-infested condition that he went to see the property where the deceased man had been living. The coroner called for the property to be closed and the Zambesi Project came into being to rehouse the other occupants.

The project targeted the residents of run-down lodging houses and the street drinkers of the area. The emphasis was to provide good quality, safe and secure accommodation and board in a 'wet' house – alcohol is allowed in the project. People who had lived on the streets or had moved around the hostel circuit came to the Zambesi Project – and didn't want to leave. That was the problem: the project 'silted up' and we were unable to offer help to others who needed it. The residents had to be moved, but initially we didn't know how. The resettlement of older people is challenging; they are not youngsters who want a place of their own and just need help to get there. Many have had a place of their own in the past but it didn't work out; others have never had a place of their own and know no other way of life. They don't aspire to a place of their own, they don't have the confidence or skills to manage independently, and there are no role models to follow.

An opportunity arose when one of our buildings became due for refurbishment. We took the plunge and dedicated the building to rehabilitation and resettlement. The approach was to be holistic; everything we did had resettlement in mind, to encourage a sense of purpose and movement, and to increase confidence and abilities. We decided on a maximum stay of 18 months. The refurbished building has eight small and four large single rooms and six self-contained 'starter' flats. People first move into the small rooms at the top of the building, then into the large single rooms, and finally into the starter flats. Meals are provided at all three stages, although there is a communal kitchen where the residents can make snacks. When ready, a resident can self-cater but retains the fallback option of buying occasional (or all) meals from the kitchens. The arrangements create a feeling of progress, of moving through, and prevents people becoming too settled in one room.

Various workshops are also being developed to enable people to brush up forgotten skills or acquire new ones. The catering workshop is successful – its activities include shopping, cooking and clearing-up. New workshops are on 'managing on a limited budget' and 'basic home maintenance'. Information from the workshops is gathered into a pack for future reference.

Given the project's aims and purpose, at the initial interview with a prospective resident it is made clear that the building is for people who wish to resettle. Having the desire is important, not the ability to do so straight away. Shortly after a resident has moved in, the first resettlement interview begins to develop an action plan. Through a two-way process, the plan is agreed by the staff and the resident, and both have roles to fulfil. Regular contact maintains the impetus. The residents are encouraged to collect items for their future accommodation and storage space is available. Support is offered throughout the process – with viewing properties, applying for grants, buying items for the new place, moving furniture, checking that all services are connected, and setting up easy-payment schemes to help budgeting. Information on the local area such as addresses of local government offices, doctors and leisure facilities is provided. Outreach visits continue for up to six months after the person is settled in the new tenancy.

Many of the residents who have moved on talk of the isolation it brings – it can be a major problem for those who have lived in communal hostels for many years. We have set up an ex-residents' support group – the *Home Alone Club* – which meets once a month and provides opportunities to get together, to chat, to exchange experiences, and to seek advice from the staff. The group meets at the project and people who are thinking of moving on can attend and discuss with those who have done it the problems and joys of a place of your own. Those who have successfully settled provide effective role models for those who are not yet ready to move on. There is also a newsletter, which has useful information.

The resettlement scheme has had a cascading effect on the rest of the project. Some residents have moved on directly from the project itself. There is a heightened awareness of resettlement among both staff and residents. The staff are more able and willing to encourage residents to move on, knowing that there is full support available, and the residents see that whatever their age or background, it is possible to move.

**Box 5.5:** The Elders Living at Home Program, Boston, Massachusetts

*Eileen O'Brien, Programme Director of the Elders Living at Home Program, Boston Medical Centre, Massachusetts, describes how vacant housing is used as temporary accommodation for older homeless people until their needs can be assessed and they are rehoused.*

Boston Medical Centre's *Elders Living at Home Program (ELAHP)* provides homeless and at risk older people with access to safe, affordable housing, and to the services that enable them to remain independent in the community. It provides temporary and transitional co-permanent housing, intensive housing casework, and advocacy work to men and women aged 60 years and more who are homeless, facing eviction or displacement, or living in life-threatening situations. It also supports people aged 55–59 years if they have a serious disability such as cancer or chronic kidney failure requiring dialysis (for these conditions make living in an emergency shelter life-threatening). The programme was established with a three-year demonstration grant from a consortium of national and local foundations.

ELAHP's temporary housing schemes using vacant units in Boston Housing Authority's elderly and disabled developments opened in May 1988. They house clients while they are helped to find permanent rooms or apartments. In its first three years, the programme expanded to 20 apartments in three different buildings. Finding a steadily increasing demand for its services, in February 1997 the programme added six temporary apartments at a fourth building, and developed a 14-unit transitional-to-permanent programme at one site. Each temporary unit is furnished with the 'basics': a bed, table and chairs, dishes and cutlery.

ELAHP provides assessment, case management, housing search and transition services. Clients are first referred to the Programme Director, and then interviewed to assess their readiness for housing and their willingness to accept services. Those who are accepted for temporary housing are assigned a case manager, and together they agree an individualised care plan that addresses medical, psychiatric, substance abuse, personal hygiene, housekeeping, and money management issues. The case manager monitors a client's progress through home visits and telephone calls, and the care plan is updated accordingly. The case manager assists the client with applications for social security, including Supplemental Security Income, and *Medicaid* (a health insurance scheme for people on low incomes), helps the client relearn shopping, cooking and laundry skills, and when required makes referrals for services to assist with these tasks.

After an adjustment period, the case manager meets with the client to discuss permanent housing options. Based on the updated assessment of the client's needs and abilities, they decide together where the client will be safest and most comfortable, and they begin a search for accommodation. The case manager accompanies the client on visits to housing options, assists with applications and documents, and helps the client through the housing interview process. Once a client has secured permanent housing, the case manager helps with all aspects of the move, including referral to furniture banks, arranging removal services, and co-ordinating the transfer of home-care and other services. The case manager may also provide support services for up to six months after the move. Most clients have been referred from mainstream services and are followed-up long-term by a primary service provider, such as a clinic social worker or a home-care case manager.

A client who is interested in the transitional-to-permanent programme must first complete Boston Housing Authority's application form. Once approved, the client is assigned a transitional apartment, and works with the case manager to develop a care plan and prepare to move in. As with a temporary housing client, the case manager monitors the client's progress, updates the care plan, makes referrals, and co-ordinates services as needed. After 12 months in the transitional apartment, the client signs the lease and becomes a permanent tenant. These clients also receive long-term follow-up from a mainstream service provider.

Since 1988, ELAHP has helped 310 homeless older people, half of whom are women. All are low-income and have some disability or health impairment. Close to 70 per cent suffer from addiction (usually alcohol) or mental illness or both, and many also have physical illnesses such as heart and lung disease, arthritis and mobility limitations, dementia and memory loss, diabetes, and stroke. Most are socially isolated and have little contact with family and friends. They can remain in ELAHP temporary housing for up to 24 months, but most move to permanent housing within 12–18 months. Transitional housing clients become permanent tenants of their apartments after 12 months. Of those who have left the programme, 78 per cent moved to permanent housing, 17 per cent left before housing was secured, and 5 per cent died while in the programme. Of those who were discharged into permanent housing at least one year ago, 83 per cent remain housed, 12 per cent have died, and only 5 per cent became homeless again.

Providing temporary and transitional housing in elderly and disabled developments enables clients to integrate into the community, regain dignity and stability, relearn the tasks necessary to live independently, and become self-sufficient. The three key points learned by ELAHP are:

- tailor the programmes and services to fit the clients' needs and abilities, rather than trying to make clients fit into the programmes. Flexibility is crucial when dealing with individuals who have existed on the margins of society for most of their lives
- measure success in small increments. Getting a client into permanent housing is the ultimate goal, but a big success can be getting someone to show up for an appointment on time, or getting him or her to change clothes and launder
- nobody is beyond help. Getting someone into a stable environment, where he can be helped to recognize his needs and abilities, allows him to identify what the best residential setting might be for him, and gives him the tools to work towards that goal.

## Conclusions

This chapter has examined the specialist help that many older homeless people require to prepare them for a move to permanent housing. All require repeated and thorough assessments of their problems and for these to be reflected in individualised care plans. Well-designed assessment instruments and a key worker system are important. The type of help needed varies from person to person. Some require treatment for mental health problems, some need help to control heavy drinking, and others need help to combat apathy and restore interests. Through evaluations and from the experience at several projects in Britain and America, it has been repeatedly shown that many of the problems of homeless people can be effectively resolved or at least controlled if specialist and intensive help is provided. The value of structured activities and counselling to raise morale, motivation and self-esteem and discourage unsettled and disruptive behaviour needs further exploration.

Many of the required interventions, such as counselling or behaviour programmes, have to be carried out by experienced and trained staff. Generalist hostel care workers often do not have the skills to provide such help. Specialists should work alongside hostel care staff to provide programmes of care, and caseloads should be small to allow for intensive input. Services have to be tailored to respond to the needs of older homeless people. It is pointless having hostels that ban alcohol consumption in a city where many older heavy drinkers are sleeping rough. Mental health workers have to be flexible and recognise that although some older homeless people's mental health problems are ill-defined and indistinct, they require more specialist help than untrained hostel staff can provide. The evidence strongly suggests that among people with coincident mental illness and alcohol addiction, treating the problems in isolation is ineffective and that many are excluded from single focused services but offered nothing better. Mental health and substance abuse teams in Britain should establish projects and train staff to work in both fields.

It is unambitious for hostels to provide no more than food and shelter. Temporary hostels should be a hub from which homeless people learn to structure their day, build or rebuild their lives, and gain the motivation to develop goals and plan ahead. Activities and rehabilitation should be integral to a hostel's life. Many innovative schemes for homeless people are developing in Britain and elsewhere, and in the USA there are several experimental programmes for homeless people with mental health and substance abuse problems. It is important that such schemes are evaluated, their outcomes monitored over a long period, and the lessons disseminated. Learning from others' experience can make an important contribution to addressing the more complex needs of homeless people.

Chapter 6

# Resettlement and continued support

This chapter concentrates on ways to resettle older homeless people and provide support when they are rehoused. Resettlement in permanent, tenured accommodation should be the ultimate goal of all service providers working with homeless people. It involves much more than finding a housing vacancy. The long-term housing requirements of homeless people differ, and many need practical and emotional support to move and establish a home, and ongoing help and support to maintain the tenancy. It is possible to resettle homeless people with long histories of homelessness, and those with heavy drinking and mental illness problems. Many older homeless people want to be rehoused, and become more motivated, more confident, and take better care of themselves when they are resettled (Crane and Warnes, 1997b; Elias and Innui, 1993). Furthermore, resettlement is necessary to prevent hostel beds becoming 'blocked' and unavailable for newly homeless people.

Since the 1970s, there have been programmes to rehabilitate and resettle in the community vulnerable people from mental hospitals (Etheringon *et al.* 1995; Higgins and Richardson, 1994). One study suggests that people tend to be happier in the community than in hospital and that many acquire new skills and form new social contacts and friendships (Cambridge *et al.* 1994). In Greece, 99 psychiatric patients were resettled into community homes between 1990 and 1994, from an asylum where most had lived for more than 20 years. When contacted four years later, seven-tenths perceived the move as positive and expressed satisfaction with their new living situation (Zissi and Barry, 1997). It is only since the 1990s that there has been an emphasis on resettling homeless people, but now programmes exist in the UK, Germany, Austria, The Netherlands, Sweden, the USA and Australia (Edgar *et al.* 1999). But the practice is not universal. In Ireland, for example, there is little resettlement preparation for homeless people or support for those rehoused (Harvey, 1998). Even in the UK, some organisations have specialist and experienced resettlement workers, some rely on generalist hostel and day centre staff to provide resettlement alongside other duties, while some hostels not only lack resettlement programmes but do not encourage residents to move.

This chapter has four sections: the first describes the process of resettlement preparation and a number of pioneering programmes, some experimental and some well established: the second focuses on rehousing older homeless people into independent and supported housing, and describes various examples of housing and support schemes: the third concentrates on resettling older homeless people with mental health or alcohol problems: and the fourth examines approaches to rehabilitating long-stay hostel residents who have become dependent upon an institution's regime and support. There are several contributions from projects in Britain, America and Australia.

## The process of resettlement

Resettlement can be defined as the planned move of a person to tenured accommodation, usually with an unrestricted period of residence and with the provision of personal and social support if needed. It is not an easy process. Many former homeless people experience problems with adjusting to settled living, managing money and claiming benefits, and with loneliness and boredom (Pleace, 1995; Randall and Brown, 1994). There is a high rate of tenancy breakdown in the first two years, particularly in the first six months (Craig, 1995; Deacon *et al.* 1993; Dant and Deacon, 1989; Duncan and Downey, 1985). This equally applies to *older* homeless people (Crane, 1997; Crane and Warnes, 1998; Wilson, 1997).

The *National Homeless Alliance* launched in August 1997 a *National Resettlement Project* to develop good practice. In 1998, the organisation published a *Resettlement Handbook* which describes 14 detailed stages to resettlement, from the referral of a homeless person for rehousing to helping that person to settle and providing a safety net after the person has been rehoused (Bevan, 1998). Four main stages to resettlement can be identified: (i) assessing the client's housing needs; (ii) preparing the client for rehousing; (iii) finding a suitable housing vacancy and planning the move; and (iv) supporting the move and the initial adjustment to settled living. These stages are described in turn.

### Assessing the client's housing needs

Resettlement should be contemplated: (i) once a person is settled in temporary accommodation and supported by services; (ii) following a careful assessment of their needs, the problems which may impede resettlement have been ameliorated or controlled; and (iii) when the client has, or is judged able to regain, the motivation, attitudes and daily living skills required to live in long-term accommodation. Preparation for resettlement again begins with assessment – of a person's competence, motivation, and requirements for long-term housing. Some older homeless people can manage in tenancies with minimal support; some are more suited to shared houses or may require supported housing while they acquire the skills and confidence to manage in independent accommodation; others are unable to live alone and are best rehoused in residential group homes with a high level of care and support. To assess a person's housing needs, information is required about:

- their housing history, including experience of managing a tenancy and living alone, the reasons for homelessness, and past resettlement attempts and outcomes
- past and present mental and physical health states, benefit entitlements and claims, family and social contacts, drinking habits, and other addictions (drugs or gambling)
- personal care and daily living skills, i.e. ability to look after personal appearance and hygiene, and to cook, shop, budget, pay bills, and manage a home
- motivation to be resettled, and housing preferences and requirements.

It can take several weeks to compile a person's history and assess his or her housing needs. Information should be gathered from the client, from the hostel workers where the person is temporarily living, and wherever possible from other agencies. Some older people are unable or refuse to disclose information and, for some, there are no alternative sources.

## Preparing the client for rehousing

At this stage, the objective is to ensure that the person has the means, skills and attitudes to settle in the intended accommodation. He or she needs to be competent to manage personal and domestic tasks, bearing in mind that skills and confidence may improve after resettlement. Being resettled is a major step, particularly if a person has never managed a home or has not had a tenancy for years. Some people are anxious about leaving a familiar homeless community, about the considerable changes to their lifestyle, and about the responsibilities of a tenancy. Some return to the streets when housing options are proposed or when accommodation becomes available. Others become anxious in the weeks before they move, neglect their appearance, isolate themselves, and drink heavily. Homeless people therefore need to be prepared mentally as well as practically for a move. They require reassurance, and to be forewarned about the issues that may arise and how they can be overcome. The preparation may extend over many months and should progress at the client's pace. An inappropriate resettlement can be extremely stressful and demoralising for a client and have long-term repercussions. It is also costly and time-consuming for a housing provider to repossess a tenancy if a person abandons accommodation without formally relinquishing the tenancy. It is estimated that each tenancy failure costs a housing authority £2100 (Audit Commission, 1998).

## Finding a suitable housing vacancy and planning the move

Resettlement requires the careful selection of suitable housing to meet a person's preferences and needs. For those older homeless people who can manage in independent or supported housing schemes, referrals are made to housing associations and local authority housing departments for fully independent tenancies, sheltered accommodation with assistance from wardens, or shared houses with non-residential daily support workers. For those who are unable to live alone, referrals are made to local authority social services departments, who make their own assessments of care needs and fund long-term placements in residential group homes. Unlike most housed people, who have furniture, furnishings, kitchen utensils and other possessions that they have accumulated over years, and often relatives and friends who help with the move, homeless people generally have no belongings and no one to help. The resettlement worker therefore plays vital roles in accompanying the client to view the property and assess its suitability, and in making other preparations for the move.

If a person is moving to an independent flat or an unfurnished tenancy, the resettlement worker helps with applying for a community care grant, purchasing furniture and furnishings, and making the connection arrangements for gas, electricity and other utilities. Discretionary community care grants are available from the Department of Social Security (DSS) to enable people with a low income who are moving out of institutional and residential settings to establish a home (George *et al.* 1997). No stipulated amount is paid, and claims can be made for furniture, furnishings, household equipment, connection charges and moving expenses. Some people who are ineligible for a community care grant are entitled to a loan from the DSS.

## Supporting the move and the initial adjustment to settled living

The final stages in the resettlement process involve assisting a person through the move and monitoring his or her adjustment to settled living and a new home. Resettlement staff or housing (or community) support workers usually undertake this. Helping with the initial adjustment involves:

- ensuring that gas and electricity are connected, and that payment arrangements such as key-meters or budget schemes have been set up
- ensuring that the person understands how to use key-meters or to pay for electricity and gas through budget schemes, and how to operate the heating system
- ensuring that the person is receiving an income, usually a state pension or benefit entitlements, that rent or housing benefit is being paid to the landlord, and that the person understands the tenancy agreement
- training in budgeting for food and bills, cooking on a low income, paying bills, and other basic domestic tasks

- ensuring that essential items of furniture and domestic equipment have been acquired
- ensuring that needed support services such as home-care are arranged
- helping the person to get to know the local shops and post office, and to register with a local general medical and dental practitioner.

Rehousing often involves moving to a new area and losing social and support networks (however tenuous) at hostels and on the streets. Many homeless people have minimal contact with relatives and have few friends, and their isolation is commonly compounded when they move because they find it difficult to socialise and are unlikely to become acquainted with neighbours or to access community facilities. Once he or she is rehoused, an important role of the housing support workers is to assist the person to socialise and to provide emotional support. It has been suggested that after about eight weeks 'the pleasure of a new home may be replaced by apprehension at managing greater or more complex financial responsibilities, or people may be at a loss as to how to spend their time ... the transition between lifestyles is often accompanied by an emotional low' (Dant and Deacon, 1989, p.35).

The long-term adjustment to settled living involves accepting the accommodation as 'home', and that implies ceasing to use day centres for homeless people and mixing with homeless people on the streets. It also involves rebuilding a socially integrated and purposeful life. Returning to work may be a feasible objective for some in their fifties who have been homeless for just a few months and have recently worked. Organisations such as *St Mungo's* have employment and training schemes to help homeless people to return to work. Many older people will not however return to work, but can be encouraged to use community centres and libraries, to develop or renew interests and activities, to form new social relationships and roles, or to restore estranged kin ties.

## The requirements of resettlement workers

Resettlement workers need to:

- be proficient in collecting detailed housing histories from homeless people and carrying out comprehensive assessments of their housing needs
- be well informed about current housing legislation and tenancy agreements, and about local housing providers, to which clients can be referred, and of their eligibility and referral procedures
- be skilful in negotiating with local authority social services departments and NHS

mental health teams for community care assessments and placements in high-care group homes
- be aware of the procedures for arranging community care grants or DSS loans, rent payments, utility connections and payments, and changes to welfare benefits once the client has moved
- have good practical knowledge of the local facilities that are useful for homeless people who are rehoused, e.g. second-hand or cheap furniture stores and day centres, and voluntary organisations that will provide some help during the settling-in period, e.g. with fitting carpets, gardening and decorating
- have the time to develop wide-ranging links to local housing providers, and to help a client with all aspects of the move.

## Specific resettlement programmes

Some organisations have programmes, courses and manuals for homeless people who are to be resettled. *Bridge Housing Association*, London, has a resettlement handbook for service users that explains the process of rehousing, the housing options, and the procedures to follow when moving into a new tenancy, including how to claim benefits and grants (Bridge Housing Association, 1999). Each client has a 'resettlement contract' which outlines the type of housing that has been agreed for resettlement, waiting times, and the tasks that should be undertaken by the worker and the client prior to moving. Each client also has a 'support contract' which specifies both the help that the client will get from the resettlement worker and other agencies when rehoused and who will deal with benefits and utilities.

A few organisations arrange resettlement courses for homeless people. Bridge Housing Association has four such courses on: (i) budgeting and bills, including how to read a meter; (ii) nutrition and food hygiene; (iii) personal safety in and out of the home; and (iv) the maintenance of heating, water, and electrical appliances. Another course, 'A rough guide to managing your own place', is organised at a local college through *Nottingham Hostels Liaison Group's Resettlement Scheme*. At *Valley Lodge*, New York City, a 'housing readiness' course is held over 15 weeks which covers the types of housing available and prepares the residents for interviews with housing providers. At *Edward Alsop Court*, a *Salvation Army* Centre in London, seminars are held as part of the resettlement programme on budgeting, debt, first aid, cooking and food hygiene, general health issues such as eating and smoking, dealing with stress and change, problem-solving, anger management, self-motivation, and relationship building. Box 6.1 describes a resettlement training programme developed by the *Simon Community*, in Glasgow.

**Box 6.1:** Resettlement training service, Simon Community, Glasgow

*Julia Albert-Recht, the Resettlement Manager for the Simon Community in Glasgow, describes a training programme that has been established for homeless people who are to be rehoused. The programme has been developed particularly for exceptionally vulnerable people.*

The Simon Community in Glasgow has been running a resettlement training service since January 1998. We have developed a needs-led programme for homeless people who are to be rehoused, and raised awareness among other agencies of the nature and importance of resettlement work. Our programmes help the clients understand the nature of resettlement and its practical requirements and come to terms with the emotional changes involved, and enhance self-development and the quality-of-life. The underpinning aim is to build or rebuild the confidence of homeless people so that they can recognise and take advantage of wider opportunities.

It is essential that the service is easily accessible. We accept referrals on forms and by telephone as well as self-referrals. We send out posters advertising our three-monthly programmes to over 150 agencies. Almost all participants are unemployed and many have a history of one or more of: rough sleeping, psychiatric hospital admissions, prison, and sexual, mental or substance abuse. Many have had bad experiences or poor teaching at school, have missed out on productive training opportunities, experience difficulties in accessing and taking up learning resources, and prefer an informal learning environment. A significant number have learning difficulties or numeracy and literacy problems.

The training area is well lit and has comfortable chairs. Tea, coffee, biscuits and a generous lunch are provided, and travel expenses are reimbursed at a flat rate. The course uses various techniques and has regular breaks, enabling participants to relax and the group to gel. We use group learning techniques: by drawing on the breadth of experience within the group, the participants acquire new knowledge and develop confidence. The trainers' role is to motivate the participants, enable them to re-evaluate their experiences, and become aware of alternative approaches to future situations. As well as applying principles from resettlement work and group therapy (although we are clearly not running therapy groups), the training service draws on frameworks that encourage motivation and promote the formation of realistic goals and new coping skills.

The main three-day course concentrates on the emotional and practical support that a person may need during the resettlement process, and aims to improve an individual's ability to adapt to changes in his or her lifestyle. The trainees can then opt to attend one- or two-day workshops on special topics, such as 'coping on your own', 'housing choices', and 'dealing assertively with situations'. In the diverse materials that have been developed to aid learning, the language and imagery have been designed to be accessible to all including those with poor literacy. Handouts linked to the sessions take people through the issues step-by-step. These can be taken away by the trainees, who can do further work on their own or with help from their key workers. Specialists and guest speakers contribute through short presentations and question-and-answer sessions. We also allow time for a surgery, for one-to-one private consultations.

The training is not off-the-shelf or routine, but is a sensitive and skilled interactive process, for the staff have to manage their own feelings while helping a disadvantaged and often damaged group. The trainers need to have time and support to develop their group-work skills. This is done by having regular sessions with a training consultant who is also a qualified psychotherapist. The opportunity for the trainers to explore some of their own concerns about and reactions to working with the group has already had a positive influence.

Because our work also focuses on prevention, the service can be adapted to other client groups, e.g. those with mental health problems, offenders, and individuals leaving care. We are currently compiling a resource pack which will: (i) raise awareness of the importance of such training; (ii) facilitate the transfer of knowledge and skills to other agencies involved in individual or group work; (iii) promote good practice and standards; and (iv) increase the number of people who can benefit from this work.

Setting up such an innovative project has been an exciting challenge for the team. The style of training and the general ethos of the project have been based on our previous experiences of working with homeless people and on our observations of their resilience in dealing with difficult life experiences. We believe that the service meets the needs of individuals who are implementing positive changes in their lives, and have designed an evaluation system to monitor the service's impact on people's lives.

There are many examples of the training's beneficial impacts. Since June 1988, 130 people have attended the main course and 241 the workshops. The evaluation forms completed three months after the course have showed that 48 per cent made housing applications, 56 per cent made changes to the way in which they manage their money, 52 per cent contacted agencies for support, 44 per cent sought help with getting furniture or applying for a grant, and 67 per cent had enquired about joining clubs or had considered a training scheme or adult education.

## Resettling older homeless people into independent and supported housing

Many older homeless people want to have their own tenancies in independent or minimally supported housing. The option is feasible for some but others require a more supportive environment while they acquire the skills and confidence to manage independently. Various models of staged, transitional and supervised accommodation for homeless people have been developed across Europe and North America. In the UK, some homeless people are rehoused in furnished shared housing with daily visits from support workers. The tenants are responsible for household chores and paying subsidised rent, but not for paying utility bills or the general maintenance of the accommodation. Although this type of tenancy introduces people gradually to settled living, it means that they neither learn the responsibilities of maintaining tenancies nor practise living within their means, e.g. budgeting for electricity and gas. Another British model was described in Chapter 5, of rehabilitation or 'training' flats being established alongside or attached to hostels.

In Sweden a model of progressive housing independence, the 'Staircase of transition', has been developed. It promotes incremental increases in housing standards and responsibilities that parallel progressive decreases in the provision of services and support. The 'staircase' is from group homes, through training flats and transitional accommodation, to independent tenancies. *Walenburg* is a similar 'step model' in Amsterdam for older homeless men. There are concerns about this type of provision. A critic of the Swedish scheme pointed out that it asserts discipline, exclusion and supervision rather than assistance and empowerment. Clients can move down the staircase as well as up, which may adversely affect their morale and motivation, and the behaviour required of tenants is so demanding that it is almost impossible for some to progress. Some clients' problems are inconsistent with the expectation of progressively lower levels of support (Edgar *et al.* 1999; Harvey, 1998).

Resettlements in independent tenancies require the most careful selection of suitable housing and thorough preparation for the move. There are many instances of older homeless people being rehoused without adequate preparation and planning. On occasion they are moved into accommodation that is filthy and damp, or lacks necessities such as heating, a bed and a cooker, with the all-too-common consequence that they give up the tenancy shortly afterwards (Crane, 1999). In many cities, voluntary groups and charities supply free or cheap second-hand furniture and furnishings to homeless people who acquire tenancies. Some housing associations now provide furnished or part-furnished accommodation, which may be useful for people who have been homeless for years and have no belongings. *Notting Hill Housing Trust* in London offers new clients the choice of both a furnished tenancy and the furniture, the cost of which is recovered over four years through a service charge (Ellenby, 1999). Help with providing furniture, laying carpets and in other ways may also be available through local groups of *Age Concern*, *Help the Aged*, and the *Soldiers', Sailors' and Airmen's Families Association* (the latter for those who have been in the armed forces or merchant navy). An innovative idea by Ealing Council's Mental Health Housing Team in London employs a handyman to help new tenants with 'do-it-yourself' jobs in the home (Ellenby, 1999).

One obstacle to adequate planning and preparation for resettlement is the pressure on housing providers to fill voids; it happens too often that a prospective tenant who has viewed and accepted a property is required to move in without delay even if they have no furniture. It takes at the very least several days to be allocated a community care grant and to acquire necessities. Most homeless people rely on Housing Benefit to subsidise their rent, but this can only be paid on one property, i.e. either the hostel or a tenancy. There is no leeway, and if the tenancy is not immediately occupied, it may be offered to another. Some temporary hostels for older homeless people in the USA do not require the residents to pay rent but expect them to save for when they are rehoused, e.g. Valley Lodge, New York City, and *The Dwelling Place*, Washington DC. Similarly, at the *Zambesi Project* in Birmingham, the residents of the rehabilitation house are encouraged to collect items for their new accommodation (Box 5.3). The *Over-55s Accommodation Project* in Leeds has a supply of fold-up beds, electric hot plates, kettles, crockery, and bedding that can be loaned to people when they move (Box 6.2).

---

**BOX 6.2:** RESETTLING OLDER HOMELESS PEOPLE INTO INDEPENDENT

HOUSING, LEEDS, YORKSHIRE

*Richard Sharp works at the Over-55s Accommodation Project in Leeds, the principal commercial city of West Yorkshire. He describes the process involved in resettling older homeless people into independent tenancies.*

The Over-55s Accommodation Project was developed in 1991 by *St Anne's Shelter and Housing Action* to resettle homeless people aged 55 years and over. The project extended to Sheffield in 1998. When a person is referred to the project for resettlement, he or she is interviewed and information collected about his or her background, problems and needs, ability to budget and manage self-care and household tasks, and housing requirements and preferences. It is important to find out why previous tenancies have failed, and whether the person is committed to resettlement. Information may be collected at one interview, but most people are initially reticent and it is first necessary to build a relationship between the worker and the client. As this strengthens, more detailed information is usually provided.

Once the necessary information has been collected, an individualised care package is prepared with the client. This describes the help that can be expected from the project, the next steps in the resettlement process, and the tasks that will be fulfilled by the resettlement worker and the client. The client is made aware of realistic housing options and timescales, and may be taken to view different housing schemes before the most appropriate type of housing is decided. This way of working means that the client is part of the resettlement process and encourages independence, motivation, and empowerment. It helps the client to acquire the skills that will be needed to live independently and to access mainstream services.

Housing applications are completed with the client. The client has the final say about where he or she wishes to live, subject to the availability and location of vacancies. Close liaison is maintained with the housing agencies to ensure that the client's housing application is dealt with swiftly and that the client is offered a suitable tenancy. Once an offer of housing has been made, the worker accompanies the client to view the accommodation. Through experience and because the worker knows the local neighbourhoods, they may point out possible problems with the property or the area. The client is thus able to make an informed choice about the accommodation. If the client does not like the property, then the worker accepts this and helps the client find other vacancies. At the end of the day it is the client's decision, for he or she is choosing a home, in most cases for the rest of their life.

Once a property is accepted, the worker accompanies the client to sign for the tenancy and helps with the application for a community care grant or a bridging loan. During 1999, it became increasingly difficult to get a community care grant for a client. The worker also helps the client to obtain charitable donations of furniture or to purchase carpets, curtains, second-hand furniture and a cooker and a fridge. The worker checks the property to make sure that the heating is working and that there are no problems, and reports anything that needs repair. The worker takes meter readings for the gas, electricity and water before the client moves in, forwards these to the appropriate companies, ensures that the utilities are connected and working, and helps the client set up budget-payment schemes. We use a standard checklist of the tasks that should be carried out before the client moves in.

The worker regularly visits the client during the first few weeks after the move, and ensures that all the necessary paperwork has been completed, e.g. housing benefit and council tax forms, and that various services have been informed of the client's change of address, e.g. the local post office and benefits office. The worker also makes arrangements with any services that the client needs, such as day centres, to help them integrate into the community.

The first four to five weeks are critical for the transition to settled living. Throughout this stressful period the client receives practical and emotional support from the worker. Once the client has settled, the worker provides a safety net should difficulties arise. The project does not deem a resettlement successful until a tenancy has been sustained for six months without major problems, e.g. rent arrears. Moving house is stressful for most people and particularly so for these clients. In the past, there has generally been little or no support available to help homeless people sort out problems after they are rehoused. The normal attitude has been – here are the keys, now get on with it.

The Over-55s project has successfully helped individuals in ways that are generally beyond the capacity of the statutory agencies. Although a strong relationship is normally formed with the clients, the aim is that they make their own choices and decisions, cease to be dependent on their resettlement worker, and build support links in their local community.

## Housing with various levels of support

There are several types of low support housing for homeless people, including shared houses and grouped or 'clustered' self-contained accommodation. They offer different levels of support, independence and companionship, and each has advantages and disadvantages. In shared houses, three or four people live together, they have their own bedrooms, a communal kitchen and sitting room, and a support worker visits daily. In some, the tenants are provided with a meal each day and are taught to budget and cook. Shared housing offers support and social contacts, and enables some tenants to develop skills and confidence before moving to independent accommodation (Cooper *et al.* 1994). But sharing a house requires tolerance, trust and at least a modicum of co-operation and some people prefer to be alone. Many with mental health, alcohol and behaviour problems are unsuited for communal accommodation (Crane and Warnes, 1997b; Dant and Deacon, 1989; Morrish, 1996; O'Leary, 1997).

For those who need support but prefer to live alone or are unsuitable for communal living, *Thames Reach Housing Association* and Bridge Housing Association have developed self-contained flats adjacent to a hostel or a group home, with the tenants in the flats receiving support from the attached project (Crane and Warnes, 1997b; O'Leary, 1997). One Bridge HA scheme is specifically for older homeless men and women, and comprises a 25-bed group home and adjacent flats for 13 men and women. Tenants from the flats have access to the home's dining room and communal facilities. Another solution, developed by St Anne's Shelter and Housing Action in Leeds, has been to accommodate homeless people in grouped or 'clustered' self-contained flats. Two clusters with six and 12 flats have been developed specifically for older people, with the tenants receiving help from a visiting housing support worker (Crane and Warnes, 1997b).

Both the *Committee to End Elder Homelessness* in Boston, Massachusetts, and *Wintringham* in Melbourne, Australia, provide accommodation at which the intensity of support is adjusted to suit individual needs, thereby enabling the clients to stay on with increased support when they become frail or require extra help (Boxes 6.3 and 6.4). At *Anna Bissonnette House* in Boston, each tenant has his or her own apartment, with a kitchen and bathroom. There are also communal areas and meals are provided if preferred. Hence, the tenants have the choice each day of self-catering or eating in the communal dining room, and of remaining in their apartment or socialising with others in the communal lounges. A similar arrangement exists for older homeless people at the *Abraham Residences* in the *Seagate Community*, New York City, which house 75 and 45 tenants respectively. Each tenant has a studio flat with a kitchen and dining area, a bed-sitting room, and a bathroom, while a subsidised meal is available every day.

**Box 6.3:** Housing and support services for older homeless people in Boston, Massachusetts

*Janice L Gibeau, the Executive Director of the Committee to End Elder Homelessness in Boston, Massachusetts, describes the various housing and support schemes that her organisation has developed for older homeless people to meet their different needs.*

The Committee to End Elder Homelessness (CEEH) was established in 1991 by a group of professional women who were committed to eliminating homelessness among older people in the city. The Committee provides housing and social services to men and women aged 60 years or more who are homeless or at risk of becoming homeless. It develops and runs its own housing sites and has four schemes designed to create a sense of community and promote independence among people who have often been isolated, untrusting, and hesitant to change entrenched patterns of behaviour. Most had been considered 'unhouseable'.

The first project, *Bishop Street*, is a shared house (congregate living programme) in a residential area for nine homeless women. Each tenant has her own bedroom and shares a kitchen and living room. It has disabled access, a lift, and a garden. Staff are on-site 24 hours and a daily communal meal is provided. The services include case management with care plans (service and treatment plans), and assistance with personal care, the activities of daily living and life-management skills. Five of the nine current tenants are eligible for professional nursing, social work, and home-maker services, all funded by the *Massachusetts Department of Medical Assistance* through the Group Adult Foster Care Programme (GAFC). The goal of this programme is to provide an alternative to and, where possible, prevent admission to a nursing home.

The *Symphony Shared Living Programme*, funded by the *Massachusetts Department of Mental Health*, has 11 apartments for mentally ill older people who were previously homeless or at risk of homelessness. The programme aims to promote the highest possible level of autonomy by providing stable housing in which the tenants are helped to develop or improve their life-management skills, and to widen their social networks both within and outside of the housing community. The programme is staffed by a social worker (the director), resident assistants, an overnight live-in worker, and a nurse. The programme has been very successful in housing clients with significant behaviour and medical problems.

Anna Bissonnette House accommodates 40 formerly homeless older men and women in 22 studio apartments and 18 one-bedroom apartments on four floors. Each apartment has a kitchen and bathroom, and on each floor there is a communal kitchen, sitting room with a television, and a laundry. There is also a large living room on the ground-floor. The average age of the tenants is 66 years, and almost one-third are women. While many of the men have substance abuse problems, many of the women are mentally ill. It is staffed 24 hours, with a social worker (the director), a nurse, a substance abuse worker, resident assistants, personal care assistants, an activities co-ordinator, and a resident overnight manager. A doctor and a psychiatrist visit regularly.

The aim of the project is to promote independent living while providing needed support. Two meals a week are currently provided at the project, but plans are underway to offer one hot meal daily. Hence the tenants have the choice of self-catering or eating in the communal dining room. Activities are a key feature of the project, with regular exercise and social groups, and education, literacy, health promotion and nutrition classes. The on-site nurse provides health screening services, and 'alcoholics anonymous' meetings are held at the project.

The fourth and newest site, Ruth Cowin House, is scheduled to open in January 2000. It is a restored house in Brookline, Massachusetts. With nine apartments, a common community room, a newly installed lift and a sunken garden, this site completes the range of housing options in CEEH's continuum of care. The organisation has now reached a point in its development that allows staff to 'match' the size and characteristics of each site to the characteristics and special needs of each older homeless person.

**Box 6.4:** HOUSING AND SUPPORT SERVICES FOR OLDER HOMELESS PEOPLE, MELBOURNE, AUSTRALIA

*Bryan Lipmann, the Chief Executive of Wintringham in Australia, describes the innovative housing and support services that his organisation has developed for older homeless people.*

Wintringham is a specialised not-for-profit welfare company in Melbourne, Australia that is committed to providing elderly homeless men and women with high quality services. The vision of social justice that drives Wintringham is that older homeless men and women should have the right to affordable and secure housing and receive care services of the same standard as the rest of the community.

Wintringham believes strongly that realistic strategies to prevent older people from becoming homeless include the provision of a range of practical housing and care services. Importantly, all of the housing and residential care facilities that we have built are unashamedly beautiful buildings. In setting new standards of housing for older homeless people, some of these buildings have won international acclaim. People adapt to their environment in ways that we are only beginning to understand. Wintringham believes that providing a dignified and enhancing home assists residents not only to feel positively about themselves, but also to be valued members of society.

While our buildings are all different and reflect the repeated evaluation of our previous efforts, they do retain features of traditional Australian architecture and styles, which older people relate to, and help create a home-like environment. A residential care scheme that continues to work well is in a bay-side region of inner Melbourne. It has six houses, each providing a home for five to seven residents. Each resident has his or her own bedroom, ensuite toilet and shower and verandah all centred around a lounge room, and a staff house-carer to meet day-to-day needs such as menu planning and personal care.

All of the buildings are set in beautiful landscaped gardens, a feature being a fishpond. In addition, there is a centrally located recreational facility called 'the shed', with an adjacent barbecue area. Wintringham works on a belief that environment shapes behaviour and self-image. Providing dignified personal space that a resident can claim as his or her own raises self-esteem and positively affects that person's perceptions of the world around him or her. The aim is to offer residents privacy, personal space and opportunities for interaction. The design of the buildings helps to create small communities in each of the houses and exemplifies how a non-institutional, domestic model of residential care can be delivered to independent-minded residents who need varying degrees of care and support.

### The process of moving people into new accommodation

Homeless elderly people are invariably powerless and withdrawn. The survival skills they have developed over many years involve patterns of behaviour that minimise their risk from violence or harassment. This frequently results in their acceptance of appalling housing or shelter for fear of what the future could hold. As a consequence, simply to offer quality housing alternatives does not guarantee its acceptance. Some readily take the opportunity to escape from homelessness: for others a worker will require a lengthy period of contact in order to win their trust and confidence.

Wintringham places great importance on the formation of this trusting relationship and sees it as the single most important factor in ensuring that a formerly homeless aged person makes a successful transition to permanent housing. Our housing alternatives now extend from full nursing home residential care to independent apartments. The quality of the units does not vary, but the level of support is adapted to needs. The notion that people can stay 'until stumps', or open-endedly, is critical to the resident establishing his or her identity and sense of home. A lifetime of movement and the constant threat of eviction creates its own expectation of vulnerability, but as new residents become aware of the possibilities and benefits of permanent housing, they begin to create their own friendships and their own supports. This process is actively encouraged.

The uncertainty and anxiety associated with moving from night shelters, dormitories or sleeping rough to private single-room apartments with fully equipped kitchens, stocked fridges, heating, carpets and ensuite showers should never be underestimated. There have been instances where formerly homeless men found the apartments too big and imposing and so dragged their beds out of their bedrooms and slept in the lounge or kitchen. But interestingly, within a week or so, they became accustomed to their new surroundings and returned the bed to the bedroom. With a sense of permanence comes growing confidence and assertiveness and a level of self-dignity that is inspiring to witness.

## Support and adjustment to settled living

The need to provide low-level flexible support services to vulnerable people in the community has been recognised by British social housing providers since the mid-1990s, as shown by the increased employment of support workers to offer advice and assistance to their tenants (Ellenby, 1999; Goldup, 1999; Morrish, 1996; Quilgars,

1998). The monitoring of and support for rehoused homeless people is crucial. The *Homeless Mentally Ill Initiative* teams found that most tenancy breakdowns occurred shortly after the teams withdrew their support (Craig, 1995). Although some formerly homeless people may require support only for the first few months, the support needs of others do not reduce over time. Well organised monitoring and support requires: (i) reliable and flexible ways of keeping in contact with those who are rehoused; (ii) ways of assessing and adjusting counselling and instrumental support; (iii) approaches and instruments that reliably detect critical levels of 'residential distress', loneliness and low morale; and (iv) regular liaison between the resettlement agency, the landlord and the support services.

The type and intensity of help that is available to rehoused homeless people varies. Some organisations deploy community support workers for only the first 6–12 months after a person has been rehoused, and dissuade ex-residents from keeping in contact with their former hostel. The rationale is to reduce dependency and promote integration in the community. Other organisations offer long-term support, maintain contact with ex-residents, and encourage them to seek help from the staff if they are experiencing difficulties. The Over-55s Accommodation Project in Leeds has a monthly luncheon club for older people who have been rehoused, and the Zambesi Project in Birmingham runs a monthly ex-residents' support group (Box 5.3). At Valley Lodge in New York City, former residents are encouraged to return and meet with their key workers for the first three months after being rehoused. This enables the staff, who are already familiar with the clients and their problems, to monitor progress, give advice or assistance if required, and detect difficulties at an early stage. This is particularly important for those older people who will not seek help when they have problems (Crane and Warnes, 2000b).

Some formerly homeless older people, when rehoused, continue their homeless lifestyle, spend most of the time on the streets or at day centres for homeless people, and only return to their accommodation for a few hours at night (Crane, 1999). To promote self-esteem and self-worth, encourage settledness, and reduce problems such as loneliness and heavy drinking which can lead to tenancy failures, it is necessary to help rehoused people gain confidence and adjust to their new lifestyle. At the Abraham Residences in the Seagate Community, New York City, and the Anna Bissonnette House in Boston, activities co-ordinators organise diverse social, educational and other activities for the tenants. An innovative scheme in London, developed by St Mungo's in 1999, is a day centre specifically for homeless people who have been rehoused but remain vulnerable. It provides support and a range of activities to build interests and skills, including computer classes, cookery, photography and handicrafts.

# Resettling older homeless people who are mentally ill or heavy drinkers

Many older homeless people with mental health or alcohol-related problems are unable to manage in independent accommodation even with support. They require a high level of care or supervision with everyday tasks, including personal hygiene, medication, nutrition, and health care, and are most appropriately housed in residential group homes that are staffed 24 hours. There are, however, difficulties in getting the British statutory agencies to accept responsibility for vulnerable formerly homeless people. The Homeless Mentally Ill Initiative teams' attempts to resettle people with mental health problems were frequently blocked by a lack of resources and the reluctance of local authority social services departments and community mental health teams to take on the responsibility for people who needed long-term support (Craig, 1995). To be considered eligible for funding, a person generally needs to have a 'local connection' with a local authority. Some older homeless people have moved around the country for years and have no connection with any authority. Furthermore, many local authorities will not fund people in their fifties who have chronic alcohol problems to enter high-care residential homes even though their behaviour may be too chaotic for them to manage independently. The problems experienced by one resettlement worker are described in Box 6.5.

> **BOX 6.5:** RESETTLING OLDER HOMELESS PEOPLE INTO SPECIALIST ACCOMMODATION, ST MUNGO'S, LONDON
>
> *Terry Thomas was the resettlement worker at the erstwhile Lancefield Street Centre in London. He describes the intricacies involved in resettling older homeless people, particularly those who are unable to live alone and require specialist accommodation.*
>
> I was employed by St Mungo's as the resettlement worker at the *Lancefield Street Centre* from April 1997 until its closure in December 1998, having previously had experience of resettling older homeless people from a cold-weather shelter in London. The safe, secure and trusting environment of Lancefield Street allowed older homeless people who had lost their trust in the 'system' to rebuild confidence in welfare staff. It allowed me to work constructively with the clients towards the final goal – the provision of secure permanent accommodation in conventional or special needs housing with an appropriate balance of personal and social support. A resettlement worker can successfully help and rehouse clients only once this initial trust has formed.
>
> Successful resettlement means balancing the preferences of the clients with their lifestyles and needs. For example, there are some older homeless people who want to live independently in a flat but their housing histories and their conduct in hostels demonstrate that they would be unable to manage living alone. There is then the difficult task of informing them that they cannot be rehoused in independent

accommodation but could be offered supported housing. Some clients with physical or mental incapacities need and qualify for high-care group homes. These are staffed 24 hours and funded by local authority social services departments. I did not find it particularly difficult to advise residents that this was the form of support they needed even though their weekly disposable income would fall, because most of their social security entitlement would be expended for their care. Most residents did not seriously question the need for them to live in such a setting.

Finding the most appropriate accommodation for each resident is an important part of resettlement. Apart from places in St Mungo's stock of supported housing, high-care homes and specialist projects, I sought accommodation from other housing organisations. Networking and talking to colleagues both inside and outside of my organisation and following diverse leads often uncovered seemingly unlikely sources of permanent housing. Colleagues in housing associations were willing to offer accommodation to clients who were capable of living independently. By discussing with other specialist and hostel workers the problems of finding appropriate accommodation for certain residents, they were able to offer advice on organisations that might help, and this in turn led to additional housing opportunities.

There are many difficulties with resettling older homeless people, not least because many are heavy drinkers and suffer from memory loss. This causes problems when trying to compile personal housing histories – an accurate housing history is the bedrock of resettlement planning. Those who are ashamed of their past housing failures may be evasive and withhold important information. Some do not wish information to be gathered from other agencies and one resident left the hostel complaining that he considered the questions pried into his personal affairs. Anxiety is another problem. Many clients become extremely anxious prior to being rehoused and starting a new life. One client had 'hidden' mental health problems which only surfaced when he moved into a sheltered flat – his mental health state deteriorated, he began to drink heavily, could not sustain his tenancy, and had to return to the hostel for further assessment. With the help of staff, the majority of residents can, however, manage through this period of extreme stress.

For those clients who need high-care group homes, the places are funded by local authority social services departments (SSDs). Although many SSD care managers were helpful and promptly assessed a client's needs and arranged funding, there were difficulties in negotiating assessments and obtaining funding from some local authorities. Where I could establish the location of 'normal residence', I sought out the local authority with the area responsibility. There is however 'parcel passing' among SSDs when a request is made for a community care assessment (which carries the prospect of expenditure on a long-term housing placement). If, moreover, a resident has alcohol and mental health problems then the issue of 'dual diagnosis' comes into play. An effective mental health condition cannot be diagnosed until the resident is sober, yet this is sometimes difficult to achieve. Some clients were referred to the SSD substance misuse teams, who then referred on to their disabilities section, only for the clients to be passed back to the original team. This can be frustrating and time-consuming for the client and the resettlement worker. One local authority took a whole year to decide which team was responsible for a client who had been diagnosed as having a severe personality disorder. Some older homeless people are heavy drinkers and their behaviour is so chaotic that they could not manage in independent or minimally supported housing projects, but many local authorities will not fund such clients in high-care group homes. At Lancefield Street, several of this group had to return to all-age generalist hostels when the project closed.

Despite the difficulties, funding was agreed with local authority social services departments for 18 Lancefield Street residents to be rehoused in high-care group homes. A further 34 residents were resettled in independent tenancies or shared houses.

## Housing for older homeless people with special needs

Organisations in London, Glasgow, Nottingham, Aberdeen and elsewhere have developed residential group homes (with 20–30 beds) for homeless people with severe mental health and alcohol-related problems who need high levels of care and support. It is generally found that such people do better in environments that tolerate relatively high levels of disorganised behaviour, have modest expectations of improvement, and are highly supported by staff who have a good understanding of the problems (Craig, 1995). *Aspinden Wood*, London, for example, is a group home for 24 residents aged 40 years and more with histories of heavy drinking and who have found it difficult to manage tenancies. In most areas of the country, however, such accommodation is scarce. Instead of providing separate homes, some organisations in London have established a high-care unit within an existing large hostel. One drawback is that the image and stigma remains of being attached to a large institutional setting. Boxes 6.6 and 6.7 describe projects in London and Manchester that are working in innovative ways to support formerly homeless heavy drinkers in the community.

---

**BOX 6.6:** SUPPORTED HOUSING FOR OLDER HEAVY DRINKERS, BRIDGE

HOUSING ASSOCIATION, LONDON

*Connie Stapleton, the team leader at Green Lanes, north London, a long-term supported housing scheme for older heavy drinkers, describes the help and support that is provided to the tenants, and the changes that the tenants and staff have experienced since the project opened in May 1997.*

*Green Lanes* provides long-term supported housing to men and women who have long histories of homelessness and heavy drinking. The scheme, funded through the *Rough Sleeper's Initiative*, is managed by Bridge Housing Association. It has 15 furnished one-bedroom flats, each with a separate living room, kitchen and bathroom. There is a lift to its three floors, a garden, and a staff office on the ground-floor. Two staff are based at the project; we work mainly during office hours but also some evenings. The staff at another Bridge HA hostel nearby can provide out-of-hours advice and emergency assistance to the tenants, but it has rarely been required. Our prime task is to provide housing management and tenancy support, which is done by working intensively with the tenants, and responding to needs and issues as they arise. We help the tenants to access specialist services, and advise on life-skills such as cooking and financial management and the new or expanded responsibilities of managing a tenancy. We offer a programme of education, focusing on what responsibility means in practice and how it affects their own life, and how their actions affect others. These issues are usually discussed informally in the tenant's flat.

Since the project's inception, we have been through several transitions. The majority of the tenants had been in hostels and slept rough for years, and were accustomed to a street homeless lifestyle. Some had had tenancies in the past but were unable to manage them. When the project opened, the tenants had 'hostel attitudes' and were dependent on a high level of support. For our part, we were used to doing things for residents. It was appreciated that there would be a long settling-in period for both the tenants and us, and that the tenants would need a high level of support in the early months.

Most of the tenants arrived together, which encouraged peer understanding and mutual support. The reality of having a flat, a home and new or different responsibilities soon became apparent. This provided some with the motivation to buy possessions for their flats and create a home. Their attitude was, 'I've got my flat now and I don't want to go to day centres or do anything that is institutionalised'. Occasionally they needed assistance with bills or re-lighting boilers, and more general support was needed to deal with problems with other tenants, tenancy breaches and hygiene issues. The residents also needed encouragement to take control of their own affairs, e.g. ringing the electricity company and making social contacts outside the project.

Others felt 'stalled' – obtaining a flat had disrupted their lifestyles and aspects of their identities. Adjusting to their new accommodation and responsibilities had exhausted their capacity to absorb anything new. They also realised that their situation was no longer 'temporary' and that some things could no longer be conveniently put off. We offered constant reassurance, responded to spontaneous needs, encouraged independence, and basically ensured that they could 'tick over' until they were able to accommodate further change. Some found it difficult to adjust to the changes in their social contacts brought about by the move. A few tenants had once mixed with street drinkers but felt that they no longer fitted into the street culture. To alleviate loneliness, some brought street drinkers to their flats, but the visitors disturbed the other tenants and put their own tenancies in jeopardy. They wanted company but were not in control of the situation. We dealt with this problem by strongly emphasising to the tenants their responsibilities, and explaining clearly how they could manage these difficulties and the choices that they had.

At the same time as each tenant faced individual changes, one problem affected them all. Neighbour disputes caused disturbances and would occasionally lead to violent incidents. Through empowering and sensitive support, the tenants were able to deal with disturbances from their neighbours more assertively and constructively. It is important that the needs of other tenants are considered and that a safe environment is provided for all, including neighbours and staff.

Although Green Lanes is a 'wet project', dilemmas occur when tenants choose to reduce their drinking. One implication is that they have to review their social activities and networks; if they continue to socialise with the other tenants, there is the temptation to start drinking again. They need to be distracted from this, but their confidence to pursue other activities is not always high. There is also a tension between wanting to move away from a drinking environment but not to give up the flat. Finding a balance proves difficult and we are all learning through experience how to manage these issues.

The attitudes of both tenants and staff have changed considerably since the project opened. The tenants are learning to be independent and the staff are learning to encourage this adjustment. A few tenants have been reluctant to accept individual responsibility and continue to rely on the staff, but these dependent attitudes are progressively declining. We try to keep up with a tenant's changing attitudes, to present the right options at the right times to facilitate informed choice, to spread the realisation that any decision produces consequences that may or may not be acceptable, and to offer support for their choices. The key support is that the staff are consistently available at the project. We chat, pass the time of day, and help the tenants get through the challenges that present day-to-day: difficulties that would be trivial to the outsider can be highly problematic to a tenant. With lots of contact, we are able to promote self-esteem, stability and confidence among the tenants. This enhances their growing independence and their ability to maintain their tenancies.

## Box 6.7: The Heavy Drinkers Project, Methodist Housing Association, Manchester

*Yen Ly, the former manager of the project, describes how older people who have been long-term heavy drinkers, including some who have been 'crude' drinkers (of methylated and surgical spirits), are supported in long-term housing in the community. Her contribution details the intensive help that the clients receive.*

The *Heavy Drinkers Project*, Manchester, was established in 1985 by *Peterloo Housing Association*, and is now run by *Manchester Methodist Housing Association*. The aims are threefold: (i) to allow the residents to live in the community as independently as possible; (ii) to help them gain control over their own lives; and (iii) to minimise the harm done by long-term alcohol consumption. The project comprises a group home for seven men, and nine small dispersed houses nearby. The core house offers a high level of support to the most vulnerable residents, with 24-hour staff cover, and staff from the core house support the clients in the dispersed houses. The houses nearby each accommodate two clients who have their own bedrooms but share other living spaces (originally they each accommodated three tenants, but there were frequent arguments among them).

The clients have various medical and mental problems related to alcohol abuse, poor nutrition and physical neglect and many are progressive. Excessive alcohol consumption can lead to multiple health problems including liver and kidney failure. The damage to mental health is less tangible, but the common symptoms are memory loss, depression, and low self-esteem. The clients tend to have few social skills, which in turn affects their ability to access services. We work in close partnership with other service providers, including the City of Manchester's Social Services alcohol team, the community mental health team, community psychiatric nurses, the local health centre, and local hospitals. All clients have a care manager from social services, and regular reviews and assessments take place with the project staff and the care manager.

We have a key worker system and each client has an individualised care plan. Their needs are varied and complex, the most basic being for long-term, safe and secure accommodation. Another priority is for ongoing health care. We ensure that the residents are registered with local GPs, accompany them to appointments when necessary, and seek referrals to specialist services as appropriate. With the clients' agreement, we dispense their medication to maximise compliance. Providing a balanced diet with flexibility over meal times helps to ensure that the residents eat well, which in turn helps to keep them fit and healthy and reduces the effects of heavy drinking. Many need help and encouragement with personal hygiene.

We work hard with the clients to control and in some cases to reduce their alcohol consumption and to stop them drinking crude spirits, which are extremely damaging to their health. Many enter into budget agreements by which they spend a small amount each day on alcohol rather than binge heavily once a week. On occasions, the staff may purchase alcohol for the clients to ensure that it is of decent quality. Drinking schools are discouraged in the group home. A minority eventually decide to give up drinking alcohol and when this happens we wholeheartedly support them. In some cases they are successful, but this is not a realistic outcome for most clients.

The tenants in the dispersed houses receive a great deal of assistance. Two support workers assist them with personal hygiene and bathing and generally attend to their well-being. Every weekday a food package is prepared at the core house and distributed to the tenants in the dispersed houses. The package has a frozen meal, sandwiches, eggs, fruit, bread, sugar and tea. The tenants pay for this each week, and it ensures that they receive adequate nutrition. A cleaner is employed 20 hours per week for the satellite houses and helps the tenants to clean the kitchen and change their beds. Each house has an alarm connected to Manchester Social Services for out-of-hours emergencies, and there are always staff at the group home to help the tenants. One room at the core house is used to provide respite care if a tenant in one of the satellite houses is ill or not coping and temporarily requires support or supervision. This room is frequently used.

Most residents are able over time to reduce their drinking or to drink better quality alcohol. Most stop drinking crude spirits. In the past, most have been arrested and charged on numerous occasions for drinking and causing a disturbance in public, but this no longer happens and the men are now 'out of the legal system'. For some, there has been an improvement in their physical and mental health, and most have learned to manage their own money and attend to their personal hygiene. In summary, they have gained dignity and self-respect.

**The way ahead**
The project works creatively and innovatively with a group of men who have previously been excluded from services. We are constantly seeking ways to improve our service by working with statutory and voluntary agencies to identify unmet needs. An additional six self-contained flats for the project are being developed, to enable us to offer a choice of single accommodation to our clients. Should a resident wish to abstain from alcohol, he could do so without the temptation and pressure from his co-tenants. Equally important, this development will enable us to provide accommodation and support to women who are heavy drinkers and who cannot be accommodated in our existing shared houses. A steering group is currently examining methods of service delivery to meet the needs of women who are heavy drinkers.

It is always difficult to measure success in a project where every outcome is individual. However, the project is providing 'care in the community' in an individual and practical way and we believe gives good value for money. From the residents' point of view, the project is preferable to the alternatives of street life or institutionalisation.

## Resettling long-stay hostel residents

Some older people have lived in temporary hostels for more than 25 years and have become dependent on the setting (Crane and Warnes, 1997a). As a few schemes in Britain, Germany, America and Australia have demonstrated, it is possible to resettle some from this group. When successful, the individual gains independence, confidence and motivation; becomes more sociable, drinks less and eats better; improves self-care and hygiene; and some renew contact with relatives (Crane and Warnes, 1997b; Elias and Inui, 1993; Hallebone, 1997). In Bielefeld, Germany, 26 elderly homeless men were rehoused from a traditional hostel into converted flats in three houses nearby. Their average duration of homelessness was 13 years, and many had poor health, were heavy drinkers, and had never previously held a tenancy (Harvey, 1998). An evaluation of the scheme found that many of the men had become more independent, had engaged in new activities and social relationships, and some had renewed family contact. Many had learned to manage their own accommodation and finances, although approximately one-third continued to need help. The scheme demonstrates well the long-term savings that successful resettlement achieves, for there were 6.5 full-time equivalent hostel staff at the traditional hostel but only 0.5 fte in the housing scheme. Box 6.8 describes the comparable experiences and reactions of older homeless men in Melbourne, Australia, who were resettled from a Salvation Army hostel into supported housing.

**BOX 6.8:** MOVING FROM AN INNER CITY INSTITUTION TO SUPPORTED

CLUSTER ACCOMMODATION

*In this contribution Major Graeme McClimont, Assistant Director of the Research and Development Unit of the Salvation Army in London, reports his experiences of resettling into supported tenancies older men who had lived for years in the organisation's homeless hostel in Melbourne, Victoria, Australia.*

The front door of the flat was closed, and we had to knock to enter. We were greeted at the door by Ray, one of the tenants, who introduced us to three other gentlemen sitting in the lounge. They had all been residents of the now defunct *James Bray Salvation Army Hostel* for homeless older men in the inner city of Melbourne. They had moved to *James Barker House*, which provides supported 'cluster' accommodation for financially disadvantaged older people. It was a new experience to be greeted at *their* front door as we entered their lounge.

At James Bray each of the 45 residents had had his own small room while all other facilities were shared. Meals were at set times and there was a generally rigid separation of the roles of personal carers, cleaners, kitchen and administration staff. The facility was adjacent to a crisis accommodation service for up to 120 homeless men and diagonally opposite a day centre for the homeless, in a part of the inner city well known for its homeless sub-culture. Establishing the new accommodation had taken the Salvation Army three years from conception to birth. It is in Footscray, a thriving cosmopolitan community and suburban transport hub, three miles from the former haunts of most of the residents, and its location just off the High Street is busy by day but quiet at night.

The physical design is as important as the model of care. James Barker House accommodates 45 people, is purpose-built, and each occupant lives in a flat or cluster with six or seven other residents, initially all male. There are three ground and three first-floor flats. Each resident has a large room with private facilities and a view of the garden or the street. Older homeless people are good 'watchers' and the opportunity to see the world pass by needed to be retained. Each flat has a kitchen, lounge, dining area, large balcony or garden area and laundry. There are central office, staff, personal care, recreational and barbecue facilities. There is no central dining area or kitchen. The unit arrangement means that when behaviour problems occur, they are limited in impact to that unit.

The residents are aged between 44 and 88 years. Two-thirds have physical health problems, around half a diagnosed mental illness, and a similar proportion an alcohol dependency problem. Almost half have diagnosed brain damage, usually alcohol-related, and most present behaviour problems. The service operates a social, not a medical, model of care. Residents can rise when they want, get their own breakfast, and make themselves snacks and assist with meal preparation. Different meals are provided in each unit and at different times. The principles behind the social model of care include:

- this is the occupant's home and, as his or her needs change, services are increased rather than the person moved on, i.e. the occupant may 'age in place'
- independence, empowerment, and normalisation
- creating a sense of place and a homelike and safe environment
- access to services, quality health care, and participation.

The staff have general 'home-making' roles and assist in personal care, cooking, cleaning, laundry and programmed activities. They have nursing, mental health and social services backgrounds. The service, while providing a relaxed living environment, also prepares care plans with strategies to achieve specific goals. The care plans set out needs assessments and goals across 40 items, including personal hygiene, eating and sleeping, communication, medical problems, social relations, special therapy needs and behaviour. Daily programmes attempt to link the residents to a broad range of services in the local community, be they health, social, employment (in a few cases) or welfare. Key additional services include a recreational programme that links residents into the community, and an alcohol worker who supports both the residents and the staff by minimising the disruptive and harmful impacts of alcohol abuse.

### Outcomes of the move and lessons learned

- On the first morning when the men were admitted, a wave of anger swept the facility: 'it was not right that they had to get their own breakfast, they were paying good money and expected to be waited on as in the past'. Within two weeks this attitude had changed. The men are now cooking their own special dishes, and preparing meals for their mates who need help.
- A concern was that the residents would drift back to their old patch. None has done so and, when asked if they would like to return, the usual response is a polite 'no thank you'.
- After having been cut off from the community, many have been welcomed by the local *Elderly Citizen's Club* and the *Returned Soldiers League*. Many join in celebrations, as at Melbourne Cup time, and the Friday afternoon dances that women from a nearby hostel attend. This 'busyness' encourages social interaction and helps to minimise alcohol abuse.
- The provision of a high quality, homelike environment markedly improves the residents' self-image and behaviour. At James Bray hostel one man would not speak but remained silently in a corner, but at James Barker House has come out of his shell and is animated.
- A large group (in this case 42) of residents can be moved in a group if they are well informed and have had the opportunity to participate in the development. They will have some idea of what to expect.

Resettling older homeless people who have lived in hostels for years is not easy. They are likely to be apprehensive and the preparation might extend over many months. In London, 25 homeless men over the age of 60 years were rehoused from *Arlington House*, a large direct-access hostel managed by Bridge Housing Association, into a purpose-built supported group home nearby. Most men had lived in the hostel for more than 20 years. The preparation lasted eight months and involved regular discussions between the staff and the men, who visited the project frequently as it was being built and were involved in selecting the furnishings and furniture (Crane and Warnes, 1997b). The experience of six older men who, after 15 months' preparation, were resettled from the *Fyffe Centre* (a direct-access hostel) in Lowestoft, Suffolk, into a purpose-built supported group of flats is described in Box 6.9.

---

**Box 6.9:** Resettling older homeless men into supported housing, Lowestoft, Suffolk

*Lana Ward has been a resettlement worker at the Fyffe Centre, Lowestoft, Suffolk, since 1994. She was involved in resettling six older men who had been in the hostel for years into supported housing. This contribution describes the intensive preparation that was given to the men in readiness for the move.*

The Fyffe Centre is a direct-access hostel, managed by the *St John's Housing Trust*. It opened in 1985 and accommodates 26 single homeless people. Funding was obtained in 1994 for my post as a resettlement worker. One of my first priorities was to address the housing and support needs of six male residents who had been in the hostel between two and eight years. The men had become institutionalised, were unable to practise everyday skills, and were not functioning well. Furthermore, six bed spaces were 'blocked' and we were unable to admit people who were homeless.

Five of the men were over 60 years of age and one was in his late forties. They all had mental health or alcohol-related problems, and had been homeless and unsettled for many years. Within the hostel, the men lived as a group, always eating meals and socialising together, and generally looking out for each other. To attempt to divide the group would have caused a great deal of distress and probably further emotional and social problems. Their preferences, needs and lifestyle meant that mainstream older people's accommodation, such as sheltered housing or a residential home, would have not been suitable.

After several months of intensive meetings between *St John's Housing Trust, Waveney District Council Social Services* and *Suffolk Heritage Housing Association,* funding was obtained to build three two-bedroom flats specifically as 'move-on' accommodation and to provide long-term support. When all the funding was in place and a site (Sandringham Road) was secured, there were approximately 18 months to prepare the men for the move. Many feared that the men would simply not be able to cope with the change. I gave each man the news individually, and all coped surprisingly well.

As the move was not to be for a year and a half, there was no immediate 'threat'. Rather, the men's main concerns were: (i) will we be together? (ii) will there be someone on duty at night? (iii) will there be a cook? and (iv) how will this affect us financially?

During the subsequent 18 months, there were inevitably times of great apprehension. It was therefore important that all staff were positive, encouraging and supportive but also entirely candid. It was explained, for example, that while there would not be a cook, they would be given every assistance. I felt that it was important for the men to have a sense of 'ownership' of the project, and so involved them in many aspects of its development – without overwhelming them and creating unnecessary anxieties. I worked closely with two social workers and we met the men regularly. Each man had a 'project folder' with plans of the new building, photographs as it was being built, and a plan of the local area which marked local shops and other amenities. Additional information was added throughout the 18 months. The men, with help from the staff, selected the colour schemes for their flat and chose their own carpets, curtains and furniture. This could have been daunting, so no one was pressured into doing things, and the men contributed as much as they felt comfortable with and at their own pace. They showed interest, attended all the meetings, and had pride in their project folders, which they showed to other residents. A characteristic comment was, 'this is where we're going, great isn't it'. To make the transition as smooth as possible, the project staff were appointed four weeks before it opened. The manager was based at the Fyffe Centre for this time and the support workers visited regularly to build up familiarity and rapport with the men.

The Sandringham Road project has been running for three and a half years. Staff provide cover seven days a week. Night cover was provided for the first six months and ceased once the men's confidence had increased. All of the men settled happily and each progressed in his own way. One man had been at the Fyffe Centre for eight years and for five had never left the building. He had been very withdrawn and communicated little with the other residents, but within weeks of moving to Sandringham Road, he was going to the local shops to buy tobacco, initiating conversations, and helping to prepare meals.

I believe that the two factors that contributed most to the success of the move were: (i) having sufficient time to prepare the men emotionally and practically for the move; and (ii) the high level of support that was given. In addition the project demonstrated the practical importance and value of empowerment, of enabling the men to participate in improving their own circumstances. It was this that increased their motivation and self-confidence.

## Conclusions

The value of following good practice in resettling homeless people into permanent accommodation is increasingly recognised. This chapter has described several innovative schemes that have successfully resettled older people with complex problems and long histories of homelessness. Resettlement programmes are multiplying but are unco-ordinated and unevenly developed. Schemes differ according to the experience and qualifications of staff and the range of interventions, and by the type and intensity of follow-up support. Few resettlement programmes in Britain have been evaluated (Randall and Brown, 1994), and there is little evidence of the direct outcomes, not even of the number who remain housed after several months, and even less on the factors that influence success. Only a few studies have contacted former homeless people who have been rehoused (Dant and Deacon, 1989; Duncan and Downey, 1985; Duncan *et al.* 1983). In contrast, several evaluations have been undertaken of the resettlement of both mentally ill people from long-stay hospitals and of those with learning disabilities (Etheringon *et al.* 1995; Higgins and Richardson, 1994). The cost-effectiveness of such moves has been examined (Dockerell *et al.* 1995; Knapp *et al.* 1994), and the progress of those resettled has been monitored for up to five years (Trieman *et al.* 1998; Francis *et al.* 1994).

Many rehoused people either cede tenancies or are evicted and return to homelessness. Information is required about the factors that are associated with successful and unsuccessful resettlement. Personal factors, programme content, and the characteristics of the new home could all be implicated. One study in London found that many rehoused people had problems with paying bills, budgeting and sorting out grants and housing benefit payments, and that many accumulated rent arrears (Randall and Brown, 1994). Another study of rehoused hostel residents in Leeds found no connection between tenancy failure and either their prior experience of managing household chores and paying bills or their contact with relatives and friends (Dant and Deacon, 1989). Resettlement tended to be least successful for those who had been in the city less than six months.

Many homeless people are rehoused without adequate planning and preparation because they are required to take up their tenancies immediately. Yet the negative effect of moving into a tenancy hastily and ill prepared are rarely acknowledged. Heavy drinking, mental health problems, and loneliness also influence the success of resettlement, particularly if people are rehoused in independent accommodation without adequate support. Some older homeless people have lost tenancies because they drank excessively and did not pay the rent (Crane, 1999). More information is required about the effectiveness of different programmes of monitoring and support. One recent study in New York City found that mentally ill men who were given additional support when rehoused from a temporary shelter were less likely to become homeless than those who received the customary level: the benefit continued even after the enhanced support ceased (Susser *et al.* 1997).

The 1990s saw a growing interest in the contribution that resettlement can make to the prevention and alleviation of homelessness in Britain and many other countries, and many effective housing and support schemes have developed. These require evaluation, and the lessons should be disseminated to other service providers working with homeless people and other vulnerable groups. There are still far too many homeless people being resettled ineffectively and returning to homelessness. This is costly for society, harmful to the subjects, and demoralises and debilitates the efforts of homeless services staff. As this chapter has shown, there are sufficient demonstrations of good practice to know that we can do better.

# Section II

# Establishing services for older homeless people

# Chapter 7

# Frameworks for service development and support

This chapter aims to provide both a general understanding of and some practical guidance in using the current frameworks in the UK for developing and running effective services for homeless people. Detailed points about the development and provision of services through individual projects are reserved for the next two chapters. The first section summarises the elaboration of central government policies and funding programmes during the 1990s and the changed priorities of the post-1997 Labour administration. The following section surveys the intricate and variable mesh of responsibilities and practice among statutory and voluntary agencies at the local (city or county) level. If more and more local initiatives are being enabled by central government funds, their capacity to help is related to their linkages with established specialist providers. The task of fitting into a spectrum of local provision is, however, complicated by the rapidity of change in social housing and the National Health Service as well as homeless services policy. The third section therefore focuses on the new opportunities for developing health care services for homeless people associated with the changes in primary health care, while the fourth describes the role of voluntary organisations in providing local homeless services. The chapter concludes with a selective and reflective account of contrasting frameworks and approaches in other countries.

## Central government programmes

### The Rough Sleepers' Initiative and other programmes: 1990–99

Since the late 1980s in the UK, central government has played an increasing and more directive role in the development and funding of services for homeless people. It has been responding both to the welfare problems of the increase in the number of young homeless rough sleepers in central London, and to strong pressures for action from the media, tourism, retail companies and the general public, for many were (and are) both discomfited by street sleepers and cannot understand why, in an increasingly affluent society, young people live that way. Because neither voluntary organisations nor the local authorities had the resources to tackle the problem, in 1990 the Conservative Government launched the *Rough Sleepers' Initiative (RSI)*, '[to make] it unnecessary to have to sleep rough in central London' (DoE *et al.* 1995, p.5).

Over three three-year phases, more than £255 million has been allocated through the RSI for temporary and permanent accommodation for single homeless people, for outreach and resettlement workers, and for a programme of winter shelters that provide free accommodation and support from December to March each year. In its third phase from 1996, the RSI was extended to 28 other towns and cities, including Bristol, Brighton, Southampton and Nottingham (DoE *et al.* 1995; 1996).

The RSI initiated radical changes in the roles of central government, local government, other statutory agencies and voluntary organisations in homeless service provision. These continue, most recently with the growing contributions of 'registered social housing providers' (which may now be for-profit organisations), and prospectively in a developing role for primary care NHS trusts. While previously central government had funded a nationwide network of direct-access hostels – the (misleadingly named) Resettlement Units – and provided some financial support for other temporary hostel provision, until this initiative the primary responsibility for homelessness was allocated to local authority housing departments (Drake, 1989). The RSI placed for the first time the control of funds for specific local projects with central government. The procedure is that the Department of the Environment, Transport and the Regions (DETR, formerly Department of the Environment) invites non-statutory organisations to submit project bids which have been approved by the local authorities. Although at the outset the stated aim was to return the responsibility for housing rough sleepers to local authorities, the prospect was explicitly abandoned in 1996.

Supplementary funding programmes for specialist services have complemented the RSI initiatives. The Department of Health and the Mental Health Foundation launched the *Homeless Mentally Ill Initiative (HMII)* in 1990 to coincide with the RSI and as a response to the increasing number of mentally ill people sleeping rough in central London (Craig, 1995). Its purpose was to provide short-term accommodation and support while resettlement was arranged in conventional or supported housing. Over £20 million was made available for outreach teams and specialist hostel places (Department of Health, 1992; 1990). In parallel with the third phase of the RSI, the HMII was extended with a budget of nearly £2 million over the three years (DoE, 1996). The DETR also allocated £8 million a year to voluntary sector organisations through section 180 grants for the prevention of homelessness among single people. *Drug and Alcohol Specific Grants* from the Department of Health fund services to help rough sleepers who are substance abusers – they require 30 per cent matching funds from the local authority. In 1997–98, £720,000 was allocated to 20 schemes. Through a resettlement programme, the Department of Social Security has funded approximately 4300 beds in hostels and move-on accommodation, costing about £18 million a year (Social Exclusion Unit, 1998).

During 1990–99, a total of around £300 million was invested by the government in services for homeless people. Much provision has, however, been short-term and insecure, e.g. the winter shelters operate for just a few months each year and many other projects for just two or three years. This sits uneasily with the time required to set up projects, to identify effective ways of working, to fit into a spectrum of local provision, and to settle and rehabilitate vulnerable people. And despite these substantial programmes, the problem of homelessness had not been curtailed when the Labour Government was elected in May 1997.

## The Rough Sleepers' Unit and Homelessness Action Programme: 1999 onwards

Following the Labour Government's election, the *Social Exclusion Unit* was set up in December 1997 and the following summer it published its objective – to reduce the number of people sleeping rough by two-thirds – and its strategy for tackling rough sleeping (Social Exclusion Unit, 1998). There will be more spending (£145 million for London and £34 million for the rest of England during 1999–2002), better co-ordination of the work of central government departments, local authorities and voluntary organisations (the 'joined-up' approach), and more attention to prevention and resettlement.

The RSI was reconfigured in April 1999 as the *Homelessness Action Programme (HAP)* and *Rough Sleepers' Unit (RSU)* within the DETR, the latter initially for London but by late 1999 with a policy and programme direction role for all England (homeless policies are a devolved responsibility in Scotland and Wales). The first steps for London have been: (i) to create a *Rough Sleepers' Unit* within the DETR and the appointment of Louise Casey (formerly the deputy director of *Shelter*) as the Head of the RSU, (ii) the consolidation as a single budget of the various programme funds provided by different central government initiatives, and (iii) the allocation of £39 million in grants to 26 housing associations for new and improved hostel facilities and support services (DETR, 1999b). Outside London, the first steps have been: (i) the allocation in February 1999 of £27 million to voluntary organisations for 156 new and 98 continuing projects that tackle and prevent homelessness; (ii) an administrative order to the local authorities with a significant rough sleeping problem to appoint a co-ordinator of local action (other local authorities are being pressed to do the same); and (iii) the issue to local authorities of guidance on effective strategies for preventing rough sleeping (DETR, 1999a; 1999c). The 156 new projects have been funded for up to three years. Since September 1999, the programmes for rough sleeping in London and in the rest of England have been integrated within the Rough Sleepers' Unit under the direction of Louise Casey.

Further strategies to tackle the problem were announced by the Rough Sleepers' Unit in December 1999 (DETR, 1999d). Within central London, 'Contact and Assessment Teams' (CATs) will work with rough sleepers in selected geographical areas. Each CAT will be managed by a single agency, and will be responsible for referring rough sleepers firstly to temporary accommodation or specialist services, and secondly to permanent housing. Outside London, this work will be carried out from day centres. In London, other changes will include additional temporary and move-on accommodation; 'rolling shelters', which will provide basic services similar to the cold-weather shelters but which will be open throughout the year; specialist workers for rough sleepers with mental health and addiction problems; a night centre in central London; and six 'Tenancy Sustainment Teams' to support rough sleepers once they are rehoused. The teams will be organised geographically.

## Current priorities

As stated in the foreword to the *1999 Report on Rough Sleeping* (DETR, 1999a), 'the central issue that government departments seek to address is that of prevention'. The target groups are clearly set out in the introduction (para.1.2): '[we must] stem the flow of people arriving on the streets every year [particularly among] care leavers and other vulnerable young people, ex-offenders, and ex-Service personnel'. Chapter 5, 'Better prevention', has extended comments on the ways in which 'national standards of resettlement' and schemes to support the entry or return to employment can reduce the number becoming homeless among these groups. There are however few comments on older homeless people.

A point of controversy first mentioned in the Social Exclusion Unit (1998) report is that the new approaches prospectively involve coercion. A North American influence is likely, for assertive, restrictive and 'low tolerance' approaches towards street people have been vigorously implemented during 1999 in Toronto and New York, generally with the approval of business and property interests but also to the dismay of some church and neighbourhood groups. The power to insist that rough sleepers accept hostel beds will be considered if needed (section 4.23), and the possibility of restricting hostel places only to people who are willing to participate in an employment or training programme may be considered (section 4.27). This has not been raised in the DETR's annual report (1999a). Through a spate of broadsheet newspaper interviews and articles in mid-November 1999, Louise Casey elaborated the principles of the Government's more goal-oriented and prescriptive approach.

Other specific practical measures have been announced. As discussed in Chapter 4, many rough sleepers are not receiving social security or housing benefits and have no proof of identity, which leads to vulnerable people being turned away from hostels and providers losing revenue (Harrison, 1996). The Government intends to make housing benefit payments to hostels during 'a period of grace', a time allowance for a new resident to produce proof of identity and information about earnings (DETR, 1999a, p.22). This will mean that people who have been sleeping rough for years and have neither had contact with services nor claimed benefits will not be excluded from hostels. There is also to be explicit geographic targeting of the Government's efforts. According to street counts, in June 1998 'only Birmingham, Brighton, Bournemouth, Bristol, Oxford, Manchester and Cambridge (in England) had 30 or more rough sleepers on any one night', but 'we welcome evidence of a problem in other areas and where justified would help to organise a count'.

## Local government responsibilities and involvement

In the UK, local authority housing and social services departments have a statutory duty to help vulnerable people in priority need if they have a local connection with that authority. People in priority need include vulnerable children, older people, and the mentally ill, physically sick or disabled. According to the *Local Authority Agreement* (1979), a local connection implies being resident in an area for at least six of the preceding 12 months (Lowe, 1997). Through the *Housing Acts 1977* and *1985*, local authority housing departments had a responsibility to secure accommodation for homeless people in priority need, provided that they had not made themselves intentionally homeless, and permanent accommodation was normally found. By these rules, many single homeless people were excluded.

Recent legislation has diluted these responsibilities. Under the *Housing Act 1996*, local authority housing departments have now to ensure that 'advice and information about homelessness, and the prevention of homelessness, is available free of charge to any person in their district' (Housing Act 1996, section 179(1)). To avoid homeless people having preferential treatment over those on housing waiting lists, the duty is to provide only temporary accommodation for two years, with discretion to continue if the applicant still meets the criteria (Lowe, 1997; Niner, 1997). If suitable private, rented housing or hostels are available in the area, local authorities need only advise and assist homeless people to secure that accommodation. Through the *National Health Service and Community Care Act 1990*, local authority social services departments have a duty to carry out assessments of care needs for vulnerable people, and appoint case managers to arrange care packages to meet these needs. The social services departments are responsible for funding the care, and work with other statutory bodies and voluntary and private sector social care organisations to provide the care.

There are several gaps in the framework of services provided by local authority housing and social services departments through which some vulnerable homeless people fall (Rummery, 1998). Statutory services respond to presented need but only exceptionally are required to find unmet need: the assumption is that people are competent to initiate a housing application or to come to the attention of a GP or social worker. The extent to which housing officers should and could have 'welfare surveillance' or care responsibilities has been an issue for decades (Central Policy Review Staff, 1978). It is also the case that many statutory agencies lack the resources or capacity to respond to presented needs. Individuals with alcohol problems, for example, are competing for social services against children and older people in need. The former are often seen as people whose problems are self-inflicted, and 'peripheral to the work of social services departments' (Harrison *et al.* 1996, p.258). Many departments are unable to help people aged under 65 years who need care but whose problems are linked to alcohol abuse.

Several changes are taking place within local authority housing and social services departments that provide opportunities for the development of intensive and innovative services to meet the complex needs of vulnerable people. The recent White Paper, *Modernising Social Services*, describes new programmes and improved inter-agency collaboration (Department of Health, 1998a). The *Better Services for Vulnerable People* initiative requires all health and local authorities to draw up plans for services, such as rehabilitation schemes, that promote independence and improve people's health and social functioning. A budget of nearly £650 million will be available over the next three years to foster partnerships between health and social services. The *Better Government for Older People* programme aims to simplify older people's access to services, and improve linkages among the providing agencies. A report of December 1998, *Supporting People*, introduced a new policy and funding framework for support services in England (DETR *et al.* 1998). A cross-authority fund will be introduced to deal with the needs of people such as rough sleepers who move around and lack an unambiguous affiliation to a single local authority area.

## Area strategies and the co-ordination role

In the early 1990s some local authorities, having detected an increase in single homeless people or shortages of appropriate accommodation and support services, developed single homeless strategies. The practice was not widespread (only 60 of 402 local authorities responded to a survey and declared a strategy) and the comprehensiveness of the plans varied. Among those produced by Cardiff, Reading, Richmond-upon-Thames and Eastbourne (McCluskey, 1997), some included single homeless people of all ages, while others focused on young homeless people or those with mental health problems. Some were developed by the local authority housing and social services departments, and some by a combination of statutory and voluntary sector agencies. A second survey of local authorities outside the RSI zones found that just 28 of 242 authorities had a strategy to address rough sleeping, even though many more were aware of rough sleepers in their locality (*Crisis* and Shelter, 1998). Where strategies existed, a local assessment of needs was more likely to have been undertaken and to have guided the development of new services. They were also associated with the better use of existing resources and new funding, improvements to existing provision, new projects, better co-ordination and improved inter-agency working (McCluskey, 1997).

As mentioned, from 1999 local authorities have faced pressure to be involved in the planning and co-ordination of services for single homeless people. Local authority housing departments outside London are required to develop rough sleeping consortia involving key voluntary and private sector organisations, and to work in conjunction with the Rough Sleepers' Unit to deliver an effective strategy. When allocating HAP grants to voluntary organisation projects in February 1999, priority was given to schemes that were supported by their local authority as part of a local strategy for preventing and dealing with rough sleeping.

Local authority social services departments receive funding for mental health services from the Department of Health through the *Mental Health Grant*, but the majority of mental health services are provided, albeit very unevenly, through NHS community health, mental health and acute hospital trusts. The provision of community psychiatric services, and the extent to which they serve rough sleepers or the temporary hostel population, is exceptionally variable. As has been remarked of London, 'with increased sectorisation of mental health services, limited resources and very narrow purchaser–provider agreements, only short-term emergencies can be treated for out-of-catchment patients. Often individuals who do not have a fixed address fall out of the safety net of post-discharge support and planning. In addition, the services are often … inflexible, inappropriate and the individuals may not seek help early enough or find the help they are offered appropriate … [and] an additional problem is the inflexibility resulting from the provision of community services only in office hours (Bhugra, 1997, p.125).

Given that mental health service provision is idiosyncratic even for the general elderly population (Philpot and Banerjee, 1997), 'joining-up' services for the homeless and temporary hostel populations will require exceptional effort and resource. That may be forthcoming, for it has recently been announced that from 2000 the Department of Health will require local authorities with an identified problem of rough sleeping to target funds on specialist services for mentally ill people on the streets. They will be required to nominate a senior manager with clear responsibility and accountability for mental health services. Their task will be to work jointly with housing departments and other agencies on measures to reduce the level of rough sleeping. The intention is to ensure that there is a co-ordinated response to the mental health problems of rough sleepers, focused on the local authority's rough sleeping strategy (DETR, 1999a).

## Opportunities in the health services

The special problems of delivering health care to homeless people have been recognised since at least the early 1980s. Many GPs are reluctant to register homeless people, particularly those sleeping rough, for a combination of reasons: their lack of a permanent address and tendency not to stay in one area; their multiple health problems and high needs for treatment; deficiencies in remuneration; and the relatively high frequency of problematic behaviour in the group, e.g. not keeping appointments, poor compliance and disruptiveness in the surgery (Pleace and Quilgars, 1996; Williams and Avebury, 1995). The problem is compounded by the passivity of many homeless people, who have low self-esteem, are poorly motivated to seek medical care, or fear illness and doctors. Following the *Acheson Report*'s recommendation of 1981 that NHS funds should be made available to meet the unmet health needs of homeless people in Inner London, primary health care projects have been developed for homeless people in several towns and cities. They have included 'walk-in' medical clinics staffed by nurses, doctors and other professionals, and peripatetic teams of nurses and allied workers who provide health care at several hostels and day centres. Targeted primary health care projects are reported to be more effective in gaining the trust of homeless people and linking them to mainstream services, but they segregate homeless people, most do not provide out-of-hours cover, and they have difficulties in recruiting staff (Bayliss, 1993; Connelly and Crown, 1994; Williams, 1995).

The current vigorous shift toward a primary care-led health service could support innovations in medical services for special needs groups and new ways of tackling unmet need (Department of Health, 1997). *Primary Care Act Pilot Sites (PCAPS)* are trialing flexible contractual arrangements for GPs and allied staff to deliver personal medical services to under-served groups such as homeless people. In April 1998, 88 PCAPS were established to explore ways of improving services and access to them (Department of Health, 1998b). One south London example, the *Edith Cavell Practice*, has a nurse-led multidisciplinary team that targets refugees, homeless people and those with mental health and substance abuse problems who are marginalised from mainstream health care services (Lewis *et al.* 1999). The nurse visits local services including hostels to inform residents about the practice and to encourage registration. In October 1998, £5 million was made available for a second wave of PCAPS to start in October 1999 (Department of Health, 1998b).

*Primary care groups (PCGs)*, the precursors of trusts, were inaugurated in April 1999, but progress in developing the needs assessment and commissioning roles for both the general and special needs populations has been slowed by poor data and contractual and remuneration issues (Audit Commission, 2000). Additional funds are also available for GPs who work in deprived areas and want to develop local schemes to target specific patient groups (Department of Health, 1998c). Other changes in the delivery of primary health care services include the April 1999 *Health Improvement Programmes*, which will promote the planning of services in relation to local health care requirements through flexible partnerships between primary health care teams and local authority social services departments. They are required to provide services that are co-ordinated and easily accessible to vulnerable people (Rummery, 1998). The partnerships involve housing, environmental health, education and town and country planning agencies and departments, and the police (Poxton, 1999). The potential therefore exists for health care to be delivered more reliably to marginalised populations in innovative and flexible ways.

In an earlier contribution, a nurse practitioner who works in a hostel with homeless men described the value of providing health care in this way (Box 4.1). At the *Lancefield Street Centre* in London, many older rough sleepers were admitted with severe and untreated health problems. In the project's second year, the *Kensington & Chelsea and Westminster Health Authority* funded a local GP practice to treat the residents. A clinic at the surgery was arranged four afternoons each week, at which the residents (and other patients) were seen without appointments. This arrangement had several benefits: the clinic was particularly useful for those who were reluctant to use surgeries and accept treatment; unarranged consultations suited those residents who initially refused but later were persuaded to attend; and the residents had 24-hour medical cover.

## Voluntary organisations' responses

Voluntary organisations for more than a century have played the dominant role in service provision for single homeless people and there are several indications that their role in housing and supporting the most disadvantaged and vulnerable social housing tenants will continue to elaborate. The relevant voluntary organisations are however exceedingly diverse, from the church-based or neighbourhood groups that provide clothing, food and other practical expressions of concern, to the corporate-style non-profit housing (or housing and social care) organisations that operate throughout the country. The distinction is blurring between the for-profit housing management company which is primarily responsible to its shareholders, and the non-profit housing association pursuing a humanitarian and welfare mission. The former are increasingly securing contracts from the *Housing Corporation* and local authorities to deliver 'accommodation plus'.

Neither the organisations providing services to homeless people nor their roles and the way in which these interface with the statutory housing, social and health services can therefore be simply characterised. A description of a few 'extreme' cases will set the scene. The *Salvation Army* is the most distinct and most involved with helping homeless people. During recent years it has displayed impressive dynamism in upgrading its hostels and in developing move-on and supported housing, as well as individualised resettlement schemes. Some of its developments (as generally in the homeless sector) have been funded variously by the Housing Corporation, the RSI and, most recently influential, the *National Lottery Charities Board*. To its credit, the Salvation Army is one of the few *housing* providers to have a social services director and department. Another type of provider is the Victorian philanthropic organisation that became a substantial supplier of non-profit, low-cost housing for the 'respectable' working classes. *The Peabody Trust* and the *Guinness Trust* are the best known and they, with a multitude of more modest provincial equivalents, continue to witness their humanitarian origins through initiatives to provide special needs housing. In contrast are the many voluntary associations that are established every year in response to a neglected local problem of homelessness – some in the most unexpected places. Among the invited contributions are fine examples of the valuable services that local initiatives provide.

The two most characteristic types of voluntary organisations in the field are however the specialist charities that provide services to homeless people through multiple projects in either London or other large cities (only a few have taken a national brief), and the non-profit but not primarily charitable housing associations that to a large extent operate as agencies for the Housing Corporation. The plethora of specialist homeless organisations can be seen in the social welfare recruitment pages of the broadsheet newspapers. Only the largest charities, like Crisis, *St Mungo's* and *Thames Reach* are household names (at least in London). Similarly, the increasingly influential role of housing associations in social housing is displayed on the hoardings that front their countless housing rehabilitation, restoration and new construction projects. Their provision of 'social housing' increasingly includes shared and supported schemes for special needs and vulnerable groups.

Charitable foundations, large and small, also play a very important role in raising funds with which they support gap-filling and innovative services provided by other organisations. The *Charities Handbook* lists numerous charities that will donate funds to help homeless people. Among the most recent and most active, reflecting its exceptional capacity to raise donations, is *Help the Aged*. In 1997 it launched an 'Elderly Homeless' appeal and, in collaboration with Crisis and the *Housing Associations Charitable Trust*, has already awarded grants to many day centres, hostels and resettlement teams around the country.

The elaboration of the role of the voluntary organisations as providers of special needs housing began in 1964 with the creation of the Housing Corporation and its subsequent funding of non-statutory housing associations. It was accelerated greatly by the Conservative governments during 1979–97, both as a by-product of their relentless drive to reduce the role of 'council housing', and by the RSI and its companion homeless sector programmes. The trend has continued because of the net gains attributed to the transfer of housing management from direct local authority control to the specialist and increasingly professional housing associations (although, to be fair, the former strengths of city housing departments were systematically undermined by starvation of funds and incessant castigation).

The creation of a competitive market of social housing providers has produced dynamism and efficiencies in special needs housing management but has had its down side. Dependent organisations will normally bid for and provide only what the government requires. This has not entirely stifled innovation, for the Housing Corporation, the DETR and the RSI have, it seems, been open to many new ideas. The reliance on charitable and fixed-term project funds normally provides support for up to three years, but rarely guarantees finance over many years. In other words, there are structural contradictions between a competitive social housing market of independent providers and the provision of professional, tenacious and holistic social work and mental health services with vulnerable and damaged people.

As the specialist homeless organisations have been required to expand their provision from basic needs to rehabilitation, job training and resettlement, they have had to acquire new skills. Their role has progressively shifted from being lodging house landlords to becoming social work managers and even providers of palliative mental health services. This demands both close liaison with specialist providers and the elaboration of roles and responsibilities among the organisation's staff. It becomes increasingly inappropriate to rely on little-trained, non-professional staff who will work assiduously for low wages for humanitarian and ethical reasons. Voluntary organisations are likely to remain the dominant providers of services for homeless people, and they can play a prominent role in developing more effective and specialist help. How well they do in this may depend as much upon changes in the frameworks and structures of financing and inter-agency collaboration as upon the dexterity and application of their management and staff.

## Frameworks and programmes in other countries

As with Great Britain, in Australia, the USA and Denmark, governments have intervened directly to address single homelessness, and have acknowledged that the way forward is not just to provide basic shelter and food, but to provide specialist and supportive services that encourage rehabilitation and enable independent living. In Australia, the *Supported Accommodation Assistance Program* was introduced in all states and territories in 1985. This provides joint Commonwealth and State or Territory funds to non-governmental organisations and has emphasised the provision of 'transitional' accommodation with support, counselling and living skills training, improved access to health care, and training and preparation for long-term housing and employment. Over three years to 1991–92, the available funds exceeded Aus$407 million (Purdon, 1991).

In the USA, the *Stewart B. McKinney Homeless Assistance Act 1987* was the first comprehensive legislation pertaining to homelessness (Daly, 1996). An *Interagency Council on the Homeless* was established to co-ordinate the activities of federal agencies responsible for housing assistance programmes and grants. This has supported the creation of small transitional and specialised 'shelters' which offer care and support to homeless people, and funded health care, job training and counselling. Besides federal aid, state and local governments fund private and voluntary groups to provide services. In Denmark, the state government has created a *Social Development Fund* to address the needs of the socially excluded (Lipmann, 1995). It provides grants to around 1600 projects, ranging from alcohol rehabilitation services to community-based psychiatric services, and includes diverse projects for homeless people. In contrast, in Ireland no central government department has direct responsibility for the homeless, and most services are provided by church-based and private voluntary agencies (Edgar *et al.* 1999). In response to the increasing problem of homelessness in Dublin, the Department of the Environment established a unified framework for collaboration among statutory authorities and the voluntary sector and through which to plan and co-ordinate services for homeless people.

In other European countries, the responsibility for initiating and providing services for homeless people normally lies with local authorities. In Greece, Athens City Council has developed a women's refuge, a day centre for street homeless people, and a night shelter (Sapounakis, 1999). In Finland, local authorities and voluntary organisations jointly make up the *Y-Foundation*, a nationwide organisation that provides housing and support to homeless people in 46 municipalities (Edgar *et al.* 1999). Finally, and incidentally to put into perspective the scale and nature of the problems of homelessness in Britain and western Europe as well as the merits of a mixed economy welfare approach, it is salutary to read accounts of the massive scale of indigence and homelessness in Moscow, St Petersburgh and elsewhere in the former Soviet Union and of the paucity of state or local government help (Beigulenko, 1999; Bodingen, 1994).

## Conclusions

This chapter has described the frameworks and programmes that exist for homeless people, principally in the UK. It has highlighted current changes at the national and local levels in housing, health and social services, and the opportunities and challenges which these present to the organisations that provide services to homeless people. As more demands are placed upon them and they are required to carry out more intensive and specialised work, there is a growing imperative for effective partnerships and collaborative working with the health, social service and social housing providers. Current policy trends do seem likely to lead to more ambitious and effective services for homeless people. The new requirement upon local authorities to lead consortia of key agencies that will plan and develop services for rough sleepers should target resources into needed and effective services, help to avoid wasteful duplication, and promote the more rapid identification of unmet needs.

Chapter 8

# Appraising local provision and developing services

This chapter examines and makes recommendations about the development of a service for homeless people. It is not a comprehensive template but a guide to the key tasks, which have been identified from the experience of the *Lancefield Street Centre* and by the contributors to this book. It is important that *no* service is implemented until an appraisal has been carried out of the needs in an area, and its contribution to and links with the local network of provision has been defined and gained broad acceptance. The chapter's first section describes the purpose and methodology of a service appraisal, while in the second section attention turns to the main steps in planning a service, from the initial proposal to the search for a building and specifying its furnishing and facilities. The discussion is supported by three contributions from the managers of innovative schemes in London, Melbourne and Boston, Massachusetts.

Until recently in Britain (and doubtless elsewhere), the availability of help for homeless people in a city or district has depended to some extent on idiosyncratic local and organisational factors. These have moulded what services exist, the experience, attitudes and motives of the providers, and the inter-connectedness of provision. These attributes have in turn influenced, for example, whether rehabilitation and resettlement services are in place, and the continuity and stability of local projects. Individual services have often been established in response to a perceived need but without a thorough assessment of the aims, accomplishment and effectiveness of existing provision. This has contributed to the uneven availability of even the key services and, in a few places, to wasteful duplication and the dissipation of scarce enterprise and willingness to help. While the majority of projects meet the needs of homeless people, there are instances of ineffective services and of some that inadvertently help to sustain homelessness.

The situation is changing. Not only are more and more organisations and projects operating in most cities – raising the importance of complementarity and liaison – but also the good sense of working within a wider network and towards 'niche' roles is increasingly accepted and has recently been explicitly promoted by the British Government. In 1999, its *Rough Sleepers' Unit* made clear its determination to encourage rational and co-operative provision, and a requirement that local authorities take an active co-ordination role. The merits of new project proposals are increasingly judged on their compatibility with, and contribution to, a 'local homeless service development strategy'.

## Appraising local needs

A local appraisal of the need for homeless services begins with estimates of the size and 'throughput' of the 'official' and 'unofficial' homeless populations and then describes their broad characteristics, problems and needs. The *Department of the Environment, Transport and the Regions* collects quarterly statistics from local authority housing departments of the number of households who are officially homeless, including those who are in priority need because of old age. Information is also required about the number of 'unofficial' or single homeless people in the locality, and whether they are sleeping on the streets, in hostels, or in other temporary accommodation. Their circumstances will determine the type of service that is needed. Outreach workers and drop-in centres are required where there are people sleeping rough; resettlement workers and move-on accommodation are necessary for the occupants of temporary hostels. Details are therefore required about single homeless people who are:

- in hostels, night shelters, bed-and-breakfast hostels, squats and other temporary accommodation, and who are not registered as homeless with local authority housing departments
- sleeping rough and using day centres, drop-in centres, and soup runs for homeless people
- sleeping rough but not accessing services.

### Enumeration and population estimates

There are several problems and pitfalls in estimating the size of a local single homeless population, but with care and application serviceable figures can be produced. When assembling the numbers using different facilities, double counting can readily occur, e.g. some homeless people will visit more than one day centre in one day. Some patrons of day centres and night shelters and some occasionally sleeping on the streets do have homes or hostel places. Nonetheless it is relatively straightforward to estimate the number of clients of existing services in comparison to the problems of appraising unmet need. The most common difficulties are the 'hiddenness' of many single homeless people, and definitional and 'boundary' issues. Where local services wish seriously to address prevention, as *St Anne's Shelter and Housing Association* has done in Leeds, it is necessary to identify the most vulnerably housed in independent tenancies, bed-and-breakfast accommodation and lodging houses and squats. For these broader categories of need, it can take a long period of surveillance and practical work to estimate both the 'flow' (the numbers becoming homeless over a period) and the 'stock' (the size of the at risk populations).

The number of single homeless people and their sleeping arrangements also fluctuates seasonally and from night to night. Regardless of the season, some homeless people alternate between hostels and sleeping rough, while others move between towns, and some shift from sleeping in observable locations (as in city centres) to secluded and generally unobservable places (as in abandoned buildings). There are also incessant if fluctuating flows of people becoming newly homeless and of homeless people being rehoused. In several British towns, cold-weather shelters operate between December and March each year, when there is generally a decline in the number sleeping rough.

The mobile and irregular habits of many single homeless people mean that 'snapshot' enumerations and appraisals provide only a partial and sometimes a distorted picture of the local problem. It is widely accepted that the findings of the single-night counts of rough sleepers for the 1991 British Census and in other British and American inquiries were misleading (Homeless Network, 1995; Oldman and Hooton, 1993; Wright and Devine, 1995). A two-month survey of homeless people in Kentucky concluded that the information collected on the first day excluded virtually all cases in rural areas and many in the towns (Burt, 1995). Slight differences in methodology and definitions can produce significantly different survey results. It is therefore necessary to estimate the 'turnover' or flow of cases over a period, and to map as fully as possible the numbers following various pathways into and from the observable locations and service contact points. The chief requirements of a valuable count or survey are good organisation, planning and co-ordination among the local providers and the enumerators, and the most thorough briefing of all concerned. If the exercise is tackled seriously in this way, it should also be possible to collect 'profile' information as well as to undertake the count.

## Profiling the 'types' and needs of homeless people

Homeless people have different problems and needs, and therefore details are needed about their characteristics, i.e. age, sex, duration of homelessness, transient behaviours, and the nature and severity of mental illness and alcohol or drug addiction. The services required for young homeless people differ in certain respects from those required by their older counterparts. Those who are transient and move from town to town need outreach workers to seek them out and easily accessed drop-in centres to encourage them to use services. People with long histories of homelessness or severe mental illness or alcohol problems require specialist support and the most intensive help.

Information for appraising local needs should be gathered from several sources, the quality and comprehensiveness of which varies enormously. Some areas have recent surveys and well-conducted research, others little more than anecdotal evidence. Information may be available from local authority housing and social services departments, hospital accident and emergency departments, the police, the probation service, voluntary and religious organisations, and others who work with homeless people. In some areas, fuller information will be required from new surveys and interviews with homeless people and service providers. Information about hostel users can be gathered directly from providers. Profiles of rough sleepers in an area should be sought from several sources, including:

- day centres and drop-in centres
- outreach teams and soup runs who work on the streets
- homeless people, for information about isolated rough sleepers
- churches, convents and other religious establishments
- the staff of public services, as at bus and train stations, toilet attendants, libraries, betting shops, cafes, park keepers, and newspaper vendors.

The most productive and cost-efficient ways of gathering the information will itself require experimentation. With the Government's intention to reduce the number of people sleeping rough by two-thirds, there is understandably a premium on 'rough sleeper counts', with the odd consequence that enumerators have sat in cars for hours observing derelict buildings thought to be sleeping sites. The value of using people's time in this way and of establishing, for example, whether two or six people are in a building is questionable. The more useful information is the approximate number of rough sleepers in a locality on one night, its seasonal fluctuation, and the flow of homeless people over a period. If the various local sources of information are deftly used, it is possible to build a picture of the groups of homeless people in a locality, their distinct problems, and of the services that they need.

## Service utilisation and the location of unmet need

The mobility of homeless people and the response of welfare agencies to the existence of dedicated services mean that there are special difficulties in mapping the sources and distribution of unmet need. A general tendency for single homeless people to congregate in large cities is taken for granted, but the underlying rule that 'the location of provision influences the distribution of utilisation' is less widely appreciated. A fine demonstration of the rule has recently been reported in Boston, a small market town and port in Lincolnshire. In 1992, the local Methodist Church became aware that people were sleeping rough in the area. It collaborated with other churches through *Centrepoint Outreach* and set up a drop-in centre for homeless people. Subsequently effective rehousing services have been added and the demand for its help has increased, to the point that homeless people are both self-referring and being referred by housing, health and social service agencies from surrounding towns, such as Sleaford and Mablethorpe, up to 25 miles away. The unmet need is not in Boston but in the other towns that presently have no equivalent services.

## Appraising local service provision

An appraisal of local services has three components: an inventory and two comparisons, one with the evidence of local needs, the other with normative models of a service spectrum. Compiling the inventory is relatively straightforward but should include for each service its accessibility and eligibility rules, the interventions and help that are provided, and whatever utilisation, performance and outcome indicators are available to indicate their capacity and effectiveness in meeting needs and alleviating homelessness. As a simple example, a temporary hostel with 25 places may have been operating in a town for the last year, but it will have performed very different roles if, on the one hand, 35 people have stayed in it and none had been rehoused or, on the other, there had been 60 residents and 20 had been resettled in long-term accommodation. Information should also be collected on organisations' plans for new or redeveloped projects. Where all this information is collected, there will be a substantial evidence base for the identification of unmet need, and that will make a strong foundation for a case to potential funders for new or elaborated services.

A pragmatic model of the range of services that are required to help single homeless people along the pathway from street living to being settled in long-term accommodation is offered in Chapter 2, Figure 2.1. The model was developed by the authors on the basis of the experience of Lancefield Street and its various service teams, but its origins are earlier, in the models of provision in New York on which Lancefield Street was based (Cohen *et al.* 1993; Doolin, 1986). The included services are consistent with several of our contributors' recommendations about the services that are required to offer sustained, step-by-step or progressive and individualised help.

Comparison of local provision with local needs requires careful interpretation of the evidence and should be a collective exercise rather than being undertaken by a single organisation. As an example, the 'real' reasons why people are sleeping rough or living in temporary hostels in an area may not be immediately evident: it may be that the need for hostel places outstrips supply; or that there are no or insufficient outreach workers to persuade homeless people to use hostels. Alternatively, hostels may be excluding specific groups such as heavy drinkers; or the hostels are not being used because of their poor conditions, strict regimes, or fears of violence. Where there is an apparent shortage of hostel places, it is important to determine whether that is partly because the hostels do not encourage resettlement, and if so, whether that is because there is insufficient intermediate or 'move-on' accommodation. A careful examination of the success of resettlement should also be undertaken. In a town with a high failure rate, there may be sufficient day centres and hostels but a shortage of well-trained staff to carry out effective rehabilitation and support work. The required response would be to provide more staff and more effective resettlement packages in existing projects, not more day centres or hostel places.

The recommended audit process should identify duplicated services, gaps in local service provision, and the types of new services that are required. In London and some provincial British towns, established networks and co-ordinating agencies would offer informed advice. The best starting point would normally be the local authority, especially now that they are being required by the Rough Sleepers' Unit to take on the co-ordinating function. In some large cities of the UK, services are remarkably unaware of each other, and the compilation of an overall view of service provision will require considerable time and effort. It was however found possible to compile a serviceable overview during one-week visits to Liverpool and Glasgow (Crane and Warnes, 1997a).

## The role of local single homelessness strategies

The scale and nature of homelessness in an area change over time, so repeated reappraisals of needs and service provision will be required. Wherever the resources and co-operation to carry out an appraisal are assembled, it makes sense to take the further step and commit to a regular review, and the short logical next step is to join a consortium that will produce a local strategy for the development of services for single homeless people. This should be regularly updated and reviewed. From the opinions, discussions and practical descriptions that have been presented earlier in this book, the aims, content and functions of such a strategy can readily be set out:

- to monitor the scale and nature of homelessness locally
- to regulate the establishment of services so that resources are targeted efficiently into high quality and effective service provision
- to promote the efficient co-ordination of services
- to identify gaps in service provision.

*Tai Cymru* (the *Housing Corporation* in Wales) has proposed the following stages in the development of a strategy:

- agree objectives and the process to be followed
- agree overall aims and values
- assess overall needs
- audit provision and evaluate policy and procedures
- review resources, with an audit of existing and future housing and support provision, and assessment of the funds likely to be made available in the next three years
- develop and implement the strategic objectives
- monitor and review (cited in McCluskey, 1997, p.12).

There are several examples of the partial development of local strategies. *West End Co-ordinated Voluntary Services for Homeless Single People (WECVS)* was established in 1973 to co-ordinate the work of five charities working in London (WECVS, 1990). Now known as *Homeless Network* and with a membership of 39 agencies in 1999, it has played a lead role in the formation of 'RSI consortia' in central London and in supporting their work. The consortia bring together homeless voluntary organisations, local authority housing and social services, the DETR, the police, local businesses and residents (Homeless Network, 1994–95). It also co-ordinates six-monthly street counts of rough sleepers in the central London boroughs, and pilot schemes of innovative ways of working with rough sleepers and hostel residents. In Glasgow, the *Glasgow Council for Single Homeless* is a multi-agency forum that raises awareness of the interests and needs of single homeless people, and promotes good practice and inter-agency co-operation. It has produced two directories on services for homeless people, one covering the statutory, voluntary and private sector housing, social service and housing agencies, and the other concentrating on the provision by housing associations that work with homeless people and special needs groups (Glasgow Council for Single Homeless, 1996a; 1996b).

One city in England has benefitted from a well-integrated network of local services for an unusually long time. The *Nottingham Hostels Liaison Group* was set up in 1981 with funding from the city and county councils to support voluntary sector agencies working with homeless people. Since its inception, it has:

- fostered close links between the local authority housing and social services departments, health services and the probation service
- co-ordinated responses to issues affecting homeless people, such as social security benefit changes and community care initiatives

- in 1986 developed a 'resource team' which has researched local needs, provides a welfare rights advice service to hostel staff and homeless people, and includes a training officer who organises courses, and a peripatetic project worker who provides cover when a service is short-staffed
- in 1988 instituted a 'resettlement scheme' to provide practical and emotional support to homeless people who are rehoused for six months, and to maintain contact with housing providers and promote access to available provision. The scheme instigated a course for homeless people who are to be rehoused which is run at a local college and covers the practicalities of setting up a flat
- in 1989 developed a 'mental health support team' to provide care to homeless people in hostels, at day centres and on the streets
- in 1994 commissioned research into a local appraisal of the extent of single homelessness, the accommodation needs of single homeless people, and service provision. This resulted in a comprehensive and instructive report that describes how the evaluation was undertaken and the extent to which the needs of homeless people in Nottingham were being met (Vincent *et al.* 1994).

There are few examples of comprehensive local strategies in Britain or any other country and, despite the current British Government's enthusiasm for their adoption, there are several reasons why they are unlikely to become widespread in a short time. In the largest 'world cities' like London, New York and Tokyo where the problems are greatest, the sheer number of agencies and projects and the dynamism of the problem make an overall strategy very hard to achieve (as opposed to a set of measures to achieve limited symbolic targets). On the other hand, in small towns or districts where the problem is largely hidden or known to be small scale, the pragmatic view often prevails that a single project or intervention will be adequate. Homelessness may at times excite the media and public consciousness, but in the day-to-day business of delivering health and welfare services in 'an average town' it is normally a peripheral concern.

## Developing a service proposal

A model procedure for designing a service proposal would begin by recommending the establishment of a planning group with representatives from the local specialist homeless organisations, social housing providers, and statutory health and social service agencies. The group would then carefully consider the aims and objectives of the service, how it would complement and network with existing services, the location of need, the target clients, which organisation should or could provide the service, the other agencies that should be involved, and how the service might be funded. It is sensible to be guided by the experience of comparable projects in other places, so information should be gathered from published and unpublished reports and evaluations, and from national advisory organisations such as (in Britain) the *National Homeless Alliance*.

## Setting the aims and objectives

The aims and objectives should specify the rationale for the service, the interventions and help that will be provided, the group to be targeted, and expected outcomes. It should be noted that since the late 1980s it has been recognised that services are often most effective if they have specific goals and work intensively with one group, such as young homeless people or 'entrenched' rough sleepers, or on specific problems, such as mental illness or heavy drinking. Difficulties sometimes arise if a service targets homeless people of all ages, both sexes or drinkers and non-drinkers, e.g. a hostel or day centre may be dominated by one group to the detriment of others.

Every proposed new service should be conceived within a network or system of services, and the anticipated 'inflows' and 'outflows' or referral pathways must be carefully specified. To illustrate, in an area where there are many heavy street drinkers, a hostel that disallows drinking will not meet the need. Similarly, if there are many rough sleepers in an area, an outreach team cannot help people on to a pathway towards settled living unless there is direct-access temporary hostel accommodation with liberal admissions policies and adequate vacant places. And thirdly, it will be of little value to create thorough resettlement preparation schemes and 'move-on' or transitional accommodation unless there is a first-stage hostel where people can be helped with their problems and prepared for long-term housing (resettlement from day centres is less common because generally there are insufficient hours and staff to engage adequately with an individual).

Decisions have to be made about the size of the project, the number of clients that it will serve at any one time, the length of time that it will operate, and the ways in which people can be referred to it. The characteristics of the local area and its homeless people must be taken into account. In a rural area with poor public transport and a problem of scattered rough sleeping, it may be more beneficial to provide temporary accommodation in small projects or single flats in several locations than to develop a single large hostel. The benefits of small hostels and schemes that enable individualised and intensive work to be undertaken with the clients are widely documented and have been illustrated in this book by the contributions from Cardiff, Lowestoft and Birmingham. Although short-term projects are ill advised for homeless people with entrenched problems and who require progressive rehabilitation and 'reskilling', it is prudent for 'move-on' or 'transitional accommodation' projects to be particularly alive to the tendency for some staff and clients to put off the next move to another day. In summary, a proposed service has to be: (i) responsive to local needs and complementary to existing services; (ii) attractive and accessible to potential users; (iii) flexible to meet the distinct and changing needs of the users; and (iv) adequately funded in the short term and with reasonable prospects of continued funding to enable stability, continuity and reliability.

## Establishing networks and partnerships

Having established the aims, functions and responsible organisation for a new service, a priority is to identify the other agencies that must be involved. Specialist support from general medical practice, mental health and social service providers is invariably required, and both prevention and long-term resettlement requires the active co-operation of social housing providers and sometimes private sector landlords. Inter-agency partnerships among statutory health and social care agencies and voluntary organisations to tackle homelessness have proliferated during the 1990s. Some come together at the start of a project, others are created when a service runs into 'referral-on' blockages or financial difficulties. The former is well illustrated by *Hopkinson House* in central London, a project that provides housing, health care and resettlement to street homeless people with alcohol dependency problems. It was developed in 1998 through a partnership between *Westminster City Council, Kensington & Chelsea and Westminster Health Authority, Riverside Mental Health NHS Trust*, the *DETR*, the *Look Ahead Housing Association* and the *Drinks Crisis Centre* (now *Equinox*). The Joseph Cowen Healthcare Centre in Newcastle upon Tyne, which began in 1981 as the Bridge Medical Centre sponsored by *Homeless North*, illustrates the rescue case. In 1996 it faced liquidation, and its health and housing services are now provided by a partnership of *Byker Bridge Housing Association*, which owns the building, employs the welfare staff and manages the project; *Newcastle City Community Health NHS Trust*, which employs the nursing staff and provide supplies; and *Newcastle & North Tyneside Health Authority*, which contracts the GP service (Crane and Warnes, 1997b).

It is essential that there is close collaboration among agencies at an early stage in planning a project. Many homeless people require above average levels of medical treatment, and there will be a high demand for psychiatric and alcohol services. Health care planners, purchasers and commissioners should therefore have an early input. If a scheme is to target older entrenched rough sleepers, the involvement of a local social services department is essential, for some will require community care packages or need to be accommodated in registered care homes. Networking should be started at the planning stage of a project and intensified once the scheme opens. If for any reason there is insufficient time to make these arrangements before a service opens, complications are likely to arise, as was found by *St Mungo's* in the early days of the Lancefield Street Centre (Box 8.1).

---

**BOX 8.1:** DEVELOPING SERVICES FOR OLDER HOMELESS PEOPLE – THE IMPORTANCE OF PARTNERSHIPS

*Mike McCall is Operations Director of St Mungo's, London, an independent homeless services organisation (originally a 'community trust') which has provided accommodation and resettlement services for single homeless people since 1969. He describes the importance of developing collaborative ways of working and partnerships with local organisations when setting up services for homeless people.*

St Mungo's prides itself on its holistic range of services for homeless people. Few of these services would have started or survived had it not been for the goodwill and commitment of many other agencies, for very little can be achieved in the sector without partnership working. Services for older homeless people can be unusually complex, involving several health, housing and social care organisations each with its own agenda. Where these agendas conflict, establishing a service will inevitably be challenging, especially when local, regional and national priorities conflict. Setting up the Lancefield Centre was a prime example. The urgent need for the project had been established through painstaking research: London has many entrenched isolated older rough sleepers and needed a drop-in facility with hostel beds attached. An approach to a national charity based in London quickly secured the bulk of the funding for a pilot scheme, but then the problems started.

St Mungo's (and other specialist homelessness organisations) searched for a suitable building. The new service was strategically important for London but the power over the change of use of any building or any new development lies with the local authorities, the Boroughs. When a building suitable for conversion was found in Southwark, the Borough council's support was lukewarm. After all, why should the *London Borough of Southwark* host a project that would be a 'magnet' for all London's older rough sleepers? They bowed to local resident and councillor opposition and turned down our request for planning permission. At the time the London Borough of Southwark had little contact with St Mungo's. Our work was known but face-to-face links were few, and we had no track record in the Borough as a service provider.

Our links with the City of Westminster[1] were, however, very strong. At the time we ran ten housing projects in Westminster, and had built a good reputation with its housing and social services departments through joint working and problem-solving on various community care and homelessness issues. This had created confidence which, coupled with Westminster's recognition of its high level of rough sleeping, made it willing to support St Mungo's temporary use of a former social services hostel (for people with learning disabilities) which had been decanted and was awaiting demolition. Although a few miles away from the commercial 'west end' and not therefore ideally located, the building was a purpose-built hostel, had sufficient communal space for a drop-in centre, and adequately met our needs. Westminster offered the building for one year – we wanted it for two. Fortunately the plot was being sold to the *Network Housing Association*, which we knew well through extended joint working. They agreed to postpone their redevelopment plans for a year. Recognising the regional significance, the Housing Corporation provided funds towards the refurbishment and running costs which with the charitable funding enabled the project to open in January 1997, six years after it was initially proposed.

In operation the scheme ran smoothly. But the haste with which the building was prepared meant that the elements of its services that depended on other agencies were initially piecemeal and took time to develop fully. The most important were the primary health care and rehousing services. Our advocacy for the clients sometimes put a strain on well-established relationships with the service providers. If we had had more time to involve them at the planning stage, we would have had fuller co-operation and a better quality of service for the users would have been provided from the start.

Time, patience and perseverance are all required in abundance to get a new service started. Finding other people who share your agenda and are willing to make an effort to make things work is essential. The more they have a sense of ownership of the project, the more likely its success. At Lancefield Street, St Mungo's directly provided a spectrum of services, from street outreach, through drop-in centre management, housing management, support and care, to resettlement. We are aware that with the introduction of 'Best Value',[2] our 'comprehensive' approach will be subject to closer scrutiny; and if there are elements of the service that can be better provided by other agencies, we should directly engage them. We know that we need to start evaluating all aspects of our work from this perspective and recognise that joint working will in future be even higher on our agenda.

*Notes*
1. Administratively another of London's 32 boroughs, but with the 'City' name for historical reasons. In 1999 the Rough Sleepers' Unit of the DETR assumed responsibility for co-ordinating homeless services in the capital. When the London Metropolitan Authority is created, there will a strategic town and country planning body.
2. A programme initiated by the Government, which requires local authorities to apply the 'Best Value Performance Management Framework' to their activities in supporting vulnerable people. It is designed to achieve continuous improvements in services and greater local accountability. The key elements are establishing objectives, challenging performance targets, local performance plans, independent audit and certification, and intervention by central government if necessary.

## Obtaining suitable premises

Decisions have to be made about the location and type of premises for a service. When, for example, the intention is to help a hostel's residents to learn shopping and cooking skills and to integrate with a local community, it would be inappropriate to select a location in a remote or unserviced rural area. The needs of the client group determine the requirements of a building. If, for example, a hostel is for older rough sleepers, many of whom have physical disabilities and illnesses, a lift or ground-floor bedrooms are essential; while, if a project is to accommodate both heavy drinkers and others, there must be separate communal areas for the two groups. If a hostel is for women and men, there should be segregated sleeping and bathing areas.

Homeless service organisations in Britain have many difficulties in finding suitable premises and obtaining both the agreement of lessors and planning (or change-of-use) permission for their projects. When a homeless persons' project is proposed, there are often objections from neighbouring residents and businesses. To obtain their co-operation, it is prudent to meet with local tenants' groups and businesses and to give full details of the project and its intended clients – this may allay some concerns and will foster good relations. As implied by St Mungo's experience of its planning application in Southwark (Box 8.1), established working links with a local authority and discussion of a project with its housing and social service departments may secure their support for a proposal. They can seek the opinion of the planning officers on the likely outcome of a planning application. They in turn may advise that the use is inappropriate (non-conforming to the local plans), or that local opposition is unlikely to be assuaged, and that it would save fruitless expenditure and everyone's time to look for another building: on the other hand, if they believe that approval is likely, their advice on the presentation of the application will increase its chance of success.

To attract clients to a hostel and encourage them to stay, the premises need to be welcoming, clean and hygienic, decorated, in good repair, and heated well. The building and the rooms should be fit for their purpose and the client group, and the decor and furnishings should maximise 'homely' and minimise 'institutional' characteristics. Most single homeless people, like most adults, prefer single rooms and many will not accept shared rooms or dormitories. If the project is first-stage accommodation for rough sleepers, then shared bedrooms will deter usage. Likewise, if it is intended that a hostel is to prepare residents for independent living, the provision of self-catering facilities or rehabilitation flats is an advantage. Good quality temporary hostels in the early 2000s will require single bedrooms for which the residents have keys, a dining room (or self-catering facilities), plentiful toilet and bathing facilities, at least one sitting room, and laundry and recreational facilities. There should be sufficient space for the residents not to be crowded. Bryan Lipmann of *Wintringham* in Melbourne, Australia, argues strongly that where quality accommodation and furnishings are provided, the morale and behaviour of the residents show significant improvement (Chapter 6 and Box 8.2).

## Box 8.2: Restoring pride and motivation – lessons from Melbourne, Australia

*Bryan Lipmann, Chief Executive of Wintringham in Victoria, Australia, provides summary recommendations for the development and delivery of long-term housing for older homeless people. From its expertise in architecture and environmental design and its strongly held belief in the importance of respecting individuals and 'giving them a stake' (described in Box 6.4), the company has developed a spectrum of services from outreach to follow-up support. His recommendations exemplify the fact that whatever the initial perspective of a service, responsiveness to the needs and abilities of long-term homeless people leads to recognition of the importance of an individualised approach, collaboration with other agencies, and careful attention to staff training and support.*

### Organisational

When developing effective ways to work with older homeless people, our experience is that several conditions make it easier to create and sustain a new housing and support model. In the case of Wintringham, these have been:

- the creation of a new welfare organisation that has none of the responsibilities of established welfare agencies
- the new organisation creates its own objectives and programmes and is solely responsible for its failure or success
- a single focus or objective is adopted which does not replicate the generic responsibilities of most welfare agencies. In Wintringham's case, the company works with only one client group – older homeless people
- the organisation has a fundamental commitment to social justice and equity.

If the organisation is a separate welfare company, it is critical that its financial operations and practice ensure continuing financial viability. Permanent solutions to homelessness cannot be established if the agency providing the housing and support is forced to close its doors.

### Service delivery

In relation to the delivery of services, the lessons learned by Wintringham include the following:

- money spent on building high quality housing is never wasted. Our experience is that the better the quality of the housing and fittings, the more the residents respect and look after their environment, and the better they feel about themselves. This frequently translates into reduced drug or alcohol abuse and improved general health
- outreach and street work are a vital component of a service pathway that enables and encourages permanent exits from homelessness. Outreach workers need to have sufficient time and resources to establish support and trust with homeless people, for these are essential prerequisites for the transition to permanent housing

- it is of great importance to establish networks and linkages with other welfare agencies, local councils and government offices that are working or come into contact with homeless people
- the maintenance of such formal and informal linkages is a vital ingredient of being able to respond rapidly to crisis situations.

While environmental and building design is important, staff attitudes and commitment are paramount in creating a successful housing and support model. Staff need to share the vision of the company, which is greatly facilitated if the company has a clear and unambiguous aim. Management needs to provide continual access to training and quality improvement processes, and to provide staff with support. The social justice principles that determine the way homeless people are treated by the company must extend to its employees.

## Securing funds

It is essential that adequate funds are secured before a project opens. No service should be set up on a shoe-string in the hope of obtaining funds at a later date. Effective projects for the most difficult to help must have an extended life. The management and staff of an innovative service learn by experience, and only over time can they develop the best working relationships with specialist and long-term housing providers. When applying for funds, the distinct problems and needs of the client group should be considered. For example, a project that aims to provide intensive help to entrenched rough sleepers must recognise that money will be required for specialist workers, and for more than usual services and staff. A project that aims to resettle its clients must also consider how they will be supported in their accommodation and whether funding is required for community support workers.

The financial estimates need to include capital and recurrent costs. They must include allowances for the costs of work to meet building and fire regulations, for town planning applications and appeals, for furnishing the project, and for the recruitment and training of the staff. A characteristic of the 'mixed economy of welfare' in the homeless sector is that there is a multiplicity of potential sources of funds. Continuity of funding and operation can be achieved in two ways: by good management, which both ensures that the project's objectives are achieved and that it is adaptive to locally changing needs; and by maximising the project's contribution to the local spectrum of provision or, in other words, making itself indispensable. The greater the number of collaborating agencies who find that a project is lightening their load or patently providing a worthwhile service, the more practical help will be forthcoming in finding continuation funds. The contribution from the *Committee to End Elder Homelessness* in Boston, Massachusetts emphasises the returns from a vigorous approach to organisational networking (Box 8.3).

**Box 8.3:** Networking and orchestrating diverse funding

programmes, Boston, Massachusetts

*Janice L Gibeau, Executive Director of the Committee to End Elder Homelessness, Boston, Massachusetts, describes the reasons why the organisation was established, its objectives and how it has developed.*

Alarmed by the rapidly increasing numbers of homeless older people in Boston in the 1980s, seven professional women with extensive experience in housing, health, mental health and social services came together in 1991 to create the Committee to End Elder Homelessness (CEEH). It was in part a response to the repeated frustrations of attempts to provide home services to older people in the south end of Boston, where many were being evicted as a result of the gentrification of this historic area. Single-room tenancies (occupancy units) were rapidly being replaced by private condominiums. At the same time, many of Boston's mentally ill homeless people were ageing and increasing the population living in shelters. Other older homeless people in the shelters had a high prevalence of chronic illnesses, poverty, substance abuse, and combinations of various biopsychosocial problems. Awareness of these and other factors became a 'call to action' for the voluntary association effort to stem the rising tide of elder homelessness. Two beliefs have driven the form and function of the association's work:

- that having a home is crucial to the success of all other services for older adults, and
- solving the problem of homelessness must (i) create, integrate and co-ordinate resources in a manner that provides solutions to the problems of homeless individual elders, and (ii) intervene at a community level to prevent homelessness among vulnerable populations.

The primary mission of CEEH is therefore the eradication of elder homelessness through the provision of permanent housing and supportive services. To accomplish this mission, the Committee focuses on the following five priorities:

- to create and develop housing and service resources that address the needs of homeless older adults with chronic medical, behavioural, health and substance abuse problems
- to advocate for public and private strategies, policies, services and financial resources that reduce the level of homelessness in the community
- to develop, implement, evaluate and disseminate new service models that promote an integrative, community-based approach to elder homelessness
- to publicise the problems, scope, severity and human costs of elder homelessness
- to work closely with community residents, consumers, legislators, developers, service providers, housing management companies, the business sector, private contributors and volunteers to create community partnership models for ending elder homelessness.

The creation of housing, services and programmes for homeless older people in the USA, like most health or social services, is supported by a combination of public and private funding that includes private donations, bank loans and grants from city, state and federal housing programmes. The requirement is to gain significant rent subsidies and health services funding. Because there is no single governmental agency or spending programme to draw upon, the Committee recognised at an early stage that serving the homeless requires the intricate interweaving of housing, health and social service support. It set itself to this task and has woven such a 'welfare tapestry'.

Beginning with a $100 honorarium donated by one of its founders, CEEH now has an annual budget of nearly $2 million. It has established services that make it easier for homeless older people to progress through the several steps involved in settling into a new home. Starting with outreach services on the streets and in shelters, and progressing to the development of a relationship with a case manager who stays with the client until he or she is settled in a new home, older homeless people are helped not only to find permanent housing but also to form new friendships in therapeutic, caring communities.

**Outcomes and quality management**
Measuring performance and outcomes in such complex work is a major challenge. There have been brief satisfaction surveys that report positive feelings about the services provided at CEEH. All programmes funded by governmental sources evaluate both the processes and outcomes in meeting the objectives defined in their respective contracts. Descriptive data gathered at CEEH focuses on the average length of stay, reductions in hospitalisations for problems related to mental health and substance abuse, and higher levels of functioning. To understand more clearly which interventions create sound clinical pathways for success, however, more information must be systematically gathered and analysed. Toward that end, CEEH has received support for an exploratory study and demonstration grant from *The Medical Foundation*, with matching support from *Goddard House*, a long-term care organisation, to study the most influential factors on moving an elder homeless person along the pathway from homelessness.

## Monitoring and evaluation

A project's performance and faithfulness to its objectives needs to be monitored closely. This can be done well only if procedures for reporting, collecting, storing and organising routine 'operational data' are established from the outset. Many homeless projects do not accomplish this, and only realise the consequences when they need to document and quantify their achievements in a case for continued funding. There are three main reasons for the rarity of good quality and parsimonious routine data collection: firstly, the early establishment of the procedures requires exceptional foresight and application during the launch phase of a project when there are a thousand more pressing tasks; secondly, few people in the homeless sector have sufficient knowledge of data handling or information technology to design a system from first principles and there is little generic advice except from expensive IT consultancies; thirdly, it is by no means a simple task to train the staff (including post-launch joiners) to complete reporting forms reliably or to appreciate the importance of the exercise. Local projects and agencies cannot easily find user-friendly guidance and useful off-the-shelf packages.

## Conclusions

Developing a service for homeless people that becomes a useful and enduring addition to local provision is a complex task requiring considerable foresight and consultation. New projects should be encouraged but it is essential that they are responsive to local needs, fit into the range of existing provision, and co-ordinate with local authorities. In London and the largest American cities, homeless services are now dominated by large, well-established and professional housing and welfare associations along with the statutory housing and social service providers. While there are still large gaps in provision and there is much scope for innovative and supplementary projects, the most sensible approach to their foundation will usually be through an established provider. In the long run, to combine humanitarian inspiration and charitable enterprise with political and management experience and realism gives a service innovation the best chance of being well conceived and having a lengthy life.

There are, however, many areas in Britain and elsewhere with a problem of homelessness but hardly any specialised services. In these settings, an organisation that wishes to establish a new service may encounter more incomprehension than practical advice from the local welfare state agencies and charities. It will nonetheless be of great importance to liaise closely with the health and social services, and much guidance can be obtained from the experience of similar projects elsewhere. One or two visits to peer projects might avoid a host of mistakes and much wasteful expenditure of time and money.

In the UK, while a few organisations have developed services for *older* homeless people, no provider focuses exclusively on the age group. As a result, older homeless people are competing for services at a time when the Government's policy and funding priorities are on helping young homeless people into jobs and training schemes. The submitted contributions from Boston, Massachusetts and Melbourne, Australia describe organisations that work specifically with older homeless people. Both have found that working with a single client group significantly adds to the capacity of the local service system, and both are expanding their provision.

To summarise, several distinctive characteristics of older homeless people should be borne in mind when appraising needs and developing services. Many older rough sleepers are hidden and will not use services for homeless people of all ages, but will access and benefit from designated provision. Their distinctive or unusually prevalent needs should be noted, e.g. their poor physical health and mobility mean that some require ground-floor bedrooms or access to a lift. Long-term rough sleeping and cognitive impairments mean that some require above-average levels of help with personal hygiene, claiming benefits and nutrition. Some have deep-seated problems and require more support and a longer period for adjustment than can be provided by a winter or even one-year project. It is also necessary that links are established at an early stage with health and social services providers (for many older homeless people will require treatment for physical and mental health problems) and with mental health and social services departments (to access places and funds for special needs housing). Finally, projects for older people need a longer view of potential funding than is usual in the voluntary sector. Follow-on funds are commonly more difficult to find than support for a brand new project, but if a specialised project performs well and develops reliable and valid measures of achieved performance and effectiveness, funders will be impressed.

Chapter 9

# Good practice in service provision

This chapter sets out our views about ways of promoting good practice in services for homeless people. It opens with a discussion of management's responsibilities and tasks. The second section concentrates on staffing issues including briefing, supervision, training, and safety. The following section emphasises the importance of work with complementary providers and proposes some practical steps by which to gain their fullest co-operation. The final section examines the benefits and procedures of a well-designed assessment and monitoring system, and discusses the complex but critical task of determining and implementing the most appropriate performance and outcome measures.

While there are several codes of guidance and good practice manuals for mental health services and elderly care provision (Department of Health and Social Services Inspectorate, 1990; Warner *et al.* 1997), few deal specifically or in any depth with working with homeless people. The *National Homeless Alliance* has published two reports on good practice in day centre services for homeless people (Cooper, 1997; Llewellin and Murdoch, 1996). It has also published *The Resettlement Handbook* (Bevan, 1998), which inventories the stages of resettlement, and a short report on the role of resettlement services for homeless people (Schofield, 1999). The importance of good practice and of an 'evidence-based' approach (however imperfectly understood) is increasingly recognised. More and more service providers are genuinely keen to adopt good working standards, to learn from one another about ways to work with people who have complex needs, and to implement models that produce successful outcomes.

## Management responsibilities

The responsibilities of the organisation or management responsible for a service for homeless people are easily written but difficult to achieve. The service should be acceptable to its clients, practical for the staff, effective in meeting its objectives, and work efficiently within its budget; while the interests and expectations of the clients, funders and staff must be simultaneously served, often, of course, requiring delicate compromise. These requirements are a tall order, particularly in a voluntary sector service, which has none of the advantages of: the security of the statutory agencies; the historically or societally legitimated professional standing of medicine, professional social work or housing administration; or the emoluments of the private sector.

Services for homeless people range from single and simple interventions, e.g. dispensing food, to among the most complex and challenging of holistic welfare and support services that could be conceived. Most temporary hostels provide alongside housing at least a low level of health and welfare advice. In those that are seriously tackling personal rehabilitation and resettlement, many conventional and unconventional forms of social work, health care delivery and counselling take place. Like most residential institutions, homeless people's hostels have a multifaceted relationship with their residents, and the staff have helping, supportive, regulatory, exemplar and intra-mural community building roles. The work demands exceptional flexibility and discretion (and should attract more prestige than is normally granted), for the institutions and their staff act as landlords' stewards, *de facto* social workers, care assistants, nurses (rarely but unavoidably), and guardians. Given this complexity, and the fact that normally there are too few managers and staff and they are almost wholly engaged in essential pressing tasks, worldly realism must be applied in recommending good hostel practice.

Whatever a proposed service, its need should be undoubted, its objectives should be clear, and the project should be undertaken only if the instigators are confident that it can be done well. The move from these common sense maxims to professional management is demanding. It requires time, resources and the involvement of people with experience and appropriate skills as well as enthusiasm and goodwill. An important threshold is the formulation of a service policy and plan. It does not have to be a sophisticated document but should be full of realism and practicalities. It should identify: (i) the guiding principles and aims of the proposed service; (ii) detailed specifications of the planned interventions and how they will be monitored; (iii) the ways in which the project will serve the intended clients and will complement and liaise with other services; and (iv) the expected outcomes and how these will be assessed. An appropriate service plan is a clear statement of what is intended and how it will be done. It will inform the funders, management and staff at all stages of the establishment and implementation. It will serve as a benchmark with which to assess progress, to check deviant developments and aberrant diversions, and the baseline for convincing evidence of the enterprise's achievements. The details depend upon the nature of the project, and further comments are developed specifically for residential hostels, drop-in and day centres, and outreach teams.

## Residential accommodation

If the service is to provide temporary or permanent accommodation, responsibly fulfilling the 'landlord role' is a precondition for the welfare interventions. In a hostel, the management and welfare staff (sometimes called 'frontline' staff) have a responsibility to:

- administer and clearly explain to the residents the accommodation licences which should detail the obligations of the organisation, the licensee's obligations and rights, the house rules, and the complaints procedure
- ensure that the organisation fulfils its responsibilities to the paying residents, e.g. maintains the building and communal areas in a safe and reasonable condition, provides clean bed linen and, illustrating many small but often neglected details, replaces used light bulbs
- ensure that the residents pay rent, and therefore in many cases that they receive social security Housing Benefit and pay the weekly charges that it does not cover
- promote consideration for other residents and minimise grievances and disputes, to establish and implement 'house rules', e.g. stipulating privileges and restraints concerning drinking alcohol, noise at night, violent or threatening behaviour, visitors, keeping pets, use of communal areas and activities that may disturb others
- carry out regular checks of the bedrooms to ensure that they are in reasonable order and that health and safety regulations are not being breached
- regulate access to the hostel to maintain personal security
- supervise the ancillary staff and visitors to the hostel and their contacts with the residents
- supervise and audit expenditure on and the stocks of domestic and catering supplies.

These landlord roles can conflict with forward-looking welfare interventions and the support of individual residents. The requirements and implementation of the social welfare, rehabilitation and personal support roles have been detailed in earlier chapters. Two general requirements merit further comment, concerning the mix of residents and the mix of staff skills. Most homeless hostels have some freedom to select their clients according to personal characteristics including gender and health and behaviour problems. A number of principles that should guide a residential service have been elucidated earlier in the book, and three are particularly pertinent to decisions about the target groups: (i) the most effective interventions are individualised and specialised, (ii) a service (or the service system) is failing if it concentrates on the easiest to help; and (iii) first-stage accommodation should seek to move its residents to long-term accommodation. These principles make evident that deciding the mix or profile of the clients, specifying the consequent tasks and workload, and determining the needed staff numbers and skill-mix, are critical steps. The direct organisational and staff interests, from minimising the vacancy rate and lost revenue to promoting job satisfaction and controlling workplace stress, have to be balanced against the welfare 'ambition'. The complexity and difficulty of the tasks that are taken on have to be moderated by staff capacity and morale. A derivative issue is whether the routine reporting of the project's activity and the performance measures that are developed capture the more difficult as well as the routine work of the service.

## Drop-in centres, day centres and outreach work

The work of drop-in centres, day centres and outreach services was discussed in Chapter 3. While the problems of designing and running these services and facilities are clearly less considerable than for a residential hostel, it is still desirable for their purpose and appropriate ways of working to be clearly thought out – maybe too many run on the semi-informal basis of 'this is what we can offer, take from it whatever you can'. There are again pervasive issues of designing, matching and managing the service-mix and the client-mix: how many are helped, what groups of people they are and what their problems and needs are, and how and to what extent they are to be helped. Open-access drop-in and day centres can be extremely valuable as 'first ports of call' where people are persuaded to leave the streets, and as the setting in which individualised help and support is available. The general problem is the compatibility of these intensive forms of work with the often crowded rooms and dominant informal and group activities of a day centre. Another pervasive problem of open-access drop-in facilities is the unpredictability of and pronounced fluctuations in the types and intensity of demands upon its staff. The more ambitious of such facilities, and all those that provide a service at all times, must be able to summon additional help at short notice. That means that they should either be part of a larger facility, generally a residential hostel, or linked to out-of-hours and emergency support.

## Generic service management issues

Rules and regulations are important tools in promoting the good order of a service and are essential to ensure that it is attractive and accessible to current and prospective users and safe for the clients and staff. A service needs to develop an environment that minimises the conflicts between different groups and maximises the benefits to the users. The staff need to have the time not only to enforce rules but also to promote desirable behaviour through individual persuasion and users' meetings. A hostel has to promote good hygiene to prevent it becoming odorous and unattractive, and the bedrooms and communal areas have to be maintained to an acceptable standard to prevent them becoming a health or safety risk. Although necessary, hygiene rules can be difficult to implement and have unintended consequences. As the contribution in Box 3.4 demonstrates, it is extremely difficult to manage situations when rough sleepers are willing to move into a hostel but are filthy and lice-ridden and refuse to attend to their hygiene. Ways of resolving such situations still need to be found.

Consultation mechanisms, such as residents' meetings, are a valuable ingredient of promoting understanding between the staff and residents. A complaints procedure is valuable and should be diligently managed. Notices or circulars should set out how to make complaints and how and when they will be investigated and can be appealed. Similarly the facility's policies on confidentiality, i.e. the use and protection of the information provided by clients, and on accidents, incidents and visitors should be clearly understood and available in written form.

Adverse consequences can occur if standards and rules are flouted or if boundaries for the clients and staff are not clearly defined. Some homeless people are mentally ill, heavy drinkers or drug addicts, or have criminal or violent histories and behave in aggressive, challenging, anti-social or threatening ways. The most common consequence is damage to the main work of the facility, for a resident may leave and return to the streets because of another's behaviour. More serious problems, such as assaults on the residents or staff, or falling foul of the law can also occur.

Catastrophic problems are comparatively infrequent but not rare. Between August and November 1999, three projects for homeless people in England faced serious problems and two were forced to close. A drop-in centre in Brighton, the *Halo Centre* (Homeless and Lonely Organisation), was closed six years after opening following a raid by the police in which drugs and syringes were seized. The centre occupied the basement of the *Brighthelm Church and Community Centre* and there had been concern from the Church about 'staffing levels and supervision for a considerable time' (*Housing Today*, 1999). A night shelter for homeless men in Birmingham, the *Trinity Centre*, is to close due to high costs and concerns over the safety of the residents and the staff. The men are accommodated in dormitories, and people 'with mental health and drug problems sleeping in adjacent beds ... the younger population are preying on older men' (*Inside Housing*, 1999a, p.4). The director and day centre manager of the *Wintercomfort Bus Project* in Cambridge were found guilty in November 1999 of allowing heroin to be supplied on the premises (*Inside Housing*, 1999b, p.2).

## Staff requirements

To have continuity and dependability, projects require salaried staff with a well-judged range of skills and experience. The optimum number and skill-mix of the staff depend on the size of the project and the needs of the client group. There must be adequate staff to enable individual, flexible and intensive programmes to be carried out with the clients. When working with the most vulnerable and 'difficult' homeless people, an above average workload must be expected. This will require, for example, more staff than is normal in a general hostel and more input from an outreach worker than is generally given to recently homeless people sleeping rough. At *Valley Lodge* in New York City, expanding their social care staff enabled more intensive work to be carried out with their hostel residents, which in turn raised effectiveness (see Chapter 5). In a small or medium-sized hostel, all 'professional' or care staff should be 'key workers'. In a small hostel, key workers could also be responsible for resettling their clients, provided that they have the required skills and time for the work. In a medium-sized hostel, a designated resettlement worker may prove more beneficial. When working with older homeless people on the streets or in a hostel there are some skills that all care staff require:

- an ability to compile histories of the clients that throw light on their problems and needs
- an ability to assess the problems and needs of the clients, and plan their care
- willingness to work with older homeless people who are withdrawn, unsettled, have poor social skills, disturbed behaviour, or severe mental health or alcohol problems
- an ability to work persistently with clients who have low morale and are poorly motivated, and sensitively with confused and anxious clients
- an ability to detect pronounced physical health and psychological problems and connect the individual to emergency medical care
- a basic understanding of the care required by elderly or homeless people with health problems such as dementia, diabetes, and tuberculosis.

There are also some skills that staff need to have which reflect their particular work situations. All hostel care workers need to be able to maintain order and safety in the hostel, and intervene if a resident becomes disruptive or aggressive. In a hostel for older rough sleepers, some individual workers need to have specialised knowledge and special responsibilities:

- a detailed understanding of welfare benefits entitlements and claims, applications and appeal procedures
- the ability to detect less apparent physical and psychological health problems, negotiate with professionals for medical and psychiatric assessments and treatment, and detect adverse effects of treatments such as medication
- the ability to negotiate with social services for community care assessments and help for the residents
- knowledge of local and specialist services to which clients can be referred and of their eligibility and admissions procedures.

The skills that outreach staff and resettlement workers need are described in Chapters 3 and 6 respectively.

Individual staff should also be appointed to lead in the provision of specialist help. For example, in a project that targets mentally ill people, trained mental health workers are required. The value of structured activities and rehabilitation preparation was described in Chapter 5. No medium-sized hostel or day centre should expect generalist care workers to carry out these additional tasks. The activities co-ordinator at *Burghley Road* in London, a group home for older homeless people with alcohol dependence and other complex problems, managed by *Bridge Housing Association*, has described the time required to prepare activities thoroughly. As an illustration, planning a day trip for the residents involves finding out whether buildings are wheelchair accessible, arranging where to eat and what to do if the weather is bad, and making sure that required medication is taken and that a change of clothing is available for people who are incontinent.

All staff posts require job descriptions, which should clearly explain their duties and responsibilities. One ambiguous situation that arises in some hostels and day centres concerns the provision of personal care. A service for older rough sleepers will attract some clients whose self-care is neglected and who are filthy, lice-ridden and incontinent. If such clients are accommodated, the service must have an unambiguous policy about who will provide intimate personal care. Either some or all of the staff must be tasked to provide the care and trained in its special skills, e.g. lifting during bathing, or an agreement has to be reached with the local social services department for input from personal care assistants.

## Staff training and courses

Staff training and support needs to be integral to the service. An induction course should be arranged for newly appointed care staff at which the main topics of work should be covered, e.g. the problems and needs of homeless people, the role of key workers, developing listening and assessment skills, and the staff's responsibilities towards the clients, other staff and the organisation. The staff should receive regular supervision and support from their managers, and should be encouraged and enabled to attend relevant courses, conferences, and training programmes. In the UK, *Shelter* and the *National Homeless Alliance* arrange many courses and conferences about homelessness and allied issues. Some large voluntary organisations working with homeless people, such as *St Mungo's* in London and *St Anne's Shelter and Housing Action* in Leeds, also have their own training programmes. St Anne's, for example, has a range of courses for its staff on bereavement and loss, dealing with difficult behaviour, abuse awareness, mental health awareness, positive ageing, common medical conditions, communication skills, assertiveness and negotiation skills, stress management, personal safety, welfare benefits, food hygiene, health and safety, and emergency aid. For project managers, it has courses on managing change within systems, managing teams, and managing meetings.

The welfare and safety of staff is of great importance and is not in all circumstances possible to guarantee, as for outreach staff working on the streets, and resettlement and community support workers visiting resettled clients in their accommodation. The *British Crime Survey* found that 7 per cent of housing officers while working in 1997 were victims of violence, compared with 3 per cent of all professional workers (Forshaw, 1999). Staff should be thoroughly trained to observe safety and health procedures, and a clear safety policy should be drawn up which includes systems of reporting prior to and after street-work or a home visit. Outreach workers should never work alone on the streets, there should never be just one member of staff on duty in a hostel, and home visits should not be carried out by one member of staff if a client has a history of violence or of threatening or unpredictable behaviour.

### The roles of volunteers

There may be important roles for volunteers in some projects, but no scheme should rely on them to provide individualised rehabilitation and resettlement preparation services. In many day centres, volunteers are 'central to a project's ability to open its doors' (Cooper, 1997, p.19). They should normally complement the paid staff by providing low intensity care and companionship to the clients. If volunteers are used, they should be carefully selected, trained, supervised and supported. They should understand the organisation's operational aims and policy and its procedures regarding confidentiality, complaints, incidents and safety.

Some organisations encourage their former clients who have been resettled to work as volunteers. It was once customary in some large hostels to select ex-residents to work as kitchen assistants, porters or cleaners, and the practice continues in some day centres. An individual may switch from being a day centre user one day to a volunteer at the centre the next day. This can lead to complications and cause conflict, resentment and confusion for the individual, other users and the staff. It also does not encourage a resettled person to leave the homeless circuit. If a formerly homeless person is ready to work as a volunteer, he or she should be supported and encouraged to do so at a 'non-homeless' community project.

## Establishing working relationships with complementary providers

No homeless people's project can provide all services and operate effectively in isolation. For the majority of 'second-stage' interventions, their effectiveness will be conditioned by the quality of its links to other agencies and providers. Critical to success are well-developed communication and cross-referral procedures, and reliable arrangements for integrated work with mainstream health, housing and social service agencies, other homeless people's organisations and specialist providers.

In the USA, it has been demonstrated that where services in a city are well-integrated there is improved access to housing services and better housing outcomes for homeless people who are mentally ill (Rosenheck *et al.* 1998a). A *Social Security Administration* and *Department of Veterans Affairs Joint Outreach Initiative* was launched in 1991. In collaboration with the responsible state *Disability Determination Service*, it developed at four *Health Care for Homeless Veterans Programmes* a scheme that helped with applications for social security benefits. Two years later, this approach had improved access to disability entitlements among mentally ill homeless people (Rosenheck *et al.* 1999). At *Peter's Place*, *John Heuss House* and Valley Lodge in New York City, social workers and mental health and alcohol workers are based at the projects and work in teams. In the UK, it is common for mental health and alcohol workers to visit services regularly but rare for them to be based at the projects and offer frequent help (unless the project specifically targets mentally ill people or heavy drinkers). Social workers generally visit and provide a consultation service only in response to referrals.

There are several examples of agencies collaboratively working with homeless people in the UK (see Box 3.4). However, even when integrated ways of working are adopted it is not a straightforward process. In Bristol, *The Hub* is a multi-agency advice centre and 'one-stop shop' where voluntary sector staff work with statutory agencies, including the social, health and housing services. Although the project helps newly homeless people, only 15 per cent of The Hub's clients were rough sleepers, in comparison to 30–40 per cent at other local homeless services (Pannell and Parry, 1999). The rough sleepers were too alienated and their behaviour was too chaotic for them to cope simultaneously with multiple services from several agencies. There were also problems when staff had to deal with mainstream services, even when their staff was of the same professional background. The multi-agency approach broke down the boundaries among The Hub's specialist services, but new barriers with mainstream services were created.

It is possible for agencies to work collaboratively with rough sleepers and achieve outcomes. One interesting example involved the closure of *The Bullring* in London. This 'cardboard city', under the southern approach to Waterloo Bridge and near to the South Bank arts complex, accommodated up to 40 homeless people in makeshift shelters. Five voluntary organisations and the *Borough of Lambeth* housing and social services departments worked together to rehouse its occupants. Time was devoted to understanding the needs and preferences of the occupants and in building their confidence, though scarce resources influenced the outcomes for some people with multiple needs. It was concluded that 'agencies working together during the process of closure can be used to produce more successful outcomes than agencies acting alone' (*Thames Reach*, 1998, p.2).

Services for homeless people are not always well integrated and the resulting inefficiencies are easily seen. Frictions sometimes occur, for example when voluntary organisations believe that statutory health and social services are not meeting their responsibilities towards vulnerable clients. The *Homeless Mentally Ill Initiative*'s teams in London experienced difficulties in getting NHS community mental health teams and social services departments both to accept long-term responsibility for mentally ill homeless people who were to be resettled, and to provide the intensive contact that some clients required (Craig, 1995). Andy Shield's contribution is a case study of the problems involved in securing primary health and mental health care services for older hostel residents (Box 9.1).

## Box 9.1: ACCESSING PRIMARY HEALTH AND MENTAL HEALTH SERVICES FOR OLDER HOSTEL RESIDENTS

*Andy Shields, the St Mungo's manager of the former Lancefield Street Centre, describes the problems of organising primary health care services for hostel residents and the practical solutions. He draws on his experiences as manager at Lancefield Street and at other homeless projects.*

In Britain, older homeless people are typically a socially excluded group and have not received from the *National Health Service* the level of treatment consistent with their relatively high needs. Once they have been persuaded to move into hostels, it is therefore important and sometimes urgent to address their health problems. When a hostel is being planned, the local health authority is contacted and the proposed service is outlined together with a request for input from a GP. The response we get depends largely on which local health authority is approached; in some areas homelessness is a big issue and in others it is not. If we are fortunate, the health authority will have a scheme in place that can pay for GP sessions with the hostel residents. Failing this, we contact the GP practices adjacent to the hostel and try to find one that is willing to provide a service to the hostel.

Many GPs are reluctant to accept this responsibility because homeless people generally have multiple health problems, require high levels of care, and some exhibit challenging behaviour and cause problems in the surgery waiting room. Moreover, a practice that accepts responsibility for a hostel's residents may find itself 'out of pocket': the patients are registered as temporary residents and the GP will get a single payment for three months' medical care. A GP would normally expect to provide only one or two consultations for this payment, not recurrent health care, multiple prescriptions and expensive out-of-hours services.

If none of the local practices are willing to provide a service, a hostel may have to make an agreement with a health authority that the residents are allocated to several practices or, failing that, that the residents receive primary health care services from the accident and emergency department of a local hospital. This is neither acceptable nor cost-effective. The GP is the gatekeeper to a range of other medical services, including hospital specialties and community and mental health services such as continence advisers and district nurses. It is therefore very important for every resident to be registered as a patient with a local GP.

Mental health services are also very important in meeting the needs of older homeless people. In London several specialist teams have been funded under the Homeless Mentally Ill Initiative (HMII) to provide services for homeless people with mental health problems.[1] When planning a new hostel, contact is made with the local HMII team and its inputs agreed. These depend on the resources of the team and the expected level of need, but often the understanding is either a weekly visit from the team or that the project would make referrals as required. To ensure the necessary range of specialist support services, contact is also made with the local community mental health and social services teams.

While invariably a mental health professional will see hostel residents, it is not always possible to get the high level of input that the hostel believes is required. Many homeless people with mental health problems also abuse alcohol. If a person has these dual problems and refuses to control his or her drinking, mental health workers often say that they cannot help because the symptoms may be caused, exaggerated or masked by the alcohol.

Because of their physical or mental health problems, many older homeless people need higher levels of care than are normally offered by first-stage hostels. The procedure for accessing high care is through a local authority social services 'community care assessment'. This authorises the purchase from a community care budget of 'packages' of care, which may include residential or nursing home care. These budgets vary greatly by borough, are limited, and neither the local authority in which the hostel is sited nor the one in which the person slept rough will necessarily accept responsibility. Hostels have to advocate on the resident's behalf to ensure that the resident receives care.

Many older rough sleepers are accommodated in hostels that cannot meet their care needs. This is followed all too often by a deterioration of their health and a hospital admission. To overcome this problem many voluntary sector agencies assert a policy of not re-accepting some residents on discharge from hospital. If a hostel cannot fulfil its duty of care for a resident whose needs exceed its capacity, admission is refused until a full assessment has been carried out by social services. For obvious reasons, the policy is not popular with hospital administrators or social services departments.

**Three key lessons**
- it is essential to give local health authorities that fund primary health care services for special groups advance notice when a service for homeless people is being planned and to make clear what level of input is likely to be required
- until 'community care assessments' are more readily available for all needy homeless people (from whatever borough or local authority they came), hostels will be forced in the best interests of their residents to operate a policy of not accepting former residents with high care needs when they are discharged from hospitals

- the rights of older homeless people to health and social services should be asserted.

*Note*
1. This programme and its funds have now (October 1999) been merged with those of the *Homelessness Action Programme*.

Effective collaboration between agencies and multi-agency working is complex and difficult to achieve (McCluskey, 1997; Pannell and Parry, 1999). The problems to be overcome include:

- working with different management structures
- negotiating compromise between the different priorities, philosophies and working practices of the agencies
- overcoming suspicion, mistrust and hostility
- addressing the resource constraints of each agency
- problems of confidentiality and data protection related to information sharing
- prejudice and arrogance, as between different professionals or those working for different organisations.

It is necessary for services working with homeless people and other vulnerable groups to overcome some of these difficulties so that joint working can be achieved. Box 9.2 describes the ways in which the *Over-55s Accommodation Project* in Leeds developed information networks and increased resettlement opportunities through collaborative work.

**Box 9.2:** DEVELOPING INFORMATION NETWORKS AND CREATING RESETTLEMENT OPPORTUNITIES

*Maggie Giles-Hill and Richard Sharp work at the Over-55s Accommodation Project, Leeds, which is managed by St Anne's Shelter and Housing Action and has been resettling older homeless people since 1991. They describe methods of developing information networks with local service providers to create referral pathways and resettlement opportunities for their clients.*

The first step in developing information networks is to compile a directory of local services that may be useful when resettling homeless people, and the type of help that they provide. The directory should include a list of local housing providers and their eligibility criteria, referral procedures, and the locations of their properties. The directory should also include: (i) housing advice centres; (ii) voluntary organisations such as local groups of *Age Concern* and *Help the Aged* that provide diverse services for older people; (iii) agencies that specifically provide help during the settling-in period, e.g. with fitting carpets, gardening and decorating; and (iv) resources that are useful for homeless people who are rehoused, e.g. local second-hand or cheap furniture stores and day centres. A good starting point is the information held by the local authority housing department. Information should also be gathered about registered care homes, nursing homes, mental health services, and alcohol services.

Once the information has been gathered, the next step is to inform the agencies who work with vulnerable or older people about the project. Information can be spread through visits to local community centres and luncheon clubs, churches, hospitals and GP surgeries. Referral pathways can be created by making the work of the project known to local authority social services departments, community mental health services, hostels and day centres working with homeless people, health centres, hospital social work departments and the police. We have given talks to several of these agencies, and as a direct result they have referred older people who are homeless or at risk.

Leaflets about the service with contact names and telephone numbers should be widely distributed. Another useful device is a monthly newsletter, which is distributed to the relevant statutory and voluntary organisations. Its purpose is to update information about the project.

## Measuring performance and demonstrating outcomes

A project's faithfulness to its objectives needs to be monitored closely. Continued funding often requires unequivocal measures of performance and effectiveness, and this requires evidence-based information about the outcomes of the project's interventions. It is important that efficient assessment, monitoring and recording procedures are in operation when a new service starts, and that staff understand the value of accurately collecting the information and are taught the necessary skills. Performance indicators, outcome measures and criteria of success need to be agreed before a project opens. Afterwards they need to be regularly reviewed. The DoE (now DETR) has developed performance indicators, a 'support needs index', and targets for outreach and resettlement workers that take into consideration the length of time that a person has slept rough, his or her age (those aged under 18 years and over 50 years scoring higher), and problems that might impede successful rehousing such as mental illness, alcohol or drug abuse, learning or literacy difficulties, or a history of sexual or physical abuse (DoE *et al.* 1995; Randall and Brown, 1995). The suggestion is that an outreach worker should house 60–90 rough sleepers each year in temporary accommodation, and refer 20–30 people to resettlement programmes. A resettlement worker should rehouse in permanent accommodation 30–50 homeless people each year, depending on the clients' support needs.

The extent to which projects currently collect information varies. Most hostels record basic personal details about residents, and some carry out thorough assessments and collect detailed information about people's circumstances, problems and needs. Many day centres and drop-in centres, however, do not carry out routine assessments or record information about their users unless specific help is requested. It is much harder to gather information from people who may stay in a centre for a short while and then leave, but a consequence is that older homeless people who are withdrawn and unassertive may use a centre for a considerable time but their needs remain unrecognised. For this reason, the *North Lambeth Day Centre* in London employs a worker specifically to seek out and engage its older clients.

Services require well-designed, parsimonious and simply executed information and collection procedures that gather two types of data. Firstly, management details should be recorded of the number of people who use a service and their basic personal details, such as names, ages, dates of admission and dates of departure. The more information that can be collected on clients, the more it will produce evidence about the type of help that the clients require, the groups of people that are being helped by the project and those who have unmet needs, and changes in needs and service requirements over time. Secondly, details need to be recorded of the specific work that is carried out with the clients such as providing benefits advice, personal care, alcohol advice, referral to health services, and resettlement preparation.

## Performance indicators and criteria of success

Performance indicators, outcome measures and criteria of success are important to determine the extent to which a service is meeting its objectives and effectively helping its clients. The useful indicators range from subjective measures of the clients' well-being and quality-of-life, through objective measures of progress towards a settled life, survival and morbidity, to population and environmental indices for the local area. The latter may have direct public expenditure implications, while others are elusive if politically sensitive measures of a city's attractiveness to its residents and visitors. Outcome measures need to represent not only the immediate impact of interventions and the range of needs which have been met, but also the long-term outcomes of interventions, as whether a resettled client remains housed after one and two years. Examples of the ways in which outcome and performance indicators can be applied to a first-stage hostel are shown in Box 9.3.

**Box 9.3:** Examples of outcome and performance indicators for

First-stage hostels

**Positive primary outcomes**
• Bed occupancy.
• Percentage of residents who do not return to the streets (high).
• Percentage of residents who are resettled in long-term accommodation.

**Positive secondary outcomes**
• Percentage of residents who are registered with GP services.
• Percentage of residents with health problems who attend GP services.
• Percentage of residents with diagnosed mental health problems that are receiving treatment.
• Percentage of residents whose social security benefit entitlements have been comprehensively reviewed.
• Percentage of residents who are receiving their full entitlement to benefits.
• Percentage of residents who significantly reduce their alcohol consumption.
• Percentage of residents who renew or build family and social contacts and engage in structured activities.

**Negative outcomes**
• Bed voids.
• Percentage of unfilled staff days (as through delays in replacement).
• Percentage of residents who significantly increase their alcohol consumption.
• Percentage of residents who return to the streets.
• Percentage of residents who are evicted for violent or aggressive behaviour.
• Percentage of residents who are mentally ill and disturbed, but who are not receiving treatment.
• Percentage of residents who stay long-term and are not rehoused.

# Conclusions

Good practice depends on the commitment and experience of the staff, on the collaboration and willingness of complementary providers and specialists, and on the co-operation of the clients. This chapter has discussed the issues of promoting good practice in services for homeless people. Within this field, the search for good practice is not just a conventional exercise. Unlike residential care homes, cardiac surgery wards or housing departments, in the homeless sector, developing good practice guidelines is complex because it involves interventions relating to housing, social services, primary care and mental health services. Furthermore, the quantity of past experience is small, there are relatively few pioneers, and the development of the 'evidence base' about services that focus on rehabilitation and resettlement is still at an early stage. This chapter is no more than an introduction to good practice. Many projects are carrying out innovative and valuable work with homeless people and it is important to encourage the dissemination of the lessons learned. If providers can learn more about effective and ineffective care, their scarce resources will be directed towards efficient and high quality services.

# Chapter 10

# Overview and recommendations

## Introduction: meeting the needs

This final chapter performs three tasks. It begins with an overview of the evidence and findings from the book's empirical reports and commentaries; the second section offers some final observations on the current policy debates about services for single homeless people; and the third concludes with a summary of our recommendations for service development, organisation and delivery. This last section has drawn from the experience of the pioneering projects to develop preliminary but we hope nonetheless useful principles and models of best practice in ways of working with clients, the required staff skills and training needs, and the imperatives for inter-agency working. It is emphasised again that while our approach to the subject began with a special interest in the backgrounds, problems and exceptional neglect of *older* homeless people, for some years our attention has extended to the organisation and effectiveness of services for homeless people of all ages. Our view is therefore that the following summary and recommendations apply to services for homeless people of all adult ages, and particularly to those with long histories of housing vulnerability and homelessness associated with withdrawal and alienation from conventional domestic, family and occupational supports. This specification of the 'target client group' covers the majority of single 'unofficial' homeless people: that there are different and special problems among adolescents is clear, for many of them have never acquired the motivation or the personal and social skills that enable most of us to enter rewarding productive work, creative activities or intimate relationships with others.

The opening chapter summarised the current understanding of the biographies, problems and needs of single older homeless people. It identified a challenging threefold combination of:

- immediate needs for the basics of life: shelter, personal security, warmth, income, food and facilities for personal hygiene
- prevalent needs for medical treatment, among some of an urgent and critical kind
- deep-seated attitudinal, behavioural and addiction problems, and deficiencies in daily living and social skills.

Society's responses to street homeless people are patently clear at several levels; from the actions and expressions of the general public on the streets, through newspaper correspondence columns and radio phone lines and the utterances of politicians and other influential figures, to formal policy proposals, administrative action and funding programmes. While the responses inevitably demonstrate divergent views, they also reveal several paradoxes of an affluent society with reputedly strong, and some say over-provided, systems of social welfare. Most obviously, they show that the taken-for-granted 'safety net' has several large holes: basic social security income support does not reach many street people; current social housing policies do not deliver housing to those in direst need; the 'universal' National Health Service is not a provider to all; and community mental health services have insufficient resources to help some of those most disabled by psychiatric and behaviour problems even when they are referred.

The second chapter, on ways of engaging with and beginning to help single homeless people, provided further evidence of the laudable and lamentable features of society's present responses. On the one hand, the recent substantial rises in the general population's housing conditions and material standard of living probably lies behind the demise of the idea that destitute people are appropriately accommodated in insanitary, insecure and spartan dormitory conditions. When added to the near consensus in professional circles that containment, warehousing and incarceration are misguided as approaches to the care of disabled and seriously disadvantaged people, because they probably do more harm than good and in the long-term produce higher welfare costs, then today's concentration of capital spending for special needs housing on relatively small schemes of dispersed, grouped and supported flats is understood. Today's contested issues are about how much of this accommodation we should provide and can afford, and the forms and levels of the personal support that is required alongside to help those with 'deserving needs' without dissuading any vulnerable person or his or her close relatives from self-support or informal care. The neoliberal bogey of state-created welfare dependency has a strong purchase on third-way thought and undoubtedly influences the formulation of policies on homelessness. Beyond matters of housing amenity, there is no consensus about what it is right to do.

Our continuing ambivalence and inconsistencies about the appropriate response to street indigence are displayed time and time again. Government ministers claim that people have no need to be on the streets, but fund shelters that require the occupants to leave in the mornings. Everyone knows that alcohol dependency is a widespread problem among single homeless people, but until recently most day centres and hostels refused to accommodate heavy drinkers. Those with experience know that the rehabilitation and resettlement of the most disadvantaged and excluded people requires highly skilled personal support that is protracted and extends into social work and psychiatry, yet no voices are raised to protest to the Government or to the established welfare professions about the low priority they give to this work, about the illogicality of its financing through short-term grants, or about the need to reorganise welfare roles and professional responsibilities and, as part of that, to develop accreditation, more systematic training and a career structure for 'personal rehabilitation' staff.

# Ways of helping and supporting older homeless people

## Providing for basic needs

The middle chapters of this book focused on the development and delivery of defined services. They provided both a critical synthesis of recent policy and practice innovations, and commentaries that are in part practical guides. Chapter 3 focused on ways to engage with and begin to help street homeless people. It showed both that dedicated and individualised work with older and entrenched rough sleepers through street outreach and drop-in and day centres does work, and that these services are presently haphazardly available, insecure, and from a system perspective poorly managed and co-ordinated. Heroic projects and staff in the homeless services abound, none more so than in the outreach services. By and large, they are working from first principles, not only to develop interventions that achieve effective help but also on ways to gain the respect and co-operation of the established agencies and professions. Although in Britain the RSI and HMII have supported many well-argued proposals for additional outreach work, the applied performance indicators tend to stress the simpler aspects of the work, e.g. the numbers of rough sleepers persuaded to enter temporary hostels. It is time for their work to be given far more recognition, and for a concerted effort to develop both models of good practice and better structures of training and rewards.

Day centre and open-access drop-in provision also deserves thorough review. Day centres have an image of well-meaning but amateur volunteer help, and many do provide for only the simplest of basic needs along with liberal amounts of humanitarian concern and willingness to help. Less widely appreciated is that they serve multiple welfare functions for different groups of people. They offer nutritious meals, companionship and a point of help not only to homeless people, but also the formerly homeless and the vulnerably housed. Drop-in and day centres could be important contact points for people with a high risk of becoming homeless and, in helping them with their problems, make a significant contribution to the primary prevention of homelessness. To convert these theoretical possibilities into purposeful action, the 'housing welfare' work they are exploring needs more recognition and support from the social housing and social services organisations.

Elsewhere in the welfare services, especially at the boundaries of information provision, guidance on personal entitlements, counselling, and health care advice, changes in the definition and allocation of roles and responsibilities have recently been occurring. In general medical practice the move from single-handed practices to partnerships and health centres has elaborated the receptionist and practice nurse roles. More recently in primary care, the Government has been promoting *NHS Direct*, a telephone advice service staffed by trained nurses, as a source of advice and reassurance and a means of filtering the public's rising demands for non-medical, otherwise inappropriate and 'trivial' demands upon general practice services. The last decade has also seen myriad changes in the delivery of social services, particularly 'low intensity' domiciliary help. Some forms of domestic support have been 'recommodified' for all except those on the lowest incomes. The fact that these experiments are underway – despite the usual initial hostility of the established providers – should encourage the specialist homeless agencies that changes can be achieved in their roles, standing and relationships with other welfare agencies.

### First-stage residential accommodation, rehabilitation and resettlement

Chapter 5 brought together several accounts of and opinions concerning the best approach to the personal rehabilitation and resettlement of homeless people. There is, of course, no rigid line between providing for immediate needs and helping a person regain the aspirations, skills and confidence that they need to resettle in long-term accommodation. It is, however, increasingly recognised that preparation for resettlement involves more than sorting out state benefits and finding a housing vacancy, and one detects among homeless services (widely defined) that a concerted attempt to improve resettlement procedures is getting under way.

As could be documented for other defined homeless people's services, the norms for resettlement practice have improved considerably over the last quarter of a century. The last remnants of the pre-Beveridgean welfare state, the workhouse casual wards that became the *Reception Centres*, were taken over in 1976 by the Department of Health and Social Security and renamed *Resettlement Units*. Even then, they continued to require some users to move on after a few nights, and 'resettlement' often meant no more than providing the address of another lodging. Now a host of circumstances, not least the Government's assertion of 'joined-up' working, of social outcomes in public housing investment, and of local single homeless strategies, are directing the attention of homeless sector and social housing agencies and of local authority housing and social service departments to the ways by which enduring and effective resettlement can best be achieved.

Current hostel practice still has many deficiencies, often for lack of funds but sometimes for lack of ambition. Some temporary hostels make little attempt to resettle their residents and, although for more than two decades 'resettlement' has been the lauded goal of opinion leaders in the field and the best first-stage hostels, for the most part what has actually been done is 'moving on' or at best 'rehousing'. Most of those with experience of rehousing hostel residents know however that many of them have poor living skills and either fear or are incompetent at dealing with bureaucracies, while others have persistent problems associated with alcohol abuse and mental health. The general need is for a careful assessment of the individual's problems and capabilities, the formulation in collaboration with a client of a care and accommodation plan, finding a suitable housing vacancy, and careful preparation of the move. Resettlement requires:

- matching the person to a housing setting through careful assessment and individual care and accommodation plans
- developing the daily living skills and the motivations of the client
- thorough forewarning and orchestration of the housing provider and of the agencies or staff who will provide follow-on support
- thorough checking that the client is equipped to settle into the accommodation, and that the property and its amenities are in livable and full working condition
- diligent and responsive (but not wastefully excessive) follow-up monitoring and support services to be in place and to continue as long as they serve a useful function.

In most areas of the country, however, the availability of continuing advice and support to a resettled person is poorly funded and organised.

## Approaches to service development and improvement

Housing and social welfare theorists have bemoaned the move away from collectivist, state-managed policies, but little has been done to specify the limitations of the social welfare market of competitive agencies supported by short-term funds. Commentators have for decades been advocating pooled budgets, joint commissioning and joined-up approaches to meet needs at the interstices of social welfare, housing and health provision. What is never done is to make the co-ordinating roles influential (particularly over budgets) or secure. Without such radical steps in the field of rehabilitating homeless people, it will always be a marginal and low-status concern of the long-established welfare professions, and an area of funding vulnerable to the next round of cuts.

## The current policy debate

For all the innovation of the 1990s, homeless people's services continue to be dominated by temporary hostel places, and large hostels, sub-standard accommodation and inadequate facilities still exist. Only half of the 2588 beds in London's direct-access hostels are in single rooms (Harrison, 1996). Some hostels and most shelters require the residents to leave in the morning: most linger on the streets or use day centres until the evening, reinforcing unsettledness, low self-esteem and health problems. The focus on temporary hostel places is heightened by the RSI cold-weather shelters, which provide free accommodation for rough sleepers. Their humanitarian (and media) appeal is strong: they open just before Christmas in a blaze of publicity, attract strong private sector support, and close in March without remark. Even discounting the small proportion of the users who move to cold-weather shelters from temporary hostels, which offer more services and stability but charge rent, they offer only limited individualised help and many users are transferred to other hostels and temporary accommodation when the shelters close (CRASH, 1999).

## The service and prevention agenda for 2000–02

More emphasis is needed on outreach, rehabilitation and resettlement. Too many links in the 'complete pathway' from the streets to long-term housing are absent or haphazardly filled. The Government favours helping young homeless people to gain job skills and to get work, and they may restrict hostel places to those willing to participate in an employment or training scheme (Social Exclusion Unit, 1998, section 4.27). Training in basic living skills is also important, but the main weakness of current services is inadequate resettlement: it is unevenly available, follows an 'unjoined-up' approach, and is poorly informed by good practice. Some hostels lack resettlement programmes, for it is costly to employ resettlement workers, and there is a perverse financial incentive to minimise vacancies by retaining stable residents. Few hostels or day centres have the resources or trained staff to cope with the mentally ill or heavy drinkers, whom consequently they exclude and evict (DoE *et al.* 1995; Ham, 1996; Harrison, 1996). Many rehoused homeless people experience problems, and many resettlements fail in the first two years (Craig, 1995; Morrish, 1996; Randall and Brown, 1996; Wilson, 1997). Of 4865 tenancies created through RSI schemes, 787 (16 per cent) ended in abandonment or eviction, with a higher rate of failure in shared housing than self-contained flats (Dane, 1998). This may result from differences in the tenants' problems and behaviour, or from the conflicts intrinsic to shared living (Cooper *et al.* 1994; Crane and Warnes, 1997b; O'Leary, 1997). The issue warrants intensive research.

## Approaches to prevention

Homelessness as measured by the number sleeping rough on any one night can be prevented in two ways: through a falling rate of people become newly homeless, or a shortening duration of the episodes. A mature service system and the 'social welfare market' might substantially reduce episode duration but they will hardly affect the genesis of newly homeless people. (For example, although 4500 homeless people were resettled during 1990–97 through the RSI, 1800 *new* rough sleepers were found in central London in 1996–97 (Cripps, 1998).) It is not surprising that a policy for prevention is elusive, for there is neither a consensus on the causes of homelessness nor hardly any theoretical or practical exploration of primary prevention. Reducing the incidence of homelessness could first address the most obvious proximate causes, such as eviction from social housing and discharge from the armed services or from custody. It has been estimated that 60 per cent of London's social housing tenants in 1995 needed help with claiming benefits, budgeting and paying bills (Audit Commission, 1998). Some who are unable to manage and lack support are evicted or abandon their homes (Craig, 1995; Ford and Seavers, 1998; Morrish, 1996). Many single men leave the armed forces without help to adjust to settled living (Gunner and Knott, 1997), and at least two-fifths of prisoners are reported to be homeless on discharge (Carlisle, 1997; Paylor, 1992). Given this catalogue of vulnerabilities, it becomes clear that systems are required that can detect, anticipate and alleviate marginality among the housed. Both income levels and personal competence are intricately involved.

## Recommendations: the development and delivery of services

This final section consolidates our main recommendations concerning the objectives, development and day-to-day working of a complete pathway of services from the streets to long-term housing for older homeless people.

### 1. On the need for dedicated services

Even where there is a full spectrum of all-age homeless services, providing a pathway from the streets to independent housing, they are unlikely to meet all the needs of older and long-term homeless people. There is generally a need for dedicated services, though many can be provided alongside or as part of the generic provision. The model adopted by the *Lancefield Street Centre*, *The Committee to End Elder Homelessness* in Boston, Massachusetts, *Wintringham* in Melbourne and by others, of a set of progressive services dedicated to older people, succeeds in persuading some entrenched rough sleepers to leave the streets, and has shown the capacity to resettle many in long-term accommodation.

## 2. On the importance of contact services: outreach teams and drop-in and day centres

Outreach teams are a valuable component of a service pathway, and the workers dedicated to helping older rough sleepers make convincing claims that they succeed in persuading some to enter hostels who have previously shunned help. The intense nature of outreach work should be taken into consideration when objectives and targets are set, and measurement of its achievement should not be confined to short-term housing outcomes.

The 24-hour drop-in centre at Lancefield Street provided a unique and valuable service (Chapter 3). As a point of both first contact and last resort, the drop-in rooms provided many different kinds of help to some of the most disadvantaged and needful older people in London (as *Peter's Place* does similarly in New York City). Drop-in centres should be integrated with a hostel or other larger project. Plentiful opportunities for drop-in centre users to mix with hostel residents are beneficial. Such contacts familiarise the users with a hostel and reduce their anxieties about moving in. This can be achieved by having a communal dining room and other shared facilities.

## 3. On setting the aims and service profile of first-stage residential hostels

Some of the most important lessons from the pioneering projects that have been described are about setting the goals of a project with reference to the 'difficulty' and mix of clients. As detailed in earlier chapters, the problem is that not all types of clients are compatible in a residential hostel or day centre without careful separation and special attention. The difficulties of helping women alongside men have been mentioned. Too many heavy drinkers will sometimes deter non-drinkers or those trying to overcome the problem; and too many clients who are incontinent and have high care needs are likely to discourage use by others. The simultaneous requirements for a centre are that: it achieves positive results, it is comfortable or tolerable for all the users and staff, and it makes the best use of scarce public and charitable funds within the regulations and rules that apply. An essential basis for success is that the objectives of the project (in the sense of which client groups are to be served and the goals that are set for each) are explicit and fully understood by all the staff. Over time experience will be gained on the variations in these proportions that can occur without dysfunctional effects.

## 4. On the provision of individualised help and intensive personal care

Older homeless people require individualised assessment and care programmes to ensure that their needs are identified and addressed, and that they are helped towards resettlement. Specialist workers should also be involved. For the mix of clients that the Lancefield Street hostel and drop-in centre served, the following specialist roles are highly beneficial: a nurse practitioner, a combined alcohol and mental health worker, and an occupational therapist. These roles will bring expertise in terms of assessments and treatments, developing programmes of care and support, and linking clients to mainstream services.

Projects dedicated to older homeless people encounter a high need for intimate personal care. Many in the group have moderate or severe cognitive disorders: people of their age in the general population become residents of residential care and nursing homes. A first-stage accommodation, assessment and resettlement centre is required for people who can be persuaded from the streets, but such a facility should be differentiated from a nursing home. It must have the capacity to provide the required level of care to clients who cannot be immediately admitted to a specialist home, but the emphasis should be on prompt onward referral.

## 5. On the requirements for successful long-term resettlement

A key service at many of the projects described in this book has been the assistance in finding long-term housing solutions. The intensity and effort of their individualised approaches to resettlement have surpassed the normal levels. The resettlement worker post is vital not only to maximise the matching of a client's needs and capabilities to the various housing opportunities, but also to undertake the time-consuming work of seeking vacancies and of advocacy on the clients' behalf. The role is also important in freeing hostel beds for newcomers, and therefore in maximising the number of homeless people that a facility helps. The more that connections to housing and funding agencies are put in place during the planning period of a project, the greater will be the effectiveness of the resettlement worker. A specialist post enables a wider and more up-to-date network of contacts to be maintained.

## 6. On staff training and development

Staff training and development should be integral at projects for older homeless people. All care staff require induction and training in the special problems and needs of older homeless people, and they should receive regular support and supervision.

## 7. On links with statutory health, social care and housing providers

Services for homeless people require well-developed links, cross-referral procedures, and reliable arrangements for integrated work with mainstream health, housing and social service agencies. When planning a new project for older homeless people, statutory services and specialist providers should be involved at the outset.

## 8. On developing the evidence base

Good practice depends on the commitment and experience of the staff, on the collaboration and willingness of complementary providers and specialists, and on the co-operation of the clients. At present, many services have poorly developed data collection and monitoring systems, evaluations of their programmes are rare, and very valuable work is not recognised outside of the organisation. There is a strong case for building evaluation programmes into services so that information can be gathered about the short- and long-term outcomes of interventions, lessons learned and good practice disseminated from innovations, and providers can learn more about effective and ineffective ways of working.

This book has provided an insight into some pioneering and imaginative projects that are working with older homeless people in the UK and elsewhere. At present, many services for homeless people are working with difficult clients who resist or have been rejected by mainstream providers. They are having to work hard to gain the co-operation, support and respect of the better-funded statutory health, housing and welfare services. The contributors have willingly shared their experiences with us and have reported both their achievements in working with older homeless people and the problems that they have encountered. We urge others to share their hard-learned understanding and for there to be more dissemination and critical evaluation of experience in the homeless service field.

# References

Anderson I, Kemp P, Quilgars D. *Single Homeless People: a Report for the Department of the Environment*. London: Her Majesty's Stationery Office, 1993.

Archard P. *Vagrancy, Alcoholism and Social Control*. London: Macmillan, 1979.

Argyle M, Henderson M. *The Anatomy of Relationships: and the Rules and Skills Needed to Manage Them Successfully*. London: Penguin, 1993.

Audit Commission. *Home Alone: the Role of Housing in Community Care*. London: Audit Commission, 1993.

Audit Commission. *The PCG Agenda: Early Progress of Primary Care Groups in 'The New NHS'*. London: Audit Commission, 2000.

Balazs J. Health care for single homeless people. In: Fisher K, Collins J, editors. *Homelessness, Health Care and Welfare Provision*. London: Routledge, 1993: 51–93.

Bayliss E. Models of health care provision. In: Fisher K, Collins J, editors. *Homelessness, Health Care and Welfare Provision*. London: Routledge, 1993: 149–67.

Beard J, Propst R, Malamud T. The Fountain House model of psychiatric rehabilitation. *Psychosocial Rehabilitation Journal* 1993; 5(1): 47–53.

Beigulenko Y. Homelessness in Russia: the scope of the problem and the remedies in place. In: Kennett P, Marsh A, editors. *Homelessness: Exploring the New Terrain*. Bristol: Policy Press, 1993: 219–38.

Belcher J, DiBlasio F. The needs of depressed homeless persons: designing appropriate services. *Community Mental Health Journal* 1993; 26(3): 255–66.

Bevan P. *The Resettlement Handbook*. London: National Homeless Alliance, 1998.

Bhugra D. The homeless in London. In: Johnson S *et al. London's Mental Health. Report to the London Commission*. London: King's Fund, 1997: 118–30.

Bissonnette A, Hijjazi K. Elder homelessness: a community perspective. *Nursing Clinics of North America* 1994; 29: 409–16.

Block A, Braucht N, Crispino R *et al*. CMHS/CSAT Collaborative Demonstration Program for Homeless Individuals. *Journal of Social Distress and the Homeless* 1997; 6(4): 261–74.

Bodungen A. *Homelessness in Russia*. London: Charities Aid Foundation, 1994.

Bramley G. Explaining the incidence of statutory homelessness in England. *Housing Studies* 1993; 8(2): 128–47.

Bramley G, Doogan K, Leather P, Murie A, Watson E. *Homelessness and the London Housing Market*. Bristol: School for Advanced Urban Studies, 1988.

Brickner P, Scanlan B, Conanan B, Elvy A, McAdam J, Scharer L, Vicic W. Homeless persons and health care. *Annals of Internal Medicine* 1986; 104: 405–09.

Bridge Housing Association. *Resettlement Handbook*. London: Bridge Housing Association, 1999.

Brown R, Hughson E. *Behavioural and Social Rehabilitation and Training*. New York: John Wiley and Sons, 1987.

Burt M. Critical factors in counting the homeless: an invited commentary. *American Journal of Orthopsychiatry* 1995; 65(3): 334–39.

Cambridge P, Hayes L, Knapp M, Gould E, Fenyo A. *Care in the Community: Five Years On*. Aldershot: Ashgate, 1994.

Carlisle J. The housing needs of ex-prisoners. In: Burrows R, Pleace N, Quilgars D, editors. *Homelessness and Social Policy*. London: Routledge, 1997: 123–31.

Carter M. *The Last Resort: Living in Bed and Breakfast in the 1990's*. London: Shelter, 1997.

Casey L. The homeless czar responds. *The Big Issue* 1999; 362: 5.

Cavell I. Plots, counter plots and pecking orders. *New Statesman and Society: Gimme Shelter* 2 April 1993: 12–13.

Central Policy Review Staff. *Housing and Social Policies: Some Interactions*. London: Her Majesty's Stationery Office, 1993.

Chambliss W. A sociological analysis of the law of vagrancy. *Social Problems* 1964; 12: 67–77.

Citron K, Southern A, Dixon M. *Out of the Shadow: Detecting and Treating Tuberculosis Amongst Single Homeless People*. London: Crisis, 1995.

Coalition for the Homeless. *Crowded Out: Homelessness and the Elderly Poor in New York City*. New York: Coalition for the Homeless, 1984.

Cohen C. Aging and homelessness. *The Gerontologist* 1999; 39: 5–14.

Cohen C, Sokolovsky J. *Old Men of the Bowery: Strategies for Survival Among the Homeless*. New York: Guilford Press, 1989.

Cohen C, Onserud H, Monaco C. Outcomes for the mentally ill in a program for older homeless persons. *Hospital and Community Psychiatry* 1993; 44(7): 650–56.

Cohen C, Ramirez M, Teresi J, Gallagher M, Sokolovsky J. Predictors of becoming redomiciled among older homeless women. *The Gerontologist* 1997; 37(1): 67–74.

Cohen M. Social work practice with homeless mentally ill people: engaging the client. *Social Work USA* 1989; 34: 505–09.

Connelly J, Crown J. *Homelessness and Ill Health: Report of a Working Party of the Royal College of Physicians*. London: Royal College of Physicians, 1994.

Consortium Joint Planning Group. *The Proposed Closure of Camberwell Reception Centre and Its Implications for Services in S.E. London: a Report from the Consortium Planning Group*. Camberwell, London: S.E. London Consortium, 1981.

Cooper A. *All in a Day's Work: a Guide to Good Practice in Day Centres Working with Homeless People*. London: National Homeless Alliance, 1997.

Cooper R, Watson L, Allan G. *Shared Living: Social Relations in Supported Housing*. Sheffield: Unit for Social Services Research, University of Sheffield, 1994.

Craig T. *The Homeless Mentally Ill Initiative: an Evaluation of Four Clinical Teams*. London: Department of Health, 1995.

Crane M. *Pathways to Later Life Homelessness*. Sheffield: PhD Thesis, University of Sheffield, 1997.

Crane M. *Understanding Older Homeless People: their Circumstances, Problems and Needs*. Buckingham: Open University Press, 1999.

Crane M, Warnes A. *Homeless Truths: Challenging the Myths about Older Homeless People*. London: Help the Aged and Crisis, 1997a.

Crane M, Warnes A. *Coming Home: a Guide to Good Practice by Projects Helping Older Homeless People*. London: Help the Aged, 1997b.

Crane M, Warnes A. *The Lancefield Street Centre: an Experimental Project for Older Homeless People in London. A Report to the King's Fund.* Sheffield: Sheffield Institute for Studies on Ageing, University of Sheffield, 1998.

Crane M, Warnes A. *Lancefield Street: Achievements and Lessons. A Report to the Henry Smith Estate Charity and the King's Fund.* Sheffield: Sheffield Institute for Studies on Ageing, University of Sheffield, 1999.

Crane M, Warnes A. Policy and service responses to rough sleeping among older people. *Journal of Social Policy* 2000a; 29(1): 21–36.

Crane M, Warnes A. Evictions and prolonged homelessness. *Housing Studies* 2000b: forthcoming.

CRASH. *Survey of Users of Winter Shelters Provided in London, Brighton, Bristol and Cambridge: December 1998–March 1999.* London: CRASH (The Construction and Property Industry Charity for the Single Homeless), 1999.

Cripps A. *The Street Homeless Bulletin 1998.* London: Housing Services Agency, 1998.

Crisis and Shelter. *Street Homelessness Outside London: English Local Authority Responses.* London: Crisis and Shelter, 1998.

Crockett T, Watson P, Chandler R, Harrison M, Taylor V. *London Hostels Directory 1997.* London: Resource Information Service, 1997.

Crocq L. The emotional consequences of war 50 years on: a psychiatrist's perspective. In: Hunt L, Marshall M, Rowlings C, editors. *Past Trauma in Late Life: European Perspectives on Therapeutic Work With Older People.* London: Jessica Kingsley, 1997: 39–48.

Daly G. *Homeless: Policies, Strategies, and Lives on the Streets.* London: Routledge, 1996.

Dane K. *Making it Last: a Report on Research into Tenancy Outcomes for Rough Sleepers.* London: Housing Services Agency, 1998.

Dant T, Deacon A. *Hostels to Homes? The Rehousing of Homeless Single People.* Aldershot: Avebury, 1989.

Deacon A, Vincent J, Walker R. *The Closure of Alvaston Resettlement Unit: Summary Report.* Loughborough: Centre for Research in Social Policy, Department of Social Sciences, Loughborough University, 1993.

Department of the Environment (DoE). *Access to Local Authority and Housing Association Tenancies.* London: Her Majesty's Stationery Office, 1994.

DoE. *Our Future Homes: Opportunity, Choice, Responsibility.* Cm. 2901. London: Her Majesty's Stationery Office, 1995.

DoE. *Government Provides Further Help for Rough Sleepers.* Press release 454, 31 October 1996. London: DoE, 1996.

Department of the Environment, Transport and the Regions (DETR). Statistics of local authority activities under the homelessness legislation: England. *Information Bulletin 194:* London: DETR, 13 March 1998.

DETR. *Annual Report on Rough Sleeping.* London: DETR, 1999a.

DETR. *£39 Million to Help London Rough Sleepers.* Circular 333. London: DETR, 31 March 1999b.

DETR. *More than 250 Projects to be Funded to Tackle Homelessness Outside London.* Circular 105. London: DETR, 5 February 1999c.

DETR. *Coming in from the Cold: The Government's Strategy on Rough Sleeping*. London: DETR, 1999d.

Department of the Environment, Department of Health, Department of Social Security, Home Office and Department for Education and Employment. *Rough Sleepers Initiative: Future Plans. Consultation Paper*. London: Department of the Environment, October 1995.

Department of the Environment, Department of Health, Department of Social Security, Home Office and Department for Education and Employment. *Rough Sleepers Initiative: The Next Challenge. Strategy Paper*. London: Department of the Environment, March 1996.

Department of the Environment, Transport and the Regions, Department of Health, Department of Social Security *et al. Supporting People: A New Policy Framework for Support Services*. Hayes, Middlesex: Department of Social Security, 1998.

Department of Health. *Stephen Dorrell announces new scheme to help homeless and mentally ill people in London*. Press release 90/352, 12 July 1990.

Department of Health. *More money to help mentally ill people sleeping rough*. Press release H92/31, January 1992.

Department of Health. *The New NHS: Modern, Dependable*. Cm. 3807. London: Stationery Office, 1997.

Department of Health. *Modernising Social Services: Promoting Independence, Improving Protection and Raising Standards*. Cm 4169. London: Stationery Office, 1998a.

Department of Health. *£5 Million to Pilot New Flexible Primary Care Services*. Circular 98/417. London: Department of Health, 1998b.

Department of Health. *Deprived Areas to Benefit from a £25 Million Boost*. Circular 98/584. London: Department of Health, 1998c.

Department of Health and Social Services Inspectorate. *Caring for Quality: Guidance on Standards for Residential Homes for Elderly People*. London: Her Majesty's Stationery Office, 1990.

Digby PW. *Hostels and Lodgings for Single People*. London: Her Majesty's Stationery Office, 1976.

Dockrell J, Gaskell G, Normand C, Rehman H. An economic analysis of the resettlement of people with mild learning disabilities and challenging behaviour. *Social Science and Medicine* 1995; 40(7): 895–901.

Doolin J. Planning for the special needs of the homeless elderly. *The Gerontologist* 1986; 26: 229–31.

Douglass R, Atchison B, Lofton W *et al. Aged, Adrift and Alone: Detroit's Elderly Homeless. Final Report to the Detroit Area Agency on Aging*. Ypsilanti, Michigan: Department of Associated Health Professions, Eastern Michigan University, 1988.

Drake M. Fifteen years of homelessness in the UK. *Housing Studies* 1989; 4(2): 119–27.

Drake R, Mueser K, Clark R, Wallach M. The course, treatment, and outcome of substance disorder in persons with severe mental illness. *American Journal of Orthopsychiatry* 1996; 66(1): 42–51.

Drake R, Yovetich N, Bebout R, Harris M, McHugo G. Integrated treatment for dually diagnosed homeless adults. *Journal of Nervous and Mental Disease* 1997; 185(5): 298–305.

Duck S. *Human Relationships.* 2nd ed. London: Sage, 1992.

Duncan S, Downey P, Finch H. *A Home of Their Own: a Survey of Rehoused Hostel Residents.* London: Her Majesty's Stationery Office, 1983.

Duncan S, Downey P. *Settling Down: a Study of the Rehousing of Users of DHSS Resettlement Units.* London: Her Majesty's Stationery Office, 1985.

Edgar B, Doherty J, Mina-Coull A. *Services for Homeless People: Innovation and Change in the European Union.* Bristol: Policy Press, 1999.

Elder G, Clipp E. Combat experience, comradeship, and psychological health. In: Wilson J, Harel Z, Kahana B. *Human Adaptation to Extreme Stress: from The Holocaust to Vietnam.* New York: Plenum, 1988: 131–56

Elias C, Inui T. When a house is not a home: exploring the meaning of shelter among chronically homeless older men. *The Gerontologist* 1993; 33(3): 396–402.

Ellenby S. *Moving On: the London Housing Federation Move-On Survey.* London: National Housing Federation, 1999.

Etherington A, Stocker B, Whittaker A. *Outside But Not Inside.* London: People First, 1995.

Federal Task Force on Homelessness and Severe Mental Illness. *Outcasts on Main Street.* Washington DC: Center for Mental Health Services, 1992.

Ford J, Seavers J. *Housing Associations and Rent Arrears: Attitudes, Beliefs and Behaviour.* Coventry: Chartered Institute of Housing, 1998.

Forshaw R. Risking life and limb at work. *Housing Today* 1999; 159: 16–17.

Francis V, Vesey P, Lowe G. The closure of a long-stay psychiatric hospital: a longitudinal study of patients' behaviour. *Social Psychiatry and Psychiatric Epidemiology* 1994; 29(4): 184–89.

George C, Simmons D, Thurley D, Wright S. *National Welfare Benefits Handbook.* 27th ed. 1997/98. London: Child Poverty Action Group, 1997.

Ghosh S. Soup, sleeping bags and the culture of kindness. *Housing Today* 1999; 160: 12.

Glasgow Council for Single Homeless. *Homelessness: A Directory of Key Services in Glasgow 1996.* Glasgow: Glasgow Council for Single Homeless, 1996a

Glasgow Council for Single Homeless. *Housing Association Activity on Homelessness and Special Needs: a Directory of Key Services in Glasgow 1996.* Glasgow: Glasgow Council for Single Homeless, 1996b.

Gloag D. Occupational rehabilitation and return to work: psychiatric disability. *British Medical Journal* 1985; 290: 1201–03.

Goldup M. *An Evaluation of Five Floating Support Schemes in North and Mid-Hampshire.* Eastleigh: Rehabilitation of Offenders Co-ordinating Committee, Hampshire Probation Service, 1999.

Grenier P. *Still Dying for a Home.* London: Crisis, 1996.

Grigsby C, Baumann D, Gregorich S, Roberts-Gray C. Disaffiliation to entrenchment: a model for understanding homelessness. *Journal of Social Issues* 1990; 46(4): 141–55.

Gunner G, Knott H. *Homeless on Civvy Street: Survey of Homelessness Amongst Ex-Servicemen in London 1997.* London: Sir Oswald Stoll Foundation, 1997.

Hallebone E. Homelessness and marginality in Australia: young and old people excluded from independence. In: Huth M, Wright T, editors. *International Critical Perspectives on Homelessness.* Westport, Connecticut: Praeger, 1997: 69–103.

Ham J. *Steps From the Street: a Report on Direct Access Provision.* London: CHAR and Crisis, 1996.

Harrison L, Luck H. Drinking and homelessness in the UK. In: Harrison L, editor. *Alcohol Problems in the Community.* London: Routledge, 1996: 115–40.

Harrison M. *Emergency Hostels: Direct Access Accommodation in London 1996.* London: Single Homelessness in London and the London Borough Grants Committee, 1996.

Harvey B. *Settlement Services for Homeless People in Europe: Lessons for Ireland.* Dublin: Homeless Initiative, 1998.

Hawes D. Old and homeless: a double jeopardy. In: Kennett P, Marsh A, editors. *Homelessness: Exploring the New Terrain.* Bristol: Policy Press, 1999: 187–217.

Higgins R, Richardson A. Into the community: a comparison of care management and traditional approaches to resettlement. *Social Policy and Administration* 1994; 28(3): 221–35.

Homeless Network. *Annual Report 1994–95.* London: Homeless Network, 1994–95.

Homeless Network. *Central London Street Monitor: 16 November 1995.* London: Homeless Network, 1995.

Homeless Network. *Central London Street Monitor: 23 May 1996.* London: Homeless Network, 1996.

Homeless Network. *London Street Monitor: July 1999.* London: Homeless Network, 1999.

*Housing Today.* Drop-in centre shut down after drugs raid. *Housing Today* 1999; 145, 5 August 1999: 5.

Hunt L. The implications for practice. In: Hunt L, Marshall M, Rowlings C, editors. *Past Trauma in Late Life: European Perspective on Therapeutic Work with Older People.* London: Jessica Kingsley, 1997: 212–26.

*Inside Housing.* Safety fears prompt night shelter closure. *Inside Housing* 1999a; 5 November 1999: 4.

*Inside Housing.* Fears for homeless drug users after landmark conviction. *Inside Housing* 1999b; 26 November 1999: 2.

Iqbal B. *Still Counted Out: Older Homeless People in Greater Manchester.* Manchester: Housing Projects Advisory Service, 1998.

Jacobs C, Woods N, Crockett T. *London Day Centres Directory: Services for Homeless People.* 3rd ed. London: Resource Information Service, 1998.

Jacobs K, Kemeny J, Manzi T. The struggle to define homelessness: a constructivist approach. In: Hutson S, Clapham D, editors. *Homeless: Public Policies and Private Troubles.* London: Cassell, 1999: 11–28.

Jahiel R. Health and health care of homeless people. In: Robertson M, Greenblatt M, editors. *Homelessness: a National Perspective.* New York: Plenum, 1992: 133–63.

Johnson S. Dual diagnosis of severe mental illness and substance misuse: a case for specialist services? *British Journal of Psychiatry* 1997; 171: 205–08.

Jorgensen K, Bohan L, Jervis L, Shea K. *Valley Lodge Transitional Shelter: McKinney Emergency Shelter Grant (ESG) Project Evaluation, Summer 1994.* New York: Valley Lodge, West Side Federation for Senior Housing, 1996.

Keyes S, Kennedy M. *Sick to Death of Homelessness: an Investigation into the Links Between Homelessness, Health and Mortality.* London: Crisis, 1992.

Knapp M, Cambridge P, Thomason C, Beecham J, Allen C, Darton R. Residential care as an alternative to long-stay hospital: a cost-effectiveness evaluation of two pilot projects. *International Journal of Geriatric Psychiatry* 1994; 9: 297–304.

Koegel P, Burnam A. Problems in the assessment of mental illness among the homeless: an empirical approach. In: Robertson M, Greenblatt M, editors. *Homelessness: a National Perspective*. New York: Plenum, 1992: 77–99.

Kutza E. *A Study of Undomiciled Elderly Persons in Chicago: a Final Report*. Chicago: Retirement Research Foundation, 1987.

Lam J, Rosenheck R. Social support and service use among homeless persons with serious mental illness. *International Journal of Social Psychiatry* 1999; 45(1): 13–28.

Lamb H. Will we save the homeless mentally ill. *American Journal of Psychiatry* 1990; 147(5): 649–51.

Laufer R. The serial self: war trauma, identity, and adult development. In: Wilson J, Harel Z, Kahana B. *Human Adaptation to Extreme Stress: from The Holocaust to Vietnam*. New York: Plenum, 1988: 33–53.

Lewis R, Jenkins C, Gillam S. *Personal Medical Services Pilots in London: Rewriting the Red Book*. London: King's Fund, 1999.

Liberman R. Coping with chronic mental disorders: a framework for hope. In: Liberman R, editor. *Psychiatric Rehabilitation of Chronic Mental Patients*. Washington DC: American Psychiatric Press, 1988: 1–28.

Lipmann B. *The Elderly Homeless: an Investigation into the Provision of Services for Frail, Elderly Homeless Men and Women in the United States of America, Britain, Sweden and Denmark*. Flemington, Victoria: Wintringham Hostels, 1995.

Llewellin S, Murdoch A. *Saving the Day: the Importance of Day Centres for Homeless People*. London: CHAR, 1996.

Lodge Patch I. Homeless men in London: demographic findings in a lodging house sample. *British Journal of Psychiatry* 1971; 118: 313–17.

Lowe S. Homelessness and the law. In: Burrows R, Pleace N, Quilgars D, editors. *Homelessness and Social Policy*. London: Routledge, 1997: 19–34.

Malpass P, Murie A. *Housing Policy and Practice*. 4th ed. London: Macmillan, 1994.

Marcos L, Cohen N, Nardacci D, Brittain J. Psychiatry takes to the streets: the New York City initiative for the homeless mentally ill. *American Journal of Psychiatry* 1990; 147(11): 1557–61.

McCluskey J. *Where There's a Will: a Guide to Developing Single Homelessness Strategies*. CHAR, London, 1997.

McMurray-Avila M. *Organizing Health Services for Homeless People: a Practical Guide*. Nashville, Tennessee: National Health Care for the Homeless Council, 1997.

McQuistion H, D'Ercole A, Kopelson E. Urban street outreach: using clinical principles to steer the system. *New Directions for Mental Health Services* 1991; 52: 17–27.

*Metro London*. Mayor plans purge on homeless. *Metro London* 22 November 1999: 14.

Moore J, Canter D, Stockley D, Drake M. *The Faces of Homelessness in London*. Aldershot: Dartmouth, 1995.

Morrish P. *Preventing Homelessness: Supporting Tenants with Alcohol Problems*. London: Shelter, 1996.

Morse G, Calsyn R, Miller J, Rosenberg P, West L, Gilliland J. Outreach to homeless mentally ill people: conceptual and clinical considerations. *Community Mental Health Journal* 1996; 32(3): 261–74.

Murray R, Baier M. Evaluation of a transitional residential programme for homeless chronically mentally ill people. *Journal of Psychiatric and Mental Health Nursing* 1995; 2(1): 3–8.

National Assistance Board. *Homeless Single Persons*. London: Her Majesty's Stationery Office, 1966.

Niner P. *The Early Impact of the Housing Act 1996 and Housing Benefit Changes*. London: Shelter, 1997.

North C, Moore H, Owens C. *Go Home and Rest? The Use of an Accident and Emergency Department by Homeless People*. London: Shelter, 1996.

Oakley D, Dennis D. Responding to the needs of homeless people with alcohol, drug, and/or mental disorders. In: Baumohl J, editor. *Homelessness in America*. Phoenix, Arizona: Oryx, 1996: 179–86.

Oldman J, Hooton S. *The Numbers Game: Lessons from Birmingham*. London: CHAR, 1993.

O'Leary J. *Beyond Help? Improving Service Provision for Street Homeless People with Mental Health and Alcohol or Drug Dependency Problems*. London: National Homeless Alliance, 1997.

Pannell J, Parry S. Implementing 'joined-up thinking': multiagency services for single homeless people in Bristol. In: Kennett P, Marsh A, editors. *Homelessness: Exploring the New Terrain*. Bristol: Policy Press, 1999: 239–65.

Parkes CM. *Bereavement: Studies of Grief in Adult Life*. 2nd ed. Harmondsworth, Middlesex: Penguin, 1986.

Paylor I. *Homelessness and Ex-Offenders: a Case of Reform*. Social Work Monographs. Norwich, Norfolk: University of East Anglia, 1992.

Philpot M, Banerjee S. Mental health services for older people in London. In: Johnson S *et al. London's Mental Health. Report to the London Commission*. London: King's Fund, 1997.

Pilling S. *Rehabilitation and Community Care*. London: Routledge, 1991.

Pleace N. *Housing Vulnerable Single Homeless People*. York: University of York, Centre for Housing Policy, 1995.

Pleace N. *The Open House Project for People Sleeping Rough: an Evaluation*. York: University of York, Centre for Housing Policy, 1998.

Pleace N, Quilgars D. *Health and Homelessness in London: a Review*. London: King's Fund, 1996.

Pollio D. The street person: an integrated service provision model. *Psychosocial Rehabilitation Journal* 1990; 14(2): 57–68.

Powell P. Use of an accident and emergency department by the single homeless. *Health Bulletin (Edinburgh)* 1987; 45(5): 255–62.

Poxton R. *Partnerships in Primary and Social Care: Integrating Services for Vulnerable People*. London: King's Fund, 1999.

Purdon C. *Needs of Older Homeless People: Supported Accommodation Assistance Program*. Report to the Commonwealth Department of Community Services and Health. Turner, ACT, Australia: Purdon Associates, 1991.

Quilgars D. *A Life in the Community: Home-link; Supporting People with Mental Health Problems in Ordinary Housing.* Bristol: Policy Press, 1998

Ramsden S, Nyiri P, Bridgewater J, El-Kabir D. A mobile surgery for single homeless people in London. *British Medical Journal* 1989; 298: 372–74.

Randall G. *Counted Out: an Investigation into the Extent of Single Homelessness Outside London.* London: Crisis and CHAR, 1992.

Randall G, Brown S. *The Move In Experience: Research into Good Practice in Resettlement of Homeless People.* London: Crisis, 1994.

Randall G, Brown S. *Outreach and Resettlement Work with People Sleeping Rough.* Ruislip, Middlesex: Department of the Environment, 1995.

Randall G, Brown S. *From Street to Home: an Evaluation of Phase 2 of the Rough Sleepers Initiative.* London: Stationery Office, 1996.

Rose L. *Rogues and Vagabonds: the Vagrant Underworld in Britain 1815–1985.* London: Routledge, 1988.

Rosenheck R, Morrissey J, Lam J *et al.* Service system integration, access to services, and housing outcomes in a program for homeless persons with severe mental illness. *American Journal of Public Health* 1998a; 88(11): 1610–15.

Rosenheck R, Harkness L, Johnson B *et al.* Intensive community-focused treatment of veterans with dual diagnosis. *American Journal of Psychiatry* 1998b; 155(10): 1429–33.

Rosenheck R, Frisman L, Kasprow W. Improving access to disability benefits among homeless persons with mental illness: an agency-specific approach to services integration. *American Journal of Public Health* 1999; 89(4): 524–28.

Rossi P, Fisher G, Willis G. *The Condition of the Homeless of Chicago.* Chicago: National Opinion Research Center, University of Chicago, 1986.

Rummery K. Changes in primary health care policy: the implications for joint commissioning with social services. *Health and Social Care in the Community* 1998; 6(6): 429–37.

Sainsbury Centre for Mental Health. *Keys to Engagement: Review of Care for People with Severe Mental Illness who are Hard to Engage with Services.* London: Sainsbury Centre for Mental Health, 1998.

Sapounakis A. Urgent accommodation shelters for homeless people in Greece: who provides services and who uses them? In: Avramov D, editor. *Coping With Homelessness: Issues to be Tackled and Best Practices in Europe.* Aldershot: Ashgate, 1999: 487–509.

Schofield P. *Resettlement Works: the Role of Resettlement Services in Tackling the Social Exclusion of Homeless People.* London: National Homeless Alliance, 1999.

Scottish Office. *Statistical Bulletin: Operation of the Homeless Persons Legislation in Scotland 1986–87 to 1996–97.* Edinburgh: Scottish Office Development Department, 1998.

Scrutton S. Counselling: maintaining mental health in older age. In: Norman I, Redfern S, editors. *Mental Health Care for Elderly People.* London: Churchill Livingstone, 1997: 271–86.

Segal S, Baumohl J. The community living room. *Social Casework* 1985; 68: 111–16.

Shepherd G. *Institutional Care and Rehabilitation.* London: Longman, 1984.

Sheridan M, Gowen N, Halpin S. Developing a practice model for the homeless mentally ill. *Families in Society* 1993; 74(7): 410–21.

Snow D, Baker S, Anderson L. On the precariousness of measuring insanity in insane contexts. *Social Problems* 1988; 35(2): 192–96.

Snow D, Anderson L. *Down on Their Luck: a Study of Homeless Street People*. Berkeley, California: University of California Press, 1993.

Social Exclusion Unit. *Rough Sleeping: Report by the Social Exclusion Unit*. London: Stationery Office, 1998.

Somerville P. The making and unmaking of homelessness legislation. In: Hutson S, Clapham D, editors. *Homeless: Public Policies and Private Troubles*. London: Cassell, 1999: 29–57.

Spiers FE. The rise of St Anne's Shelter and Housing Action. In: Spiers FE, editor. *Housing and Social Exclusion*. London: Jessica Kingsley, 1999: 17–41.

Stinson N, Barini-Garcia M, Hochron J. *1998 Health Care for the Homeless Directory*. Delmar, New York: Health Care for the Homeless Information Resource Center, 1998.

Stroebe M, Stroebe W. Who suffers more? Sex differences in health risks of the widowed. *Psychological Bulletin* 1983; 93(2): 279–301.

Susser E, Goldfinger S, White A. Some clinical approaches to the homeless mentally ill. *Community Mental Health Journal* 1990; 26(5): 463–80.

Susser E, Valencia E, Conover S, Felix A, Tsai W, Wyatt R. Preventing recurrent homelessness among mentally-ill men: a 'critical time' intervention after discharge from a shelter. *American Journal of Public Health* 1977; 87(2): 256–62.

Thames Reach. *Closing the Bullring: the Last of the Cardboard Cities?* London: Crisis, 1998.

Trieman N, Smith H, Kendal R, Leff J. The TAPS Project 41: homes for life? Residential stability five years after hospital discharge. *Community Mental Health Journal* 1998; 34(4): 407–17.

Vincent J, Trinder P, Unell I. *Single Homelessness: Towards a Strategy for Nottingham*. Nottingham: Nottingham Hostels Liaison Group, 1994.

Vincent J, Deacon A, Walker R. *Homeless Single Men: Roads to Resettlement?* Aldershot: Avebury, 1995.

Warner L, Bennett S, Ford R, Thompson K. *Home from Home: a Guide to Good Practice in the Provision of Housing and Support for People with Mental Health Problems*. London: Sainsbury Centre for Mental Health, 1997.

Wasylenki D, Goering P, Lemire D, Lindsey S, Lancee W. The hostel outreach program: assertive case management for homeless mentally ill persons. *Hospital and Community Psychiatry* 1993; 44(9): 848–53.

Waters J. *Community or Ghetto? An Analysis of Day Centres for Single Homeless People in England and Wales*. London: CHAR, 1992.

Watts F, Bennett D. *Theory and Practice of Psychiatric Rehabilitation*. Chichester: John Wiley and Sons, 1991.

Welsh Office. *Welsh Housing Statistics 1997*. Cardiff: Welsh Office, 1997.

West End Co-ordinated Voluntary Services for Homeless Single People. *Annual Report 1989–90*. London: Homeless Network, 1990.

Williams L. *Addiction on the Streets: Substance Abuse and Homelessness in America*. Washington DC: National Coalition for the Homeless, 1992.

Williams R, Avebury K. *A Place in Mind: Commissioning and Providing Mental Health Services for People Who Are Homeless*. London: NHS Health Advisory Service, Her Majesty's Stationery Office, 1995.

Williams S. *Review of Primary Care Projects for Homeless People. Final Report for the Department of Health*. London: Department of Health, 1995.

Wilson D. *The First Two Years: Homeless Older People Revisited*. Edinburgh: Age Concern Scotland, 1997.

Wiseman J. *Stations of the Lost: the Treatment of Skid Row Alcoholics*. Chicago: University of Chicago Press, 1979.

Wright J, Devine J. Housing dynamics of the homeless: implications for a count. *American Journal of Orthopsychiatry* 1995; 65(3): 320–29.

Zissi A, Barry M. From Leros Asylum to community-based facilities: levels of functioning and quality of life among hostel residents in Greece. *International Journal of Social Psychiatry* 1997; 43(2): 104–15.

# List of contributors

**Julia Albert-Recht** has ten years' experience of working in the homeless field. She was employed by the Glasgow *Simon Community* to promote resettlement services and to establish a resettlement training programme for homeless people. She is now employed by the *Scottish Refugee Council* and manages their Kosovan refugee programme.

**Janice Bell** completed an undergraduate degree in social policy and administration at the University of Wales, Swansea and then trained as a registered general nurse at St George's Hospital, London. After returning to Wales, qualifying as a midwife and completing a course in special needs housing management, she became the Manager of *Grangetown PREP* when the project opened in 1992.

**Carl Cohen MD** is Professor of Psychiatry at the *State University of New York, Health Science Center*, Brooklyn, where he serves as Director of Out-Patient Services and of Geriatric Psychiatry. Since 1973, he has worked with various service programmes for homeless people and he is currently a consultant to a homeless armed services veterans programme. He has written extensively about homelessness and social psychiatry and is co-author of *Old Men of the Bowery: Strategies for Survival Among the Homeless*.

**Maureen Crane RGN, RMN, MSc, PhD** is a Research Fellow at the Centre for Ageing and Rehabilitation Studies, University of Sheffield. She has extensive experience of ethnographic research with older homeless people, and instituted a longitudinal study of the resettlement of older homeless people at *Lancefield Street* and *St Martin-in-the-Fields* centres in London, and *St Anne's Over-55s* centre in Leeds (1997–). Dr Crane initiated the funding of a 24-hour residential and drop-in centre for older homeless persons at Lancefield Street. In spring 1999, the Open University Press published her book, *Understanding Older Homeless People: Their Circumstances, Problems and Needs*.

**Janice Gibeau RN, PhD** is a nurse gerontologist and currently the Executive Director of the *Committee to End Elder Homelessness* in Boston, Massachusetts. Her experience spans the full spectrum of ageing and administration, from acute services through to community-based and long-term settings. Her principal areas of expertise include ageing policy, mental health and substance abuse, the development of integrated clinical systems, education and research.

**Maggie Giles-Hill** has over 15 years' experience of working with socially excluded people. As Project Co-ordinator for *St Anne's Shelter and Housing Action's Over-55s Accommodation Project*, Leeds, she has helped raise the profile and quality-of-life of vulnerably housed and homeless older people in the city and more widely in West Yorkshire. She now manages the recently extended project in Leeds and Sheffield.

**Portland Jones** has worked in supported housing services since 1991, and for the last seven years has managed the *Zambesi Project* and *South Road House* of *Focus Housing Group* in Birmingham, England. These projects provide accommodation and support for older homeless men, particularly those who have slept rough or been homeless and transient for years. She has particular experience in rehabilitation and resettlement.

**Michael Keen** works for *St Mungo's* and has spent 30 years developing innovative community projects, including a network of 'shoe-string' workshops in the depressed former coal mining area of the Dearne Valley, South Yorkshire, and the *Make-It-Work* project for St Mungo's in London. The latter programme encourages and facilitates purposeful activities among homeless people, with a view to easing the transition to conventional accommodation. He is currently developing a pilot project in west London that provides support to formerly homeless people who have been rehoused.

**Noreen Kerrigan** is a trained nurse who worked in the *National Health Service* for seven years before joining *St Mungo's* as a Clinical Nurse Specialist in June 1990. She provides a service to the residents at two of St Mungo's first-stage hostels for homeless people and she has an unrivalled knowledge of the patterns of health problems in the group and their difficulties in accessing conventional services.

**Bryan Lipmann AM** is the Chief Executive Officer and founder of *Wintringham*, Victoria, Australia, a not-for-profit welfare company that provides an extensive range of dignified aged care services to over 300 homeless elderly men and women in purpose-built high quality housing schemes, one of which won the 1997 *United Nations World Habitat Award*. In 1999, Bryan received the *Order of Australia* for his work with elderly homeless people.

**Yen Ly** joined *Manchester Methodist Housing Association* in 1993 after graduating from the University of Portsmouth. In 1997, she took over the management of the organisation's *Heavy Drinkers Project*, having previously managed projects for people who are HIV positive, for vulnerable young mothers and babies, and for young homeless people with substance abuse problems. In August 1999, she became the Assistant Regional Manager for Manchester Methodist Housing Association.

**Mike McCall** has worked in the supported housing sector since 1981, initially as a support worker for *Patchwork Community*, working with a wide range of vulnerable single homeless people. He joined *St Mungo's*, London's largest homelessness agency, as a Regional Manager in 1991 and became Operations Director in 1998, with overall responsibility for the management and development of client services.

**Graeme McClimont** was born in Australia and is a *Salvation Army* major and trained social worker. He spent 18 years working with homeless people in Melbourne and Perth. He has been involved in a significant transformation of services for young and older single homeless people, from institutional settings to community-based projects. He is now based in London and is the Assistant Director of the Research and Development Unit of the Salvation Army.

**Eileen O'Brien** has been working with older people with low incomes in Boston, Massachusetts since 1981, first with the volunteer organisation *Little Brothers – Friends of the Elderly* and since 1985 at *Boston Medical Center*. She has been working with homeless older people since 1988, when she became the Director of the *Elders Living at Home Program*, where she has implemented an innovative transitional housing project.

**Jeanette Reed** has worked in the fields of homelessness, substance misuse, mental health, and HIV/AIDS for 20 years. A qualified social worker, she has worked in the statutory and voluntary sectors and been active in advocacy and in assisting marginalised and entrenched groups to access primary health, mental health and other services. She worked for *St Mungo's* as an outreach worker for older homeless people in a post associated with the *Lancefield Street Centre*. Her work has focused on accessing accommodation and appropriate services for those contacted on the streets.

**Nancy Rotem** (*née* Smith) obtained an honours degree in geography at the University of Newcastle-upon-Tyne in 1996. She joined *St Mungo's* as a Specialist Elderly Outreach Worker in January 1997 when the *Lancefield Street Centre* opened, and has worked on the streets throughout London with elderly homeless people, assessing their needs and referring them to services. Prior to joining St Mungo's, she worked at the *People's Kitchen* in Newcastle as a street outreach and day centre worker.

**Richard Sharp** is a Resettlement Support Worker with *St Anne's Shelter and Housing Action's Over-55's Accommodation Project* in Leeds. He has worked closely with many vulnerably housed people who, without St Anne's co-ordinated resettlement service, would still have a very unsettled lifestyle.

**Andy Shields** has worked with rough sleepers in London since 1985 and for *St Mungo's* for the last ten years. During 1997–98 he was the manager of the *Lancefield Street Centre*, and he is now the organisation's Capacity Building Project Co-ordinator. His job entails creating opportunities for formerly homeless people to enter employment and skills training schemes.

**Connie Stapleton** has worked for *Bridge Housing Association* since 1993. She has worked in a large hostel for single homeless men and in a direct access hostel for single homeless women, helping people who are elderly, substance users, drinkers, have mental health problems, are asylum seekers and refugees. She has managed a supported housing scheme for older heavy drinkers at *Green Lanes* in north London since its opening in 1997.

**Terry Thomas** obtained a BSc in economics at the University of London and a Masters of Technology degree at Brunel University and has lived in central America for several years. He has worked for *St Mungo's* as a Resettlement Worker since 1996 and has a particular interest in the distinctive needs of older homeless people.

**Philip Timms** is a Consultant Psychiatrist and Senior Lecturer in Community Psychiatry at *Guy's, King's and St Thomas's School of Medicine* of the University of London. He has a keen interest in community psychiatry and in the difficulties that doctors have in communicating with patients and the general public. He has worked extensively with voluntary sector agencies in night shelters, hostels and day centres. He has recently co-authored several articles on homelessness, which have appeared in the *British Medical Journal.*

**Robin Vázquez** is a social worker and writer with varied experience in community-based, non-profit social services organisations. After a long career in social work and as Director of the *Service Center for the Homeless* operated by the *Washington DC Urban League,* she is changing fields and hopes soon to be teaching creative writing in a tertiary college.

**Lana Ward** has worked for *St John's Housing Trust*, Lowestoft, Suffolk for nearly nine years, firstly as a volunteer in its mother-and-baby project, then as a project worker at the *Fyffe Centre* (which provides temporary accommodation for homeless people) and for the past six years as the Resettlement Worker for the Trust.

**Tony Warnes BSc, PhD** is Professor of Social Gerontology at the University of Sheffield, Research Director for the School of Health and Related Research in the Faculty of Medicine, and Chair of the British Society of Gerontology. His major recent projects have been an ESRC-supported study of the retirement of British citizens to the Mediterranean; a study of resource allocation for 'elderly programme' services among community health care trusts in the Eastern Health and Social Service Board area of Northern Ireland, and a review of health and social care services for older people in London for the King's Fund London Commission. His books include *The Health and Care of Older People in London* (London: King's Fund, 1997).

# Contact addresses of provider organisations

## The UK

Bridge Housing Association, 233–234 Blackfriars Road, London SE1 8NW

Church Army, Independence Road, Blackheath, London SE3 9LG

Equinox, 177 Southwark Bridge Road, London SE1 OED

Focus Housing Group, Daimler House, Paradise Circus, Birmingham B1 2BJ

Glasgow Simon Community, Unit 4, Victoria Court, Hollybrook Street, Glasgow G42 7EH

Manchester Methodist Housing Association, Hopeleigh, 1–3 Fairhope Avenue, Salford M6 8AR

Nottingham Help the Homeless Association, Marmion House, Marmion Road, Carlton, Nottingham NG3 2NZ

Nottingham Hostels Liaison Group, 21 Clarendon Street, Nottingham NG1 5HR

St Anne's Shelter and Housing Action, 6 St Mark's Avenue, Leeds LS2 9BN

St John's Housing Trust, Belvedere Road, Lowestoft NR33 OPR

St Mungo's, Atlantic House, 1–3 Rockley Road, London W14 ODJ

South Thames Assessment Resource and Training Team, Masters House, Dugard Way, London SE11 4TH

Thames Reach, Bramah House, 65–71 Bermondsey Street, London SE1 3XF

The Salvation Army, 101 Newington Causeway, London SE1 6BN

Trafford Housing Aid, Crofts Bank Road, Urmston, Greater Manchester M41

United Welsh Housing Association, Ty Cennydd, Castle Street, Caerphilly CF83 1NZ

## The USA

Abraham Residences, 3915 Neptune Avenue, Brooklyn, New York City, New York 11224

Cardinal Medeiros Centre, Kit Clark Senior Services, 140 Shawmut Avenue, Boston, Massachusetts 02118

Committee to End Elder Homelessness, 1640 Washington Street, Boston, Massachusetts 02118

Dwelling Place, 2812 Pennsylvania Avenue SE, Washington DC 20020

Elders Living at Home Program, Boston Medical Center, Ambulatory Care Center, Mezzanine, 850 Harrison Avenue, Boston, Massachusetts 02118

John Heuss House, Trinity Church, 42 Beaver Street, New York City, New York 10004

Oasis Senior Center for the Homeless, Washington Urban League, 1226 Vermont Avenue NW, Washington DC 20005

Peter's Place, 123 West 23rd Street, New York City, New York 10011

Project Rescue, Bowery Residents' Committee, 30 Delancey Street, New York City, New York 10002

Valley Lodge, West Side Federation for Senior Housing, 149 West 108 Street, New York City, New York 10025

## Australia

The Salvation Army, 5 Hamilton Street, Mont Albert, Victoria 3127

Wintringham, 136 Mount Alexander Road, PO Box 193, Flemington, Victoria 3031

# Index